JUV
DC
203
.M29
1991

Marrin, Albert.
Napoleon and the
Napoleonic wars.

DISCARD

$14.99

JUV
DC
203
.M29
1991

Marrin, Albert.

Napoleon and the
Napoleonic
wars.

$14.99

NAPOLEON
and the Napoleonic Wars

*To my mind, the only immortality is the
memory we leave behind in the minds of men.
Everything on earth is soon forgotten except
the opinion we leave imprinted on history.*
—NAPOLEON

NAPOLEON

and the
Napoleonic
Wars

ALBERT MARRIN

VIKING

VIKING
Published by the Penguin Group
Penguin Books USA Inc.,
375 Hudson Street, New York, New York 10014, U.S.A.
Penguin Books Ltd, 27 Wrights Lane, London W8 5TZ, England
Penguin Books Australia Ltd, Ringwood, Victoria, Australia
Penguin Books Canada Ltd, 10 Alcorn Avenue,
Toronto, Ontario, Canada M4V 3B2
Penguin Books (N.Z.) Ltd, 182-190 Wairau Road,
Auckland 10, New Zealand

Penguin Books Ltd, Registered Offices:
Harmondsworth, Middlesex, England

First published in 1991 by Viking Penguin,
a division of Penguin Books USA Inc.

3   5   7   9   10   8   6   4   2

Library of Congress Cataloging-in-Publication Data
Marrin, Albert.
Napoleon and the Napoleonic wars / Albert Marrin.   p.   cm.
Summary: Follows Napoleon Bonaparte from his
origins as a lowly soldier to his rise to
military power and his conquest of Europe.
ISBN 0-670-83480-7
1. Napoleon I, Emperor of the French, 1769–1821—Juvenile literature.   2. Napoleon wars,
1800–1814—Juvenile literature.   3. France—History—Consulate and Empire, 1799–1815—
Juvenile literature.   4. France—Kings and rulers—Biography—Juvenile literature.   [1. Na-
poleon I, Emperor of the French, 1769–1821.   2. Kings, queens, rulers, etc.   3. Generals.   4.
Napoleonic Wars, 1800–1914.   5. France—History—1769–1821.]   I. Title.
DC203.M29   1991   944.05′092—dc20   [B]   [92]
90-42788   CIP   AC

Printed in U.S.A. · Set in 11 point Electra

CONTENTS

NAPOLEON
and the Napoleonic Wars

PROLOGUE:
NOTRE DAME DE PARIS

PARIS, FRANCE, SUNDAY, DECEMBER 2, 1804. A cold, damp morning with gray skies and biting winds. Last night's snow had already turned muddy-brown in the unpaved streets, but more was on the way.

Dawn had not yet broken as the first of the four thousand guests began filing into Notre Dame Cathedral, with its stone gargoyles glowering from the towers high above. Women, fashionably dressed in silk gowns with high waists and plunging necklines, shivered as they took their places on the hard wooden benches. Their escorts, many in army uniforms heavy with gold braid, others in skintight breeches, silk stockings, and embroidered coats, sat beside them, taking in the scene.

Notre Dame, one of the marvels of the Middle Ages, was decked out for a special occasion. Only a few years before, while the French Revolution raged, its bells had been melted down and its interior used to store animal feed. Now rows of candles sent shafts of light into every corner of the vast building. Newly restored stained-glass panels told Bible stories in shimmering reds, greens, and blues.

Everything had been arranged with the precision of a military parade. At twelve o'clock sharp, trumpets blared and a procession began to move down the center aisle, toward the high altar. There, on a magnificent throne, sat Pope Pius VII.

His Holiness had come all the way from Rome for this occasion. Yet to the assembled guests, he could have been just part of the ceremonial trappings. Their eyes were all fixed on the procession's leader.

He strode down the aisle, dressed in white silk with a purple cape studded with golden bees draped over his shoulders. As he passed, a sort of wildness gripped the audience. Suddenly guests rose from their seats, pounding the benches and shouting at the top of their voices. Their shouts filled the cathedral, echoed off its walls, and were taken up by the crowds gathered outside.

"*Vive l'Empereur!*" they cried. "*Vive l'Empereur Napoleon!*" ("Long live the Emperor! Long live the Emperor Napoleon!")

Napoleon Bonaparte was a striking figure. A man of thirty-five, he stood five feet two inches tall, had unusually white skin, small feet, and small, delicate hands with plump, tapering fingers. From the broad chest to the large head set on the short, stout neck, his body radiated power. Yet his real power, his inner strength, shined through his gray eyes. Those eyes! How they seemed to nail a person to the ground, reading one's most private thoughts!

The procession halted before the altar, where the Holy Father blessed the sword, scepter, and other symbols of imperial authority. Napoleon strode up the steps to the altar. There, on a red velvet cushion, lay a golden crown shaped like a wreath of laurel and oak leaves. Without even a bow, he grabbed the crown, turned his back on the pope, and faced the audience. Slowly, so as to savor the moment, he put it on his own head. He then picked up another crown and placed it on the head of his wife, Josephine, who knelt on the altar steps, tears of joy rolling down her cheeks.

The audience gasped, unable to believe its eyes, then cheered louder than ever. History had been made before their eyes. Never before had a European ruler crowned himself. Yet Napoleon was no ordinary ruler; for by crowning himself in the pope's presence, he showed that he ruled with God's favor and was accountable to no earthly power. He alone was master of his fate and that of the French nation.

News of the coronation spread across France, then across Europe, with lightning speed. The emperor's followers became delirious with joy. France had had many kings in her long history; but now she had an emperor for the first time in a thousand years. Yet even that last emperor, Charlemagne, could not stand by Napoleon. He was heaven-sent, a gift of God. "Napoleon," declared one admirer, "is the Face of God in the darkness." He was the "Man of Destiny," come to bring law and order to the world.

Yet others felt disappointed, even betrayed, by the coronation. In Vienna, capital of the Austrian Empire, Ludwig van Beethoven had just dedicated his third symphony, the *Eroica*, to his hero. But upon hearing of the coronation, he crossed out the dedication with such fury that his pen gouged deep scars in the paper. "So he is nothing more than an ordinary man after all!" Beethoven roared. "Now he will trample on the rights of mankind and indulge only his own ambition; from now on he will make himself superior to all others and become a tyrant."

Friends and foes were right, each in their own way. Napoleon always roused strong emotions; you either loved him or hated him, but you couldn't ignore him. One of the most complicated and talented people who ever lived, everything about him seemed larger than life. Having begun as a poverty-stricken army lieutenant with no prospects, he'd been swept up in the turmoil of the French Revolution. Rising slowly at first, through a combination of intelligence and work, boldness and luck, he'd made himself master of Europe's most powerful nation in less than a decade. His story made him the most written-about person of modern times. At last count, in the late 1960s, over 300,000 works existed on the Napoleonic era, with at least 40,000 on the emperor himself.

His followers point to a brilliant record of achievement. Determined to rescue France from revolutionary chaos, he restored its economy, reformed its laws, and created an educational system that is still in place today. Having defeated his country's enemies, he built an empire of nearly a hundred million people, ruling it with an iron hand. It is understandable why the Napoleonic legacy should be a source of pride in today's France. One has only to watch the faces of schoolchildren visiting the Invalides, his tomb in Paris, to see his influence on later generations.

Yet, as Beethoven knew, there was a darker side to Napoleon. Although no tyrant like Adolf Hitler or Joseph Stalin, he was the first modern dictator. In certain ways, he blazed the trail dictators have followed ever since. Not content merely to govern, he wanted to mold the French people into willing tools of his ambition. To do that, he tried to "brainwash" them through mass propaganda and control of the press and the arts. Although he spoke grandly of the "people's rights," in reality they had no rights save those he chose to give them. Everything else was just hollow words.

Like all dictators, Napoleon's authority rested upon force. At home, those who dared to protest found there was no law for them, only punishment as the emperor decreed. His secret police were everywhere, eager to pounce upon "enemies," real or imaginary. In the nations he conquered, his subjects were kept in line by the *Grande Armée* (Grand Army), a vast war machine that carried out his every wish.

Napoleon was, above all, a soldier—possibly the greatest of all time. Sir Arthur Wellesley, the first Duke of Wellington, who defeated him at Waterloo, was not one for giving out compliments freely. Yet, when asked who was the greatest general of his age, Wellington replied instantly, "In this age, in past ages, in any age, Napoleon."

Napoleon permanently changed the face of war, and thus of the world we live in. From his own day until the First World War, military men studied his campaigns, trying to imitate them in the age of the machine gun, high explosives, and poison gas. The result was a slaughter of millions of young men. Tough as he was, the emperor would have been horrified at such losses. From the time of his coronation until his fall ten years later, his reign was one unbroken conflict—the "Napoleonic Wars." During that time, 400,000 French soldiers died in battle. Compare this with the 542,000 Frenchmen killed during *one* battle, Verdun, in 1916.

Napoleon's influence was also felt in the United States. In 1817, cadets at the U.S. Military Academy at West Point began to study the Napoleonic Wars; they still do. The lessons they learned were applied during the Civil War, the costliest in terms of lives in our nation's history. President Abraham Lincoln's army, or "The Grand Army of the Republic," was meant to be the *Grande Armée* reborn. Generals on both sides made the French emperor their role model; indeed, some borrowed his name. George B. McClellan, head of the Union Army, was known as the "Young Napoleon." The southerner P.G.T. Beauregard took pride in his nickname: "Napoleon in Gray." Beauregard's chief, Robert E. Lee, was a lifelong student and admirer of Napoleon. While in the Philippines, General

Douglas MacArthur was called "the Napoleon of Luzon"; during the Second World War and the Korean War, he liked to compare his actions to the emperor's. There is still a Napoleonic Society of America, whose motto is *Vive l'Empereur!*

So long as people fight wars, the name of Napoleon will be honored by those who follow the soldier's profession. Our job must be to understand the man, setting him in his own time.

A BORN SOLDIER

"The Corsican, though so lazy in his own land,
works well when away and makes an excellent
policeman, warder or soldier."

—Mrs. E.R Whitwell,
Through Corsica with a Paint-Brush, 1908

Napoleon Bonaparte was born on August 15, 1769, in the town of Ajaccio, capital of the island of Corsica. Located in the Mediterranean Sea seventy miles west of Italy, Corsica is a rugged land of deep gorges and forest-clad mountains. Since ancient times, waves of invaders—Greeks, Romans, Arabs— had swept over the island, each leaving their mark on the people's way of life.

When Napoleon was born, Corsicans still lived as they had for centuries. They "spoke" a kind of Italian, using their hands as well as their tongues. Simple folk—even the nobility were poor—they lived mainly by farming and fishing. People ate well, drank deeply, and dressed plainly. Men carried weapons as a normal part of their costume, just as we wear wristwatches today. Boys grew up with swords and daggers, learning their use as soon as they could lift them. A Corsican was as likely to forget his breeches as he was to leave his weapons behind.

Weapons were not meant for show, but for protecting one's family honor. Corsicans respected the family more than any law; more, it was said, than God Himself. Family members were supposed to stick together, defending their good name against all comers. Any offense, however petty, could never be forgotten. Insults, let alone violence, triggered the vendetta, or blood feud. Instantly the warning came: "Guard thyself. I

7

am on my guard." From then on, not only the wronged party, but every member of his family was bound to attack, even kill, the offender or any member of his family. In a famous case, a priest found his enemy after fourteen years and shot him in full public view, only to be shot himself by the man's relatives. No one, including policemen standing nearby, batted an eyelash, since "debts of honor" had to be paid in blood. Feuds lasted for generations, often wiping out entire families, including children.

Nothing stirred Corsican vengeance more than foreign oppression. Only a few years before Napoleon's birth, the island had belonged to the Republic of Genoa, one of the city-states into which Italy was then divided. Although they despised the Genoese, it wasn't until the eighteenth century that Corsicans could unite against them. Under the leadership of Pasquale Paoli, a fiery patriot, they drove out the foreigners. The Genoese, however, decided to cut their losses by selling Corsica to the king of France in 1768. All he had to do to claim his prize was fight for it! And fight he did.

Paoli's men were no match for the king's soldiers, veterans who had fought in America during the recent French and Indian War. After fierce resistance, the island once again slipped under foreign control. Rather than surrender, Paoli fled to England, leaving his officers to make their own terms with the enemy.

One of his most trusted aides was Carlo Bonaparte. The Bonapartes were a minor noble family who had left Italy about the time Columbus sailed for the New World. Eventually, they bought a country farm and land in Ajaccio, upon which they built a house that can be visited today. One day Carlo met Letizia Ramolino, the daughter of an engineer. Letizia was the most beautiful girl he'd ever seen, and it was love at

Napoleon's father, Carlo Bonaparte. A minor nobleman, Carlo
fought for Corsican independence against the French. Drawing
based on a portrait by Louis Girodet-Trioson.

first sight. In 1764, when he was eighteen and she was fourteen, they married and began to raise a family. Life wasn't
easy, since Carlo, a lawyer by profession, was lazy except when
it came to talking and fighting for Corsican independence.

When the French invaded, Letizia, though pregnant, went
with him to the war. This was not unusual; for in those days
a woman's place was next to her man, whatever his occupation
and wherever he went. Women and children often followed
the armies, sharing the dangers and hardships. Years later, as
an old lady, Letizia recalled the forced marches, the nights
spent in caves, and the popping of bullets overhead. They were
pleasant memories, memories of heroic times when it was good
to be young.

With Paoli's defeat in May 1769, the couple returned to
their home in Ajaccio. There, on a sofa covered with a cloth
showing ancient heroes and battle scenes, Letizia gave birth
to the future emperor. She bore thirteen children between
1768 and 1784, eight of whom survived infancy. Joseph, the
eldest, was followed by Napoleon, Lucien, Elisa, Louis, Pauline, Caroline, and Jerome. Little did she know that each
would have a place in history.

Since Carlo was not a very good provider, Letizia struggled
to make ends meet. Always tightfisted with money, she ran
the house by cutting expenses to the bone. A warm, gentle
person, she was also firm and quick to punish. Sooner or later
all the children felt the back of her hand, or the stick she
swung like a whip. Yet, they knew, punishment was given in
love, and they took it in that spirit. No one was too old or too
important to be corrected by Mamma. A few days after his
coronation, Napoleon met her in his palace gardens. The
emperor, surrounded by his generals, playfully held out his
hand for her to kiss. She was not amused. Instead of a kiss,

he got a slap to remind him that even emperors must respect their mothers. The one thing Napoleon could count on was her love. "My mother," he said near the end of his life, "loves me. She is capable of selling everything for me, even to her last article of clothing."

Napoleon (or Nabullione, as the family called him) was a sickly child with a yellowish complexion and a head so large that it threw him off balance when he walked. Those who knew him as a child noted that he had a quick temper and a mind of his own. His needs always came first. His wishes always had to be satisfied—*now*. If not, he'd throw a tantrum that neighbors compared to that of a snarling little beast. Tears would flow in torrents; he'd whine, stamp his feet, throw things, jump up and down and roll on the floor, kicking. If he still didn't get his way, he'd sulk for days.

As Napoleon grew older, he'd run around, his stockings hanging down over his shoes, looking for trouble. "I was a mean one, always spoiling for a fight," he recalled as emperor. "Nothing overawed me. I wasn't afraid of anybody. I would pummel one boy and scratch another. They were all afraid of me." Joseph, though older and bigger, was constantly beaten, bitten, and bruised by his younger brother, Napoleon.

At the age of six, Letizia put him into a day school, where he met his first love, Giacominetta. The two would huddle in corners, whispering secrets, or walk about hand in hand. Another boy, too smart for his own good, made up a poem about them. Their classmates, giggling and pointing, once recited the poem:

> Napoleon with his stockings half off
> Makes love to Giacominetta.

Napoleon let out a howl and rushed them, throwing stones that raised black and blue marks.

It was at this time that Napoleon decided to become a soldier. How he came to that decision, we don't know. All we can be sure of is that he took soldiering for granted, something that had to be, like sunrise and sunset. For example, when he went to school in the morning, Letizia would give him a loaf of fine white bread for lunch, only to learn that he'd traded it to a soldier for a piece of coarse army bread. Asked why, he explained: "I'm going to be a soldier some day, so I might as well get used to eating this bread." Letizia saw nothing wrong with his wanting to be a soldier; indeed, she encouraged him. His favorite toy was a small brass cannon that actually fired gunpowder, which made the house shake whenever he was in a warlike mood. She even turned over an empty room to her sons to do with as they pleased. While the others played children's games, Napoleon drew soldiers in battle formation on the walls.

Meanwhile, Carlo was thinking about the future. With Paoli gone, he decided to make his peace with the French. Not only did he become their supporter, he introduced his family to the governor, Louis Charles René, Comte de Marbeuf. A lifelong bachelor, Marbeuf became fond of the Bonapartes, especially Letizia, treating her as a daughter.

The governor's friendship paid off in certain practical ways. Carlo knew he couldn't afford to send Napoleon to a military school. Besides, French military schools belonged to the king and admitted only noblemen; commoners were too "low born" to be army officers. Each year, however, a few scholarships were given to the sons of poor nobles. Marbeuf not only helped Carlo prove his noble ancestry, he used his influence to have Napoleon admitted to the Brienne Military Academy.

Shortly before Christmas, 1778, Napoleon set off for France

with his father. He was nine and a half, small for his age, and leaving home for the first time. Although he put up a brave front, Letizia knew he was scared. She took him in her arms and whispered in his ear: "Courage!"

Upon arriving in France, Napoleon found that he needed all the courage he could muster. Since he knew no French, he was sent to the Collège d'Autun, a school run by Catholic priests, to learn the language. His stay at Autun was pure misery. A stranger in a strange land, he stuck out like a sore thumb. His schoolmates, nasty little snobs with fine clothes and lots of pocket money, mocked the "Corsican savage." His manners were not those of a gentleman, and his shabby clothes were unfit for a stable boy, they said, smirking. Corsicans shouldn't be allowed among civilized people; they belonged in zoos, with the other animals.

Napoleon's Corsican blood boiled. The more they taunted him, the stronger became his love for his homeland. Corsicans, he'd shout, were more than a match for the "cowardly French"; had they not been outnumbered four to one, they would still be independent. Then fists flew, leaving more than one young gentleman with a black eye and a bloody nose.

Things came to a head when a teacher tried to punish him by having him eat dinner on his knees before the entire school.

"Down on your knees, Monsieur!" he ordered, pointing to the floor.

Napoleon burst into tears and vomited all over himself. But he wouldn't kneel. "I'll eat standing up, Monsieur, and not on my knees," he shouted. "In my family, we kneel only before God!"

The teacher, irritated at his defiance, began to use force. But as he reached for the boy, he threw himself on the floor, screaming: "Isn't that right, Mamma? Before God! Before God!" His cries brought the principal, who canceled the punishment.

By April, 1779, after a four-month stay, Napoleon knew enough French to go on to the Brienne Military Academy. Located in Champagne, a district famous for its wines, Brienne was a combination school and prison. The dormitory was a long corridor lined with rooms six feet square, about the size of a standard prison cell. Each room had a folding cot with a straw mattress, a water pitcher, and a washbasin. Students were locked in at night, while a guard paced the corridor until sunup. No one was allowed to visit his home while enrolled at the school.

Napoleon studied hard, especially mathematics, for which he had a natural ability. Although resented at first, he slowly won his schoolmates' respect. His marks were good, and he gladly helped struggling mathematics students with their lessons. He also liked to invent games based on the classes in military science. One winter he designed a system of fortifications according to the latest principles and divided the school into attacking and defending armies. Napoleon, who first led one army and then the other, treated the game as a real war, complete with bloodshed. As "general," he demanded total obedience from his "troops." When a boy disobeyed a command, he knocked him cold, leaving him with a scar for life. For ammunition he used "ice bullets," frozen snowballs packed around stones. Casualties mounted, forcing the principal to end the game.

In October, 1784, Napoleon transferred to the École Militaire de Paris (Paris Military School). Four months later, his father died of stomach cancer. Although Letizia found it harder than ever to make ends meet, she insisted that he stay in school. His education was an investment not only in his future, but in that of the entire Bonaparte family.

The École Militaire, located near where the Eiffel Tower is today, was one of Europe's finest military schools. When Napoleon arrived, he found it unlike any school he'd ever imagined. Its students lived in luxury. Each had a large, well-furnished room with a servant to take care of his every need. Unlike Brienne, where boys were thankful for a crust of hard bread and a lump of stringy meat, cadets ate the best food money could buy. They were so pampered, in fact, that Napoleon objected. In a letter to the war minister that was never sent, he warned that the school made future officers soft. If *he* was in command, he'd "have them eat soldier's bread" and do their own chores. Officers must be leaders, and leaders must be worthy of the men they commanded.

Napoleon graduated as a second lieutenant in October 1785. It is not clear why he was allowed to graduate after completing only one year of the three-year course. It couldn't have been his grades, which were just average. Perhaps the school officials, knowing his family situation, wanted to help him earn a living as soon as possible.

Second Lieutenant Bonaparte, age sixteen, didn't look very soldierly. Thin as a rail, his stringy brown hair hanging loosely over his collar, he looked uncomfortable in his uniform. His boots were so large that his spindly legs seemed lost in them. He looked so odd that two children, daughters of a family friend, couldn't contain themselves when he came to call. "Lieutenant Puss in Boots," they said, giggling behind their hands. It took a lot of effort to hold his temper, since their laughter hurt. But a few days later, to show there were no hard feelings, he gave them a copy of the book *Puss-in-Boots* and a toy showing Puss-in-Boots as a footman running ahead of a nobleman's carriage.

Napoleon's first posting was to an artillery regiment based at Valence in southeastern France. That was a lucky break, for the artillery offered the best hope of advancement. Cannons are complicated weapons that must be handled by specialists. Artillery officers had to be chosen for their ability, not because they were nobles or had friends in high places.

Napoleon was thrilled. Here was a chance to escape poverty and help his family while gaining independence! With his mathematical ability, he looked forward to becoming a captain in thirty years, maybe even a major. But there his ambition stopped. He didn't dare think of higher rank, because those positions were closed to people like him.

Before becoming a full-fledged officer, he had to do three months of basic training. He stood guard like a private, drilled troops like a corporal, and disciplined them like a sergeant. This experience was invaluable, for it showed him every part of the service. Serving in the ranks taught him how to talk to common soldiers and understand what was important to them. He learned their slang and how to swear like a trooper; even as emperor, he'd shout drill-yard curses that made veterans cringe.

In September 1786, he received a furlough. His family, who hadn't seen him in eight years, was impressed when he got off the boat at Ajaccio. Napoleon, after all, was not just another officer; he was the first Corsican graduate of the École Militaire. People fussed over him, treating him as a celebrity. Letizia, however, wouldn't let it go to his head. When he imitated his grandmother's limping walk, she asked him to go to his room to change his clothes to receive guests. Moments later, as he stood stark naked, she beat him with a stick. Mamma, too, knew something of military tactics.

His furlough over, in June 1788 he was sent to the Artillery Training School at Auxonne. During the next year, he learned all there was to know about cannons. And the more he learned, the more he came to admire them. Those engines of death, he'd say, were his *belles filles* ("beautiful daughters"). Without them the bravest troops were mere lambs led to slaughter. With them even inferior troops became lords of the battlefield.

Napoleon spent his off-duty hours in the school's library, reading about anything that took his fancy. According to a fellow officer, he was "a devourer of books." The art of war, naturally, was his favorite subject. Volume after volume of military theory was read, analyzed, and criticized. He studied the campaigns of history's famous commanders—Alexander the Great, Hannibal, Julius Caesar, Frederick the Great— refighting them in his own mind. It was from books, rather than actual battlefield experience, that he developed his key military ideas. "I have fought sixty battles," he'd say later, "and I have learned nothing which I did not know at the beginning."

In addition to military books, he read widely in history, geography, and the sciences. The beliefs and customs of the ancient world—Greece, Rome, China, India, Persia, Egypt— fascinated him. Many hours were given to biology, astronomy, and geology. He read carefully, pen in hand, taking down anything worth remembering. Notebook after notebook was filled with lists of interesting facts. A geography list ends with "St. Helena, a small island in the Atlantic. British possession." A small island indeed, but destined to become famous as the last home of the Emperor Napoleon! Altogether, his notes occupy 368 large pages in print.

The young man's favorite book was the *Social Contract*

written in 1762 by Jean Jacques Rousseau. The most influ-
ential book of its day, the *Social Contract* argued that the will
of the people should be the only source of law. The purpose
of government, therefore, is to serve the people and help them
lead moral lives; if it failed, it might be overthrown.

While at Auxonne, Napoleon entered an essay contest on
the subject of human happiness. Although his essay didn't
win, it shows that Rousseau's book had turned him into an
idealist, one with noble principles and goals. Everyone, he
insisted, is born with the need to love. Love of family, friends,
and country is natural; indeed, love is what makes us human.
And self-sacrifice, working for others' happiness, is the highest
form of love. Riches and power counted for nothing to one
who lived a good life. One's greatest pleasure should be to look
back at the end of life and say: "I have ensured the happiness
of a hundred families. I have had a hard life, but . . . through
my worries my fellow citizens live calmly . . . through my
sorrows they are gay." Young Napoleon hoped for a world
where governments ruled in their people's interests. For
France, that meant a constitution limiting the king's power
and guaranteeing human rights.

These were fine ideals; unfortunately, Napoleon's experi-
ences were to make him turn away from them as childish
"illusions." In 1789, he, like so many others, came face to
face with one of the most terrible events of modern times. The
French Revolution burst upon the land, sweeping away the
old order in a whirlwind of chaos and war. To understand how
this happened, we must first look at the world in which he
grew up.

––––––––

FRANCE IN THE CLOSING YEARS of the eighteenth century was
an unhappy land. Its society resembled a pyramid, broad at

the bottom and narrowing toward the top. At the top stood King Louis XVI. A dull, lazy man of little ability, his authority was said to come directly from God. Those who displeased him felt his anger with the *lettre de cachet* (sealed letter). This letter could order anyone arrested and jailed for as long as the king wished. King Louis, however, much preferred to shoot cats from the terrace of his palace at Versailles, or to go hunting; his diary records that, between 1774 and 1787, he shot 1,274 deer and 189,251 smaller animals. Another pastime was rolling pellets of dirt from between his toes and flicking them at anyone who came within range.

The royal family lived in luxury, spending vast sums of money on foolishness. For example, to get closer to the people, the king built a model farm where he and selected nobles "played farmer." His wife, Marie Antoinette, enjoyed playing farm maid—when she was not meddling in politics. An Austrian princess—though most often referred to as "The Austrian Witch"—she was the best customer of Paris's diamond dealers. Always at the height of fashion, in one month alone, November 1781, she bought thirty-one expensive riding costumes.

Below the royal family were the three "estates," the classes into which France's twenty-six million people were divided. The dividing line between the estates was *privilege*, the enjoyment of rights denied to others. A minority had many privileges and few responsibilities, while the majority had only responsibilities and burdens. Among the minority was the First Estate, the 130,000 clergymen of the Roman Catholic Church. Clergymen paid no taxes, controlled all education, had their own law courts, and decided what their countrymen could and could not read; every book had to pass church censors before being printed. The privileges of the 400,000 noblemen who made up the Second Estate originated in the

The relationship of the three estates—and the causes of the French revolution—as depicted by a cartoonist of the times: the crushing weight of the monarchy, supported by the aristocracy and clergy, is borne on the back of the people. AT RIGHT, Queen Marie Antoinette sits with two of her children. A popular object of hatred for her ignorance and self-indulgence, the queen would fall a victim to the Reign of Terror.

Middle Ages. Only nobles could become high government officials, hold the chief offices in the church, and be army officers. Free from taxes, they were like little kings on their estates. Anyone who lived on a nobleman's estate, or owned land that had once been part of such an estate, had to grind his corn at the lord's mill and bake his bread in his oven. During the hunting season, he had to allow the nobles to chase game on horseback across his fields, trampling the crops as they went. Wealthy nobles and clergy enjoyed a standard of living that rivaled the royal family's. They, too, lived in palaces and had scores of servants.

All other Frenchmen belonged to the Third Estate. The largest number, twenty-one million, were peasants who worked the land. Peasants' lives were filled with hardship and injustice. Farms were small and yielded barely enough to feed a family. Yet even if they had enough to eat, taxes and obligations to the nobility kept them miserable. They were a sad sight, these thrifty, hardworking people wearing rags and wooden shoes. Tobias Smollett, an English traveler, said they looked more like "ravenous scarecrows" than human beings. A cartoon of the time showed a priest and a nobleman riding on a peasant's back. The meaning was clear: idle people lived on the peasant's labor, giving nothing in return.

The rest of the Third Estate were town dwellers. Merchants and manufacturers, doctors and lawyers, though financially well off, were still dissatisfied. No matter how much money they earned, they had no voice in running the country. Taxes were collected, war declared, and laws made without their consent. They resented the nobles' privileges and wanted abil- ity, not birth, to decide how far a person went in the world.

Town workers had other grievances. Wages had failed to

keep up with the cost of living for at least fifty years. Bread, truly the "staff of life," was their basic food. The typical worker's family ate two pounds of bread per day per person, washing it down with water or low-grade wine; milk, which supposedly caused headaches and sore eyes, was drunk only by infants and the very old. Unfortunately, the price of bread kept rising, so that it used up about half a worker's wages. The rest of the diet consisted of vegetables, known as "poor man's food": peas, beans, cabbages, and carrots. Meat was too expensive for most workers to afford.

Workers found it impossible to care for all their children. Even when times were good, parents had to make a terrible choice when a baby arrived: keep it and take food from the other children, or get rid of it for the "good" of all. Newborns were sometimes killed outright, by drowning, or were abandoned in ditches and back alleys. Thousands of others were left at orphanages each year. In Paris in the 1770s, for example, one third of all babies were given away soon after birth. It was the same as killing them, for orphanages were so unhealthy that fifty percent died within the first year.

Bad as things were, they were growing steadily worse as the century drew to a close. The winter of 1788 was so harsh that sparrows froze in the trees. The spring crops were poor, forcing up bread prices. But that was only the beginning of the trouble. Since the peasants had barely enough to keep themselves alive, they couldn't afford to buy goods manufactured in the towns. Employers, seeing profits shrink, laid off workers. Town workers now faced a double crisis: bread prices shot up at the very time so many were losing their jobs. As a result, nearly half the French people were in need of relief by 1789. In Paris, 150,000 of the city's 600,000 population were unemployed.

Government officials were often unsympathetic to their hardships. Joseph François Foulon, a financial expert, scoffed at
their misery. The poor, he said, "should eat grass, like my
horses." They started the French Revolution instead.

On July 14, 1789, Paris crowds stormed the Bastille, a royal
fortress-prison in the heart of the city. News of the Bastille's
fall spread like wildfire. Throughout Europe people welcomed
the "birth of liberty" in France. In Germany, students cut
classes to hail the event. In England, the brother of Joseph
Priestley, the man who discovered oxygen, burst into his lab-
oratory, shouting "Hurrah! Liberty, reason, brotherly love forever! . . . The majesty of the people forever! France is free,
the Bastille is taken!"

A new age had indeed begun. Within a year of the Bastille's
fall, the old order was swept away. France had a constitution
that left no one above the law. No longer did Louis XVI rule
by divine right, but with the consent of the people. The Revolution's goals were summarized in the slogan "*Liberté, Egalité
et Fraternité*" ("Liberty, Equality, and Fraternity"). Never
have so few words captured the imagination of so many people.
Anyone, even the most humble citizen, could understand their
meaning. "Liberty" was the right to do as you wished so long
as you harmed no one and acted within the law. "Equality"
stood for the abolition of privilege; people should be free to
rise in the world according to their own ability. "Fraternity"
meant the brotherhood of man and the duty to help others
achieve liberty and equality.

Napoleon watched the early stages of the Revolution from
the sidelines. Somehow he wangled two lengthy furloughs to
visit his family. From September 1789 to February 1791, and
again from September 1791 to May 1792, he was in Corsica.

Between furloughs, he supported the changes that were coming about. He swore to uphold the constitution and helped form the Society of the Friends of the Constitution, becoming its secretary. Although a nobleman himself, he believed the Revolution embodied his ideals of love and happiness.

Soon after his return to France, the Revolution entered its most violent stage. "Royalists," supporters of the king, deeply resented the Revolution's reforms. Nothing, royalists believed, justified abolishing their God-given privileges. Hating any change, thousands of them fled across the border into Germany, hoping to stir up a war against the Revolution. Revolutionaries also wanted war, but for different reasons. France, they insisted, had a special obligation toward the oppressed. It was her sacred duty to stir up revolution everywhere and, in the name of fraternity, "aid all peoples who wish to recover their liberty." If that meant war, then so be it! But it would be unlike any war that had ever been fought. It would not be for loot or land, but a holy war—a crusade for the rights of man.

That promise was really a threat aimed at Europe's kings. There had been other revolutions in European history, but these had been confined to one country at a time. The French Revolution was different. By turning its cause into a crusade, it aimed at sweeping away the old order everywhere and at once. The kings had no choice. If they wished to save their crowns, they had to crush the Revolution.

On April 20, 1792, France declared war on Austria and Prussia, the leading German kingdoms. Within a year, Spain, England, Holland, and the Italian kingdom of Piedmont joined the "coalition," or alliance of France's enemies. Except for two brief truces, the war would last until 1815. It would go by different names at different times—Wars of the French

Revolution, Napoleonic Wars, Wars of the Coalitions—but it was actually the same struggle. Europe was caught in a vicious circle. Nations fought because they hated each other, and they hated each other out of fear and because they were fighting. There was no room for compromise. One side or the other had to go down in defeat.

At first it seemed that France was doomed. The Revolution had left it unprepared for war. It was short of weapons and supplies. With royalists flocking to the enemy, the army lacked qualified officers. Military discipline collapsed. The Revolution, soldiers argued, had set all men free. Now even common soldiers could do as they pleased. Before a battle, they'd vote on whether fighting was necessary. Soldiers even elected their officers. If the men liked them, they were qualified to command whether they were ignorant of military matters or not. One unit, for example, elected a sergeant as its colonel. But when he tried to discipline them, they hung him as a "despot," an enemy of liberty and equality.

The French campaign was a failure from the outset. Entire regiments surrendered or, crying "treason," murdered their commanders. By August 1792, the Austrians and Prussians had crossed the border and were advancing on Paris. Panic swept the capital. The defeats, people said (wrongly) were the result of the king's leaking army plans to the enemy. Fanatics crying *"la patrie en danger"* ("the homeland is in danger") demanded that traitors be punished. Translation: the royal family, nobles, priests, indeed anyone suspected of disloyalty, must be executed.

Meanwhile, volunteers poured into Paris from various parts of the country. Among them was a 500-man unit from the seaport of Marseilles. As they marched through the streets, they sang a song by Rouget de Lisle, an army engineer. It was

a stirring call to arms, a call to defend *la patrie* against the
foreign beasts. Here is the first stanza:

> Come, children of your country, come,
> > New glory dawns upon the world,
> Our tyrants rushing to their doom,
> > Their bloody banners have unfurled;
> Already on our plains we hear
> > The murmurs of a savage horde;
> > They threaten with the murderous sword
> Your comrades and your children dear.
> Then up, and form your ranks, the hireling foe
> > withstand;
> March on, march on.
> His craven blood must fertilize the land.

Known as the "Marseillaise," it later became the French national anthem.

Early in the morning of August 10, alarm bells rang throughout Paris. Led by the men of Marseilles, twenty thousand
people—shopkeepers, workers, women and children, the unemployed—poured into the streets. It was a blazing hot day,
which did nothing to calm their anger. They were armed with
guns and spears, knives, pitchforks, and sharp pieces of iron
fastened to the ends of clubs. Their destination: the Tuileries,
the royal palace near where the Louvre, Europe's finest art
museum, stands today. Their purpose: to overthrow Louis
XVI, who was supposed to be in the palace; he'd actually fled
to safety hours before.

The Tuileries was defended by Swiss Guards, professional
soldiers whose ammunition was dangerously low. They were
no match for the howling mob that burst through the gates
and surged up the stairs. Furniture worth more than a worker
earned in a lifetime was smashed within seconds. Government

documents were tossed into the air; sweaty people cheered the giant "snowflakes" as they came fluttering to the ground.

Anyone who stood in the mob's way was immediately cut down. The mob took pleasure in showing off its grisly "trophies." Bodies were thrown out of windows and decapitated; the heads were then stuck on the points of spears and paraded around the palace courtyard. Teenage boys kicked human heads as if they were footballs. "Ah, Monsieur," cried a man smeared with blood. "Providence has been very good to me. I have killed three of the Swiss with my own hands." Of the palace's nine hundred defenders, eight hundred died or were mortally wounded.

Napoleon had stopped off in Paris for several weeks before rejoining his regiment. Hearing the commotion, he ran toward the Tuileries. Along the way he passed a crowd marching behind a bleeding head stuck on a spear. Thinking he looked too much like a gentleman, crowd members ordered him to shout "Long Live the Nation!" He did so at once—at the top of his voice.

Entering the palace courtyard was like entering a butcher shop. Bodies, many stripped naked, lay in piles. Here and there, killers were still at work, hacking the wounded to pieces. Thanks to Napoleon, one life at least was saved. A Marseillais was about to blow out the brains of a wounded Swiss when he rushed up to him. "You're a man of the south?" he said. "So am I. Let's save this wretch." Without saying a word, the Marseillais dropped his musket and fled.

The Tuileries was a turning point for Napoleon. As a trained soldier, he expected to shed blood in the line of duty. But this was too much. It sickened him. "Never since," he recalled years later, "has any battlefield given me the same impression of so many corpses as did the sight of the masses of dead Swiss."

More importantly, it destroyed his idealism. What had become
of the ideals of the Revolution? Where were the people's humanity and respect for law? Suddenly he saw that ideals were
useless in themselves and that the people couldn't be trusted.
The people, as one Frenchman said, was really the "Great
Gorilla." Like the gorilla, it had to be chained, and led, and
made to behave. Democracy, in Napoleon's eyes, became a
dangerous force.

Napoleon's view seemed justified by events during the weeks
that followed. The monarchy was abolished and France declared a republic. Hundreds, including mothers with their
children, were jailed as suspected traitors. But as the jails filled,
rumors began to fly about Paris. Those jails, they said, were
bombs waiting to explode. A secret royalist army was working
behind the scenes to free the prisoners. Once freed, they'd
murder all patriots and hand the country over to the invaders.
There was only one way to treat these criminals. "Let the
blood of traitors flow," cried the journalist Jean Paul Marat.
"That is the only way to save the country."

And the blood did flow. During the "September Massacres,"
September 2 to 7, gangs of killers took over Paris's five prisons.
In some prisons, "courts" were set up to try inmates for treason.
Since the prisons were overcrowded, trials had to be brief,
usually five minutes, and the sentence nearly always the same:
death. Most inmates, however, didn't even have the formality
of a trial.

Defenseless prisoners, convicted on no evidence save that
they were nobles, were dragged out and killed by brawny men
wearing leather butchers' aprons. The killers took their work
seriously, pausing only to drink a cup of wine and to eat some
food for energy. To encourage them, women, some with
human ears pinned to their dresses, sang and danced the Car-

magnole, a lively folkdance. A passerby outside one prison saw "a group of butchers, tired out and no longer able to lift their arms," drinking a mixture of brandy and gunpowder "to aggravate their fury." They were sitting in a circle around a pile of corpses when "a woman with a basket full of bread rolls came past. They took them from her and soaked each in the blood of their quivering victims." Then they ate heartily. One fellow boasted of having eaten the heart of the queen's friend, the Princesse de Lamballe. We know of 1,368 prisoners, including 43 children, who were put to death at this time.

Napoleon lived through the September Massacres. Two days after they ended, he and his sister, Elisa, boarded a stagecoach for the south. Elisa, fifteen, had been attending a girls' school near Paris when it was closed by revolutionaries. It was a fine school, devoted to training the daughters of the nobility. But in 1792, having the manners of a noble could be the kiss of death. Since there was no safe place for her to live, he decided to return her to Corsica.

Traveling across France meant going through a country in turmoil. As the coach bumped along, they passed crowds armed with homemade weapons singing the "Marseillaise." God, how he hated that song!

There were a few close calls. Elisa, with her nice manners and feathered hat, attracted too much attention. During one stopover, a crowd began to shout as she stepped from the coach: "Aristocrats! Death to aristocrats!" Napoleon shouted back, "We're no more aristocrats than you!" and, snatching her hat, sent it flying. The crowd cheered. By October, they were in Corsica, glad to be out of the Paris madhouse.

This was not the Corsica Napoleon remembered. The Revolution had made it possible for "Babbo" (Daddy) Paoli to return from his English exile. Soon after this arrival, he was elected president and the Bonaparte family's troubles began.

The Bonapartes had been resented by island patriots ever since Carlo made his peace with the French. Nor did Napoleon's attitude help matters. Although he loved Corsica as much as Paoli, they disagreed on a basic issue. The old man had devoted his life to Corsican independence and would settle for nothing less. Napoleon, who was becoming more and more French in outlook, wanted Corsica to be part of a free France.

The break came with Napoleon's election as commander of the Corsican National Guard. Using the Guard as a power base, he tried to capture Ajaccio for France. But the atttempt failed and he was declared an outlaw. After some narrow escapes, he arrived home late one night. "Make ready to leave!" he told Letizia. "This country is not for us!" The family reached France in mid-June 1793. While Letizia and the younger children began life anew in Marseilles, Napoleon reported for duty.*

———

A LOT HAD HAPPENED in Napoleon's absence. France now had a new government, the Committee of Public Safety. The Committee's twelve members, known as the "Twelve Just Men," were led by Maximilien Robespierre. A lawyer by profession, Robespierre believed that people were naturally good—except when they became selfish and corrupt. Then they had to be eliminated for the sake of society. Robespierre cared nothing for human life so long as he reached his goal. And that goal was not merely to drive out the invaders. To save France, really to save it, meant eliminating all dishonesty, disloyalty, and immorality. Frenchmen must be ready to sacrifice every-

*The French eventually recaptured Corsica, forcing Paoli back
into exile. He died in England, poor and forgotten, in 1807.

thing for the Revolution. "Does not liberty, that inestimable blessing . . . have the . . . right to sacrifice lives, fortunes, and even, for a time, individual liberties?" he asked. "Is not the French Revolution . . . a war to the death between those who want to be free and those content to be slaves? . . . There is no middle ground; France must be entirely free or perish in the attempt, and any means are justifiable in fighting in so fine a cause." *Any* means, including mass murder.

To purify the nation, Robespierre created a dictatorship, the Reign of Terror. Those who served the Terror were called "Terrorists." The word stuck, becoming part of our language. Since 1793, "terrorism" has meant violence by fanatics willing to do anything to achieve their goals.

What we consider due process of law, where rules must be obeyed and trials fairly conducted, didn't exist under the Terror. The Terror was a law unto itself. Juries did not need actual proof to convict the accused; "moral proof," a *feeling* of guilt without evidence, was good enough. "For a citizen to become suspect," said one of Robespierre's aides, "it is sufficient that rumor accuses him."

No one was safe from the Terror. The man who cried "Vive le Roi" ("Long live the King"), the woman who spoke well of the Austrians, the tavern owner who sold soldiers sour wine, the shopkeeper who raised prices, the mother who wept for a son killed in the war: all were sentenced to death as "enemies of the people." Lacemakers were doomed, since lace was a luxury of the nobility. Antoine Lavoisier, the father of modern chemistry, was also doomed. He should die, said the prosecutor, because "the Republic has no need of scientists." Entire families were executed for no other reason than being related to a "traitor." If by chance the innocent were convicted, that was unfortunate. Still it was better that scores of innocents die than for one criminal to escape, according to Terrorists. Within two years, the Terror claimed no fewer than 20,000 lives.

Victims were executed singly or in batches. Hundreds were herded together and mowed down by cannon fire. At Nantes, 2,000 were tied up, towed in barges to the middle of the Loire River, and tossed overboard. But the favorite method of execution was the guillotine. The invention of Dr. Joseph Ignace Guillotin, it consisted of two posts with a triangular blade raised by a pulley. The victim was tied to a board, his neck secured by a clamp, and the pulley released. Down came the blade, and off went the head. According to Dr. Guillotin, a gentle, kindly man, victims "feel no pain—merely a refreshing coolness." His invention endeared itself to Terrorists, who dubbed it the "National Razor" and "Holy Guillotine"; executions were known as the "Red Mass."

Executions became a popular form of entertainment. Audiences took seats around the guillotine, buying wine and food from peddlers while waiting for the show to begin. To pass the time, they sang and danced; women sat by the hour, patiently knitting. As the victim was tied, they hooted, whistled, and cursed. When the blade fell, and the executioner held up the head by the hair, they cheered. The best-attended show was the execution of Louis XVI on January 21, 1793; afterward, people dipped their handkerchiefs in his blood as a memento. Marie Antoinette was beheaded nine months later.

Terrorists wanted to erase every trace of the old order. Titles were abolished in the name of equality. No longer were people addressed as *monsieur* and *madame* (my lord and my lady) but as *citoyen* and *citoyenne* (citizen and citizeness). Parents were encouraged to give their children clean, natural names, not those of Christian saints. Boys might be named Duck,

A large crowd gathers for the execution of Louis XVI. The executioner is shown performing his grisly ritual of displaying the victim's head for the cheering crowd. BELOW, Napoleon's artillery fire on the Paris mob, turning back their attack on the Tuileries in October, 1795. His successful defense of the Directory won him a promotion to major general and command of the troops in Paris.

Dandelion, or Conchgrass. Girls' names included Carrot, Rhubarb, or Cow. Liberties, Equalities, and Fraternities replaced Kings, Queens, and Jacks in decks of playing cards.

"Liberty" became the Terrorists' watchword. Patriots were expected to wear the red "liberty cap," a hat resembling a long stocking. "Liberty trees" were planted in gardens and along streets. "Statues of liberty" adorned town squares. A statue of liberty even overlooked the Paris guillotine. Upon seeing it, a condemned *citoyenne* cried: "Oh Liberty! Oh Liberty! What crimes are committed in thy name!" She realized that great crimes can be committed in the name of great principles, but they are crimes nevertheless.

The Church suffered as never before. Terrorists believed in God, but not in any particular religion. Religion, they insisted, was a pack of superstitions. Priests, nicknamed "Black Beetles," used superstition to keep people ignorant, the better to rob them. In the name of reason, religious beliefs had to be uprooted.

Religious liberty was declared and Roman Catholicism lost its place as the state religion early in the Revolution. Jews were granted equality after centuries of persecution. But Terrorists, unwilling to leave well enough alone, set out to eliminate organized religion altogether. And, since Catholicism was France's chief faith, it became their chief target. Priests underwent "de-Christianization by immersion"; that is, they were drowned in batches. Church towers were destroyed, because their height above other buildings was against the ideal of equality. Churches were closed and turned into stables and warehouses. Services were forbidden, priests' robes cut up for bandages, and golden crosses melted down in the name of the people. Busts of "martyrs to liberty" like Marat, murdered while taking a bath, replaced saints' images. "Marat" also became a popular name for boys.

The government found itself fighting a war within a war. Not only did it have to deal with foreign invaders, it had to fight enemies at home. In the Vendée area of western France, it faced peasants who still held Christianity as the true faith. These peasants repaid terror with terror. Captured government soldiers were tortured so horribly that death became a release. Napoleon knew of a peasant leader who said prayers on an altar made of soldiers' bodies. Several large cities rebelled. Toulon, France's chief naval base on the Mediterranean, drove out the authorities and invited a British fleet to give it protection.

Yet, despite the chaos, the Terror saved the Revolution. A few weeks after Napoleon's return, the Committee of Public Safety took control of the war effort. That marked the beginning of what we know as "total war," mobilizing all the nation's resources for war. Unmarried men between the ages of eighteen and twenty-five were drafted into the army, allowing the French to outnumber the enemy's small professional armies. The means of production were taken over and converted to war work. Everyone pitched in. Shoemakers and tailors produced clothes for the army. Women cut up cloth for bandages. Children were taught where to search for saltpeter, a vital ingredient in gunpowder. Hundreds of workshops were set up in Paris to manufacture muskets. These workshops pioneered in mass-production methods, so important during the Industrial Revolution. Paris began turning out 750 muskets a day, more than the rest of Europe combined.

A new spirit inspired the men behind the guns. Before going into battle, soldiers were told that they must defend the homeland and spread the Revolution's ideals throughout Europe. If they failed, Europe would enter another Dark Age of slavery for the common man. But if they succeeded, mankind would live happily ever after. Then, to the sound of warlike music, they charged the enemy.

A royalist named Mallet du Pan described them in action. He saw "fifty thousand wild beasts, foaming with rage, rush forth howling like cannibals against soldiers whose valor has not been healed by any passion. . . . Can one be surprised that such an onset shakes them and overwhelms them?" He was not exaggerating. The revolutionary armies fought with a fury unknown since the Crusades. And they won. Slowly, painfully, they drove the invaders from French soil.

Napoleon played an important role in their victories. With so many royalist officers serving the enemy, there were plenty of openings for men of ability. Young officers could now rise faster in a year of Revolution than in decades under the old order; even privates might become officers. Napoleon's skill with cannons was quickly recognized. Within two years, 1791 to 1793, he rose from second lieutenant to major.

Luck was also on his side. In September 1793, an army was sent to recapture Toulon. During the siege that followed, its artillery commander was badly wounded and had to be replaced. Napoleon was chosen for the job. It was his big chance, and he made the most of it.

The Toulon harbor was divided in two by a narrow neck of land. Several forts guarded the town, but the largest stood on the neck itself. Known as "Little Gibraltar," it was said to be as strong as the Rock of Gibraltar, Britain's fortress on the Spanish coast. Weeks of desperate fighting had produced no results whatsoever. French gunners were play-soldiers who knew little about cannons. Nor did pep talks help their infantry, who were shot to pieces when they charged the defenses.

After looking things over for a few days, Napoleon found a better way. His plan, approved by the commanding general, was so simple that officers wondered why they hadn't thought of it themselves. Since Little Gibraltar was the key to Toulon, Napoleon intended to use every French cannon against it. Once he'd softened it up, the infantry would go in to finish the job. With Little Gibraltar taken, French guns would command the harbor. The British admiral must then abandon the city or lose his fleet.

Napoleon put his talent to use for the first time at Toulon. A bundle of energy, he worked day and night, making the necessary preparations. He scoured the countryside for more cannons, found the horses to move them and, when horses were unavailable, grabbed a rope and helped haul them into position. Finally, he trained crews to use them properly, a major accomplishment in itself.

Getting a cannon into action was no easy task. Each step had to be done right, otherwise the weapon misfired or, worse, exploded in its crew's faces. Loading began with the gunpowder, which came in cloth bags called "cartridges." A cartridge was put down the cannon's barrel with a long wooden-handled spoon with turned-up sides. A wad of shredded rope was then packed tightly over it with a rammer, a large wooden knob at the end of a pole. Lastly, the shot was rolled down and rammed tight with another rope wad on top of it. To fire, a gunner poked a long needle down the touchhole to cut the cartridge below. He then poured "priming," fine-grained gunpowder, into the touchhole. The charge was set off with a slow match, a smoldering rope soaked in lime to make it burn for hours. After each shot, the burning pieces of wadding that stuck to the inside of the barrel were "sponged" with a damp mop made of sheepskin wool. Awful accidents happened when a fresh cartridge was rammed down a poorly cleaned barrel.

Cannons were rated by the weight of the shot they fired; the basic guns were four-, eight-, and twelve-pounders. Different kinds of shot served different purposes. "Solid shot" was an iron ball used to smash defenses and mow down men. Trained crews could get off two twelve-pounder shots per minute. Each ball could travel a thousand yards and punch through an earthen wall six feet thick. A ball that hit the ground could bounce for hundreds of yards, killing and crippling until it came to rest. Any fool who tried to stop a ball with his foot ended up with a wooden leg, or in a grave.

In addition to solid shot, cannons fired "canister," sixty to a hundred lead balls packed in a thin metal case. "Grapeshot" was usually a dozen two-pound balls tied in a canvas bag to resemble a bunch of grapes. Canister and grape were most effective against men in the open. When fired, they burst their containers, fanning out like pellets from a gigantic shotgun. "Shells," or "bombs," were hollow iron balls filled with gunpowder set off by a burning fuse. Exploding shells were deadly within a radius of twenty-five yards. If they didn't explode in the air, they lay on the ground, their fuses sputtering. Reckless men liked to pick them up and throw them as far as they could. The lucky ones had a hearty laugh; the unlucky ones were blown to bits.

Napoleon's gunners learned their lessons well. On December 14, they threw everything they had at Little Gibraltar. For three days solid shot slammed into its walls, sending chunks of masonry flying through the air. Soldiers, their clothes set on fire by exploding shells, thrashed on the ground, screaming. On the fourth day, French infantry took the fort with a bayonet charge. The British abandoned Toulon within twenty-four hours.

The Committee of Public Safety decided to make an example of the fallen city. Toulon's citizens were gathered together and asked to identify those who'd aided the enemy. These—men, women, children—were herded into the main square and shot. When the shooting stopped, an officer shouted that the Republic pardoned any survivors. They had only to stand up in order to have the people's mercy. Those who did stand up were bayoneted.

Napoleon watched, unable to help and unwilling to protest. In Toulon, as in Paris, he'd seen the law of the terror in action. He meant to be practical. "Since one must take sides," he wrote his brother Lucien, "one might as well choose the side that is victorious, the side which devastates, loots, and burns. Considering the alternative, it is better to eat than to be eaten."

Although he despised the Terror, he accepted its rewards. On December 22 he was promoted to brigadier general and given command of the artillery to be used in the upcoming invasion of Italy. It was a great achievement for a twenty-four-year-old, even in 1793.

———

CITIZEN BONAPARTE was doing well at his new post when matters took a dangerous turn. In July 1794, Robespierre was overthrown and executed by more moderate revolutionaries. Another government, the Directory, replaced the Committee of Public Safety, ending the Reign of Terror. Napoleon, who owed so much to the Terrorists, was arrested on suspicion of treason. But since there was no evidence against him, he was released after ten days.

The next fourteen months (August 1794 to October 1795) were the lowest point in Napoleon's career. His services to the Republic seemed to count for nothing. The army transferred him from the artillery to the infantry and ordered him to the Vendée. It was an awful assignment. He was a gunner, trained to fight real soldiers, not to chase wild peasants on foot. Seeing

it as a dead end, he took sick leave and went to Paris to try
for a better assignment.

Now a general without a post, he had to get by on half-pay.
Forced to live in a shabby hotel, he pawned his watch in order
to buy bread and wine. Day after day, he'd wander the city,
his face pinched with hunger and worry, his long hair falling
over his collar. He became so discouraged that he vowed to
leave Europe altogether. Upon learning that Turkey needed
someone to reorganize its artillery, he applied for the position
and was accepted.

Napoleon obtained his passport and was about to leave when
his luck changed again. Those who'd turned against him suddenly turned to him for help. The Directory had become
unpopular with many Parisians: royalists thought it too radical,
while radicals wanted a return to the Terror. In October 1795,
they began working together to overthrow the Directory. It
isn't clear what they intended to do if they succeeded, for,
apart from their common purpose, they were mortal enemies.
Given the chance, they would probably have slaughtered one
another.

The five Directors were frantic. Although they had several
thousand loyal troops, there was no able general to lead them.
Then Paul Barras, the leading Director, remembered Napoleon. He'd done well at Toulon and was now in Paris. Napoleon, who happened to be in the Tuileries Palace, the
government's headquarters, was brought to the Directors' offices. "Will you serve me?" Barras asked. "You have three
minutes to decide."

Would he!

No sooner was the question asked, when he presented his
plan. Cannons. Everything depended on cannons. He'd sur-
round the Tuileries with cannons and dare the rebels to attack.

Fortunately, forty eight-pounders were stored only six miles from the capital. Napoleon ordered a captain named Joachim Murat to bring them immediately. Murat, soon to become the finest cavalry leader in Europe, sped off with his horsemen.

By six o'clock the next morning, October 5, Napoleon had his cannons—and none too soon. Toward noon, a mob of 30,000 marched against the Tuileries's 5,000 defenders. The cannons were the great equalizers.

Napoleon had no intention of going the way of the Swiss Guards, slaughtered on this very spot three years ealier. He ordered his men to load with grape and canister. If the mob wanted blood, then blood it would have. Its own.

The mob advanced.

Napoleon raised his sword.

Closer it came. Closer, firing muskets, waving spears, and howling like banshees out of hell.

Down came the sword.

Cannons boomed, followed by an eerie buzzing noise. It was the sound of metal balls, thousands of them, flying in every direction. The mob halted, shocked by the bodies and pieces of bodies littering the ground. Then it broke and fled.

The government showed its gratitude by promoting Napoleon to major general and giving him command of the troops based in Paris. How his life changed! For the first time, he was prosperous. Now he wore a uniform heavy with gold braid and drew a large salary. Always a dutiful son, each month most of his money went to Letizia and his sisters. Yet there was still enough to allow him to enjoy the pleasures of the capital. He went to the theatre, attended dinner parties, and enjoyed the company of women—actually *one* woman. Josephine.

Napoleon met her a few weeks after his promotion. The

daughter of a noble family from the French West Indies, she
was born Josephine Tascher de la Pagerie in 1763. At sixteen,
she married Count Alexandre de Beauharnais, eventually having two children by him: a son, Eugène, and a daughter,
Hortense. No sooner did the couple move to Paris, when they
were swept up in the Revolution. Alexandre went to the guillotine during the Terror; Josephine, arrested with him, was
awaiting execution when Robespierre fell. After some hard
times, she found her way into Parisian high society, becoming
friendly with certain leading politicians; for a while, she was
Barras's mistress.

When she met Napoleon, she was thirty-two, six years older
than he. Five feet tall, slim, with dark brown eyes and long
eyelashes, she had a gentle, soothing voice that was like a
caress. The moment he met her, he fell in love.

Napoleon had been attracted to other women, but was usually shy in their company. It was different with Josephine. He
couldn't get her out of his mind. She haunted his dreams,
giving him restless nights. He'd pour out his heart in passionate
letters. "You have taken my soul; you are the one thought of
my life," he once wrote. "I awake filled with thoughts of you,"
he admitted in another letter. "Your image and the memory
of those intoxicating hours last night give me no peace. . . . I
shall see you in three hours. Till then a thousand kisses, but
do not give me any in return, for they set me on fire!"

Josephine admired his courage and reputation, of course.
She was flattered by his attentions, naturally. She accepted his
proposal of marriage, as he hoped she would. But . . .

"Do I love him?" she asked, anticipating a friend's question.
"Well . . . no." Her reason for marriage had nothing to do
with love. She was broke. Throughout her life she had no
sense of the value of money; anything that attracted her, she

Napoleon in Milan, 1796, and Josephine. Their marriage
ceremony was performed quickly before Napoleon took command
of the Army of Italy. TOP, an engraving from a portrait by Pierre-
Paul Prud'hon. BELOW, from the pastel by Pierre-Paul Prud'hon.

bought on the spot. During her years as empress, her closets never held fewer than 600 dresses. After being released from prison, she'd indulged her whims to such an extent that she'd fallen heavily into debt. Marrying Napoleon was simply a way to pay her bills and continue the good life.

Yet Napoleon's love also had its practical side. Josephine knew important people in Paris—people who could help his career. With his talent and her introductions, there was no telling how high he might climb.

They were married on March 9, 1796, in the town hall of one of the Paris districts. Josephine and her witnesses, among them Barras, had been waiting impatiently for the groom to appear. As the hours ticked away, the magistrate who was to perform the ceremony sat snoring near the stove. The bridal party waited, fidgeting, until they heard the clanging of a sword on the stairs outside.

"Come on and marry us—quickly!" said Napoleon, shaking the magistrate awake. Since Josephine had no birth certificate, she used that of her dead sister, which made her twenty-eight, four years younger. Napoleon, also lacking a birth certificate, borrowed his older brother's, making him twenty-seven, a year older.

Their honeymoon lasted only two days. On the morning of the third day, Napoleon set off on his next assignment: the command of the Army of Italy. As he left, he gave his wife a wedding present. It was a plain necklace with a golden pendant, a small gift, but one full of meaning to him. Two words were inscribed in the pendant: *Au Destin* ("To Destiny").

THE LITTLE CORPORAL

"The frontiers of nations are either large rivers, or chains of mountains, or deserts. Of all these obstacles to the march of an army, deserts are the most difficult to surmount; mountains come next; and large rivers hold only the third rank."

—NAPOLEON, Military Maxims

THE REPUBLIC OF FRANCE had been at war since 1792. After severe setbacks, its armies recovered and began to win victories. By 1796 it had forced Prussia and Spain to make peace; Holland was overrun and occupied. Only Britain, Austria, and Piedmont continued the struggle. But since Britain's real strength was at sea, its tiny army posed no threat to French territory. Austria, however, was another matter. A mighty land power, for centuries it had dominated Central Europe. France could never be safe so long as Austria remained in the field.

The Directors decided to end the war by a daring move. One army would cross the Rhine River and attack Austria head-on. A second army would attack Austrian possessions in Lombardy, the plain of northern Italy, and its ally, Piedmont. A victory there would place Austria in the jaws of an enormous nutcracker. Faced with invasion from the south and west, it would have to make peace. Britain must then follow suit or fight alone. The second army—the Army of Italy—was to be led by Napoleon. Not only had he proven his ability, but Josephine had spoken to the "right" people, and to their wives, to help him win the post.

Napoleon joined his army at Nice, a lovely seaside town on the Mediterranean. What he found there was anything but lovely. Of all the French forces, the Army of Italy was in the poorest shape. Its 45,000 men looked more like a gathering of tramps than a fighting team. Soldiers' uniforms were whatever they could lay their hands on; instead of boots, they wore wooden shoes or sandals of woven straw. Morale, fighting spirit, was low and discipline poor. Comrades stole from one another. Privates cursed officers, spat on the ground in front of them, and dared them to do something about it. Nor were they impressed by their young commander. They wondered out loud how such a little fellow could be a general. He was so small that they called him "Hop-o'-my-Thumb," or winked as he walked by in his oversized boots; hence the nickname "Longboots."

Napoleon quickly showed them who was boss. Incompetent officers found themselves serving as common soldiers in the ranks. Soldiers who broke rules did so at their own risk. Anyone who insulted an officer was loaded with chains and put on a diet of bread and water. Thieves were stripped naked, covered with black chimney soot, and paraded before the army. Deserters were hanged. General Charles Augereau, a tall, hard man who'd never flinched in his life, admitted, "I can't stand it—that little beggar makes me afraid."

Yet fear never made a hero. In order to build fighting spirit, Napoleon gave the army a rousing speech. The speech, delivered on horseback, appealed to his soldiers' pride as men and to their self-interest; that is, to their desire for loot. "Soldiers!" he cried. "You are ill-fed and almost naked. The government owes you a great deal, but it can do nothing for you. Your patience and courage do you honor but give you neither wordly goods nor glory. I shall lead you into the most fertile plains on earth. There you shall find great cities and rich provinces. There you shall find honor, glory, riches. Soldiers of the Army of Italy! Could courage and constancy possibly fail you? Let's go!" The soldiers cheered politely. They'd seen enough of the world to know that talk is cheap, and wouldn't commit themselves until he'd turned words into deeds. He didn't keep them waiting long.

Early in April 1796, Napoleon began one of the most brilliant campaigns in history. The odds against him seemed impossible. Enemy forces, vastly outnumbering his own, held a position that formed a V-shaped wedge 150 miles long. The Piedmontese side of the V was a line running southeast from their capital, Turin. The Austrian side ran southwest from their bases at Milan and Mantua. Confident in their numbers, they held their ground, daring the French to attack. They didn't realize what they were up against.

Napoleon had worked out his plan to the last detail. His reading had taught him that one's total strength was not what decided battles. What counted was strength on the battlefield on the day of battle. His basic rule was brief and to the point: "*Attaque! Toujours l'attaque!*" ("Attack! Always attack!") He planned to march along the coast into neutral Genoa and strike northward through a pass in the mountains. He'd then knock off the point of the enemy V, opening a gap between their forces. Once that was done, he'd throw most of his army against one enemy, defeat him, and then turn on the other with his full strength.

Napoleon's plan depended upon something new in warfare: speed. War in old Europe had always been a leisurely affair. Armies couldn't move fast even if they wanted to, which they didn't. Burdened by long wagon trains filled with supplies, they resembled overfed snakes winding across the countryside. Slowness made them easier to watch, making it impossible to launch surprise attacks. These, too, were unnecessary, since

everyone fought "by the book," according to a fixed set of
rules. Except for their uniforms, soldiers were all the same.
Drilled like robots, they were not supposed to think for themselves, but follow orders without question. Today, military
drill is for show. Two centuries ago, every quarter-turn, about-
face, and counter-march had its purpose. On command, soldiers marched in step in tightly packed units. Arriving on the
battlefield, each side formed, on command, a "line-of-battle"—a parallel line three men deep with cannons scattered
among them. The lines faced each other on flat ground, in
the open, without taking cover; taking cover was thought to
be unmanly. Then, on command, they fired massed volleys
with muskets, their chief weapon.

The musket was nearly five feet long, weighed ten pounds,
and carried a twenty-one-inch bayonet. Handling it was a
difficult job. To load, the soldier took a cartridge from a leather
box attached to his belt. Unlike a cannon cartridge, this was
a paper tube containing gunpowder and a one-ounce lead ball.
While standing—he couldn't lie down because the weapon
had to be loaded from the muzzle—he bit the cartridge open
and sprinkled some powder into the pan above the trigger;
beneath the pan was a narrow channel leading to the inside
of the barrel. He then poured the rest of the cartridge down
the muzzle, crumpled the paper into a wad, and packed everything tightly with a ramrod. To fire, he raised the musket to
his shoulder, drew back the hammer, and pulled the trigger.
The hammer struck a flint, which sent a spark into the powder-
filled pan, exploding the main charge in the barrel.

An average soldier fired two shots a minute. Still, the musket
was not a dependable weapon. In rainy weather, the flint got
wet and the powder in the pan fizzled; we still call a sudden
effort that accomplishes nothing "a flash in the pan." Even

on good days, the musket was so inaccurate that it took an estimated 450 shots to hit one enemy. The cry at Bunker Hill, "Don't fire until you see the whites of their eyes," originated not in America, but in Europe. The reason for massed firing at close range was to overcome the musket's inaccuracy. With lots of bullets flying in the same direction at the same time, someone was bound to be hit. When one side began to waver, the other charged with bayonets. Before our age of rapid-fire weapons, battles were decided by cold steel.

Napoleon threw away the rule book. Beginning with the Italian campaign, his army marched quickly rather than in order. It didn't make a very pretty sight, but it moved like lightning. It was everywhere and nowhere, appearing, disappearing, reappearing where least expected. Speed was further increased by giving up wagon trains. "War must feed on war," he'd say, meaning that his army must live off the enemy's country. Wherever it passed, peasants and townspeople had to give it supplies. Sometimes these were paid for with worthless paper money; usually they were just taken.

Napoleon met the Austrians at Mentonette, at the point of the V, on April 12. But his sudden appearance was only their first surprise. The Army of Italy fought an entirely new type of battle. Instead of forming a line-of-battle, thousands of "skirmishers" appeared in front of the Austrian line. Skirmishers were small, agile men who fought, not in formation, but as individuals. Taking cover behind trees and rocks, they blazed away at the white-clad lines. If the Austrians charged, they scattered, returning when the danger passed.

The skirmishers' task was to weaken the enemy while covering the French main force, a combination of cannons and infantry columns. Napoleon changed the way cannons are used in warfare. Rather than scatter them among the infantry, he gathered them into compact masses. Scores of cannons banged away at one section of the enemy line. For those who had to stand under their fire, battle became a living nightmare. Shells exploded overhead, showering them with hot iron splinters. Solid shot flew and rolled, bounced and skidded, through their ranks. Grape and canister tore gaping holes in the line.

At the right moment, Napoleon sent his infantry columns to finish the job. Each column was a block of men 170 across by 24 deep, for a total of 4,080. Two or three columns marched toward the line side by side, human battering rams tipped with steel points. When they were close enough, the attackers broke ranks and ran forward, shouting at the tops of their voices.

The Austrians raised their muskets and, on command, each man pulled his trigger at the same moment. Fire spurted from the pan with a loud hiss. Half-burnt powder and flint particles flew into his eyes. His ears rang. His shoulder turned black and blue from the kickback. The "fog of battle," clouds of gray smoke, enveloped the battlefield, making him cough and sneeze and wipe tears from his eyes.

The French fell by the hundreds, but their comrades, leaping over the bodies, cracked the line with their bayonets. By sheer weight of numbers they broke through, turned, and pressed the attack from the rear. The line collapsed, its soldiers either surrendering or running for their lives. Few got away. French cavalry chased after them, swinging swords at any heads that came within range.

Napoleon's victory at Mentonette was just the beginning. With the Austrians in retreat, he turned on their weaker ally. Piedmont was a pushover. Within eight days (April 13 to 21), he had three more battles: Millesimo, Dego, Mondovi. Each was a carbon copy of the other, fought with the same tactics and ending in a stunning French victory. Enemy officers could hardly believe what was happening. One evening Napoleon met an Austrian prisoner, a captain. Without revealing his identity, he asked how things were going. "Badly," the captain sighed. "They've sent a young madman who attacks right and left, front and rear. Such a way of making war is intolerable, as it violates all the traditions." Napoleon smiled to himself. Not playing by the rules was paying off.

The aftermath of each battle was similar in human terms. The dead were lucky, if they went quickly. The wounded were unlucky; most died later, in pain.

Soliders were terrified of army surgeons, fearing them more than enemy bullets. Being treated for gunshot wounds was the supreme test of courage. There were no painkillers. The patient was laid on a table by the surgeon's assistants and a stick placed between his teeth to prevent him from biting off his tongue. Then they held him while the surgeon went to work.

The surgeon's instruments were few and simple: saw, knife, tourniquet, forceps, probe, needles, and thread. Plain wounds were stitched together and the patient returned to duty or, worse, put into a hospital. Hospitals, military or civilian, were dangerous to one's health. Dark and dirty, staffed by illiterates and criminals, they killed more than they cured.

In dealing with bullets, the surgeon searched for the ball with a finger or a probe, removing it with forceps. Odd things might be taken from wounds, such as bits of leather, cloth, and braiding. Even pieces of other people's bones and teeth were extracted. Solid shot struck with such force as to blow a soldier apart, turning pieces of his body into "bullets" able to kill or cripple his comrades.

For a leg or arm wound, there was an easy remedy: cut it off. Surgeons deserved the nickname "sawbones," for amputation was their treatment of choice. Amputation was fast and neat, avoiding unnecessary loss of blood. An average surgeon, working at normal speed, could take off a limb in three minutes. The stump was then sewn or cauterized, that is, seared with a red-hot blade to stop bleeding. Such treatment caused one patient in nine to die of pain and shock. French soldiers, believing surgeons too quick to amputate, grumbled that they'd cut off your head to cure your dandruff! Chest or stomach wounds could not be treated at all; victims might be killed on the battlefield to put them out of their misery or left to die unattended.

Doctors had no idea that dirt causes infections. Wounds were washed with soiled cloths to give the surgeon a better view, or not washed at all. A surgeon cleaned his hands after operating, not before; and if an instrument fell on the ground, he wiped it on his bloodstained smock and kept working. The same instrument, unwashed, was used on scores of patients. Bandages could be anything from bed sheets cut into strips to old underwear; when bandages were scarce, they were taken from the dead and used, unwashed, on other patients. No wonder Napoleon disliked doctors. Whenever he met one, he would open with the question: "How many patients have you killed in your practice?"

When Piedmont surrendered on April 28, Napoleon invaded Lombardy. Moving swiftly, he defeated the Austrians at Lodi on May 10, crossed the Adda River and took Milan, Lombardy's main city, five days later. The capture of Milan was important militarily. But the victory at Lodi, in which he inspired men to cross a bridge swept by enemy gunfire, changed his view of himself and of his place in the world. That night he realized he was a superior being. "From that moment," he recalled, "I foresaw what I might be. I could already see the world falling away beneath me, as if I were being carried to the sky." He'd convinced himself that he could do anything. His soldiers also saw him differently. That same night the army's veterans gathered around their campfires. The logs crackled and sputtered, sending sparks leaping skyward. Solemnly, respectfully, they "promoted" him from the ranks. No longer was he General Bonaparte. To them, he was *"Le Petit Corporal"* (The Little Corporal). He'd become one of them. They loved him and would storm the gates of hell to please him.

Napoleon, however, was more interested in taking Lombardy than in fighting the devil. Three times Austrian armies came through the Alps by way of the Brenner Pass. And three times he gave them a whipping such as they had never known before. On July 29 and August 5, he fought General Dagobert Würmser's army. Würmser had a fine record but, at seventy-four, was not one for speed. Defeated at Leonato and Castiglione, he took shelter behind the walls of Manuta. General Joseph Alvintzi, sent to rescue him with a fresh army, was defeated on November 17 at Arcola, a bloody affair that cost the lives of fourteen French generals. Another effort by Alvintzi met a similar fate at Rivoli on January 14, 1797. Würmser surrendered his starving army early the next month, and with it all of Lombardy.

Napoleon was hailed as Italy's liberator. Cheering crowds greeted him everywhere. Flags and coats of arms, symbols of Austrian rule, were torn down and thrown into the gutters. Men and boys put on the tricolor badge, the red, white, and blue insignia of the French republic. Mothers held up their children for a glimpse of the great man. Girls threw flowers in his horse's path. New prayers were written in his honor. Worshipers knelt in some Milan churches to recite: "I believe in the French republic, and in its son, General Bonaparte."

Liberation proved to be an illusion. Italy at this time had more gold and silver than any country in Europe. Church taxes and the profits of trade had poured into Italy since the Middle Ages. Her churches and monasteries were decked in rich fabrics and precious stones; golden crosses shimmered in the light of golden candelabras. Her palaces and art collections, museums and libraries, were the envy of the civilized world. She was a treasure house waiting to be robbed.

The Little Corporal's campaign was not only against Austria, but a looting expedition to enrich himself and balance the French budget. For starters, he squeezed sixty million francs out of the Italians. He followed this by taking art treasures "to strengthen and embellish the reign of liberty." Thousands of statues, carvings, vases, and manuscripts were carted off to Paris. Paintings by some of Europe's greatest artists—Titian, Raphael, Tintoretto, Correggio, Michelangelo—were stolen. Napoleon gave personal attention to the works of Leonardo da Vinci. While in Milan, he seized Leonardo's scientific manuscripts and one of the most famous paintings of all time, the *Mona Lisa*, which remains in the Louvre today. Yet he was also careful to limit the damage of war. During a visit to a convent in Milan, he saw Leonardo's *The Last Supper*, a fresco, or painting done on plaster. Noticing its fragile condition, he ordered that no soldiers were to be allowed near it. That was a wise decision, for soldiers were not always art lovers: sometimes they used paintings for target practice.

The Milanese, robbed of their heritage, rebelled. Napoleon cracked down. Rebels were hung on street lanterns and the city fathers told they'd pay with their heads if trouble continued. When villagers outside Milan ambushed French patrols, he snapped an order: "Generals will send against the villages the necessary force . . . to set them on fire, and to shoot all those found with weapons in their possession." To this day, Italians have strong feelings about their "liberator."

In March 1797, Napoleon led his army into southern Austria. His veterans, certain that nothing could stop their Little Corporal, scattered the defenders and sped toward Vienna. Panic swept Vienna, as the government and nobility fled for their lives. The French "barbarians" were coming with their guillotines and firing squads! The emperor Francis II fled with his children, among them a pretty six-year-old princess named Marie-Louise, whom we will meet again. When Napoleon offered a truce, he accepted and peace talks began.

Negotiating, for Napoleon, combined the skills of both the diplomat and the actor. Every move he made was part of a carefully thought-out plan. The idea was to throw the Austrian emissaries off balance and keep them there. To win their confidence, he'd act as the perfect gentleman, calm and reasonable. The next day he'd bully and bluster in order to confuse them and weaken their determination. Once, when they objected to a demand, he swept a display of fine porcelain from the conference table. "I will break you in the same way," he bellowed. They gave in.

The talks dragged on until October, when the Treaty of Campoformio was signed. Austria gave Belgium (the Austrian Netherlands) to France, along with the left bank of the Rhine. It also recognized the Cisalpine (south of the Alps) Republic, created by Napoleon from its holdings in Lombardy. The Cisalpine Republic was Napoleon's country in a very real sense. Not only did he create it without the Director's permission, he organized it, appointing all officials from government ministers to judges.

Napoleon was now a man to be reckoned with. When he returned to Paris, the people hailed him as a conquering hero.

The Directors, however, received him coldly. They'd begun to see him as a monster they themselves had created. No longer was he the awkward boy begging for favors. A military and political force in his own right, he sensed his growing power. Today he overshadowed them. And tomorrow? Surely he'd try to overthrow them. They had to get him out of the way.

That wouldn't have been difficult during the Reign of Terror. A phony charge of treason, a rigged trial, and the guillotine would have settled his case. But one must be careful with a hero commanding 45,000 devoted troops. One must keep him busy elsewhere.

Since Britain still refused to make peace, the Directors saw a chance to kill two birds with one stone. An *Armée d'Angleterre* (Army of England) had been formed along the northern coast. Its mission was to invade Britain, a goal that Frenchmen had tried unsuccessfully to achieve for centuries. Putting Napoleon in charge would occupy him for a long time. If he failed, they could remove him for incompetence. But if he succeeded, France would be on its way to ruling the world.

After an inspection tour early in 1798, Napoleon advised against the scheme. The *Armée d'Angleterre* was too small and untrained for such a task. Worse, an invasion fleet could not slip past the British Royal Navy. If it was put to sea, every ship would be sunk and every man drowned within hours. He did, however, suggest another way to strike at Britain. The road to London lay, not across the English Channel, but through the Middle East. Through Egypt.

The idea of striking at Britain through Egypt did not originate with the Little Corporal. During the French and Indian War (1756 to 1763), Britain had taken Canada after a bitter struggle. France wanted revenge. In 1769, the year of Napoleon's birth, the French foreign minister planned an invasion of Egypt. He wanted to set up a colony there as a French power base in the Middle East. That colony would stretch clear across Egypt to the shores of the Red Sea. Warships built there, or sailed there from France, could control the trade routes across the Indian Ocean. India was Britain's most profitable overseas market; its silver paid most of the Royal Navy's upkeep. Thus, cutting Britain's lifeline to India meant crippling her as a world power.

The plan was filed away until Napoleon revived it and brought it up to date. Egypt seemed an easy target. Although part of the Turkish Empire, it was ruled by the Mamelukes, private armies led by twenty-four chieftains, or beys. Constantly at war with one another, the beys could never unite against a common enemy. Once he defeated them, Napoleon would march overland to India, a plan often described as a romantic dream. Yet there was nothing romantic about it. A glance at the map shows that the distance from Egypt to India is only slightly greater than from Paris to Moscow. An army mounted on camels and horses could have reached India in about four months. There it would have found powerful allies, native princes eager to drive out the English. The Directors jumped at the plan.

At six o'clock, on the morning of May 19, 1798, Napoleon boarded the warship *L'Orient* at Toulon. As he came on deck, a single cannon shot echoed across the harbor. Instantly the vessels anchored nearby sprang to life. Barefooted sailors, each with a long pigtail dangling down his back, raced to their posts. Five-man teams turned heavy wooden wheels, making ropes creak as anchors rose dripping from the muddy bottom. "Topmen" scurried up rope ladders to the masts towering above the decks. Holding on for dear life, they unfurled the sails. Suddenly there was a rustle of loose canvas and the *snap* of sails catching the breeze. Slowly the ships began to move, dipping and rolling and tossing foam. One by one, for eight hours, they slid past *L'Orient*, heading for the open sea. Once clear of the harbor, they formed columns and headed east.

The fleet, the largest military force ever to leave France, consisted of 400 vessels, including thirteen warships. Aboard them were 50,000 men, 700 horses, and 1,000 pieces of field artillery. In addition, they carried the Commission on the Sciences and Arts, a mini-university complete with libraries and scientific instruments. Napoleon was not only determined to conquer, but to learn everything about the land of the pharoahs. To help him, he brought along 150 experts in all fields of knowledge. There were astronomers, botanists, chemists, geologists, zoologists, and mathematicians. Historians were to study Egypt's past, archaeologists to dig into its ancient ruins. Cartographers (mapmakers) were to chart the country and artists were to make a pictorial record of what they'd seen. Engineers had a special task: planning a canal across the Isthmus of Suez to link the Mediterranean with the Red Sea. Although it was not built in his lifetime, Napoleon was the father of the Suez Canal.

The first stop was Malta (June 12), an island fortress held by the Knights of St. John of Jerusalem. Time and again, for two centuries, the Knights had withstood Turkish invaders. But their glory days were past, and they surrendered in return for pensions from the Republic of France. Napoleon gave the Maltese a French-style government, left troops to keep order, and sailed away after only five days.

A miserable voyage lay ahead. For the next two weeks, the weather was rougher than usual for that time of year. Waves crashed against the ships' sides, sending equipment flying. The troops, mostly landlubbers who'd never been on blue water,

learned sailing the hard way. Crowded below decks in filthy
compartments, they ate rotten salt meat and drank yellow water
that reminded them of latrines. "I vomited blood every day,"
an officer wrote his mother. Every soldier was seasick, including the Little Corporal. He spent days in a special bed
made with legs attached to springs to steady it against the ship's
motion. When his stomach was calm, he'd gather his experts
to discuss subjects of interest. These ranged from the meaning
of dreams to the age of the earth and the possibility of life on
other planets.

Misery was combined with danger. British spies had alerted
the Royal Navy when Napoleon sailed from Toulon. A powerful squadron under Rear Admiral Horatio Nelson, who we'll
meet later, was sent in pursuit. Nelson's orders were simple:
Find the enemy, fight him, sink him. Had he caught the
French at sea, there's no way they could have escaped. At the
very least, their fleet would have been scattered; at the worst,
scores of transports would have been captured or sent to the
bottom. That would have been the end of the Little Corporal
and of our story. But luck favored him—this time.

During the early hours of July 1, Napoleon anchored outside
the port of Alexandria. When the sun rose, the city's inhabitants rubbed their eyes in disbelief. Ships! There were ships
as far as the eye could see. Ships were so close together that
their masts seemed like a forest bobbing in the gentle swells.
"My lord, the fleet which has just appeared is immense. One
can neither see its beginning nor its end," the governor wrote
the bey of Cairo, the Egyptian capital. "For the love of God
and His Prophet, send us fighting men." But time had already
run out. The French captured Alexandria before noon. Five
days later they set out for Cairo.

They marched eastward across sixty miles of desert. It was

summer, the worst time of year in Egypt. The sun beat down without mercy. Temperatures soared to 110 degrees Fahrenheit. Winds whipped up sandstorms; each grain of sand felt like a hot needle stabbing into one's skin. The air shimmered and, through the heat waves, there appeared lakes of cool water. Thirsty men ran forward, only to drop as if felled by a bullet; for the "lakes" were mirages, illusions of water.

Those lucky enough to find a village with a well became drunk on the water. They danced, sang, and laughed in hysterical outbursts. One unit drank until their bellies swelled, then ate their biscuits, flat pieces of bread baked hard as stone. "We devoured these provisions with a ferocious appetite," a soldier recalled. "Never have I eaten a better repast. . . . That halt remains engraved in the memories of every soldier in my division as one of the happiest moments of his life." Hundreds of others, crazed with thirst, shot themselves.

Upon reaching the Nile River, the French turned south, heading upstream. Things were better now—for them, not the Egyptians. No love was lost between the two peoples. Charles François kept a diary of the campaign, *Journal of Captain François, Written on a Camel in Egypt*. François saw entire villages wiped out. A village had refused to turn over its food: all nine hundred men, women, and children were massacred "in order to teach a lesson to a half-savage and barbarous people."

On July 21, the invaders reached the village of Embaba on the Nile. From there they saw a scene out of a fairy tale. Ten miles to the southwest the pyramids, man's oldest monuments, glistened in the sunlight. Two miles to the southeast, across the river, rose Cairo's minarets, slender towers from which Muslim priests called the faithful to prayer. But today would see more fighting than praying.

The Egyptian forces, some 25,000 strong, stood between
Embaba and the pyramids. Their main striking force was the
6,000 Mameluke cavalry. The fiercest horsemen on earth, the
Mamelukes were also the most colorful. Red, green, orange,
and yellow were their favorite colors. Each wore a cotton shirt
of these colors, a silken vest, and baggy silk trousers, each leg
of which could hold a large man. Some wore turbans topped
with white feathers, others helmets inlaid with gold and precious stones.

At its bey's command, each unit took its battle position.
They formed in a long line, one next to the other, waiting.
They waited patiently, confidently, fearing no man. Each
Mameluke carried a musket, six pistols, several spears, a club,
battle-axe, dagger, and two curved swords known as scimitars.
Mounted on a sleek Arab horse, he could dash in and kill the
enemy before he knew what was happening. If things went
wrong, he'd escape, leaving behind only his tent. No matter;
he carried his fortune with him in the form of jewels, silks,
and gold coins.

As soon as Napoleon saw the Mamelukes, he gave his
orders. Trumpets blared. "Fall in," sergeants bellowed. "Fix
bayonets!" Soldiers instantly formed hollow squares six
ranks deep, bayonets pointing outward and cannons placed at
each corner. The French were tired, hungry, and far from
home; their enemy was well-rested and on familiar ground.
Yet he didn't have a chance. Though fearless, the Mameluke
fought as an individual, not as part of a team. The Frenchman had discipline, which multiplied his strength many
times over.

Those nearest Napoleon heard him say, pointing to the
pyramids, "Soldiers, forty centuries of history have their eyes
upon you." So did the enemy. Moments later, the clatter of

hoofbeats came from the southwest. The Battle of the Pyramids had begun.

The Mamelukes came like a whirlwind, shouting and waving their weapons. Some stood in their stirrups and fired their pistols; then they threw away the empty weapons, leaving them for their servants to pick up later. Others swung a scimitar in each hand while holding the reins between their teeth.

At a range of half a mile, Napoleon's "beautiful daughters" went into action. Heavy iron balls kicked up dust spouts among the attackers. Horses and riders went down in a welter of dust and blood. Riderless horses, their bellies torn open and trailing their guts, ran about wild-eyed. Men, blown from the saddle, were dragged along the ground when a foot became caught in a stirrup. Still their comrades kept coming.

When the Mamelukes drew near enough to see the "whites of their eyes," tongues of flame lashed out from the squares. By ones and twos, tens and twenties, they tumbled to the ground.

For almost an hour, the Mamelukes gave an awesome display of strength and courage. A captain named Hussein, for example, rode right into a square and, with his scimitar, cut muskets in half as if they were twigs. When he fell wounded, the French spared him out of respect. But in the end courage was no match for firepower. At least 2,000 Mamelukes died; French losses were 29 killed and 120 wounded.

The French enjoyed the fruits of victory. For the rest of the day, they stripped Mameluke bodies in seach of valuables. Some bodies had 200 to 300 gold coins, more than most soldiers had ever seen at one time. Happily, they "put on turbans still wet with blood," an eyewitness reported. "Others proudly draped themselves in sable-lined [capes] or in gold-trimmed jackets." Next day they marched into Cairo.

What a disappointment! From all they'd heard, they'd imagined a treasure city of golden palaces. They found instead a pesthole of filth and disease. Packs of wild dogs, many foaming at the mouth with rabies, roamed the streets. The streets themselves served as graveyards for Muslim holy men, buried in the middle out of respect. Beggars, blinded by an eye disease called trachoma, were everywhere, shouting and holding out their hands. An officer described Cairo in his diary:

> Once you enter Cairo, what do you find? Narrow, unpaved, and dirty streets, dark houses that are falling to pieces, public buildings that look like dungeons, shops that look like stables, an atmosphere [smelling] of dust and garbage, blind men, half-blind men, bearded men, people dressed in rags, pressed together in the streets or squatting, smoking their pipes, like monkeys at the entrance of their cave; a few women of the people . . . hideous, disgusting, hiding their fleshless faces under stinking rags and displaying their pendulous breasts through their torn gowns; yellow, skinny children covered with suppuration [pus], devoured by flies; an unbearable stench, due to the dirt in the houses, the dust in the air, and the smell of food being fried in bad oil in the unventilated bazaars.

Napoleon moved into the bey's palace and invited Cairo's leaders to a meeting. He introduced himself not as General Bonaparte, but El Kebir, "the Great Sultan." Egypt, he said, was now under the protection of the French republic. Its people were free at last. He'd respect their religion and rule according to the Koran, the Muslim Bible. But they must be loyal and obedient. If not, El Kebir knew what to do.

Things were going nicely when a message came from the coast. Napoleon's fleet, his only link to Europe, had been destroyed in a bloody battle. After missing it several times, Admiral Nelson made contact on August 1 at Abukir Bay just east of Alexandria. The opponents were evenly matched: Nelson's fourteen men-of-war to the enemy's thirteen men-of-war and four smaller ships. Toward evening, when least expected, Nelson began the Battle of Abukir Bay, also known as the Battle of the Nile.

Dividing his fleet into two sections, Nelson caught the enemy in a crossfire. The British pressed their advantage, forcing them to choose between surrender or destruction. The climax came aboard *L'Orient*, the French flagship. Admiral Brueys, the fleet's commander, had already been killed by a cannonball when fire broke out on the main deck. Spreading quickly, it ignited the mainmast, bringing it down with a crash. When the fire found barrels of gunpowder stored below decks, *L'Orient* exploded, hurling timbers, guns, and bodies skyward in a gusher of flame. Windows shook twenty-five miles away, and the flash lit up Alexandria bright as day. With their flagship gone, the French surrendered. They'd lost all but two vessels, plus 9,000 men captured or killed. The British lost no ships, but had 128 killed and 677 wounded, including Nelson, when an iron splinter gashed his forehead. A grateful King George III made him a nobleman: Lord Nelson of the Nile.

Napoleon was having lunch with his staff when the messenger arrived. "You seem to get along well in this country," he said, interrupting their meal. "That is very fortunate, because we have no more fleet to take us back to Europe." But not to worry! Every setback was also an opportunity, if used properly. The sea might separate them from home, but it couldn't keep them from India.

The army moved into the Mameluke barracks and settled down for a long stay. Like soldiers anywhere, they learned to amuse themselves. Men visited the pyramids, leaving behind graffiti that can be read to this day. Charles François scratched his name, birthday, rank, unit, and date of visit on the wall of the king's chamber in the great pyramid of Cheops. A Frenchman, it was said, shot off the nose of the Sphinx, a huge stone figure with a human head and a lion's body. Off-duty hours were spent courting the local girls and drinking wine; since Muslims are not allowed to have alcohol, the French made wine from dates.

Wine helped them bear Egypt's bugs and heat, which wore men down faster than anything else. A major wrote home: "When you have finished sightseeing, you return to your house. No comfort, not a single convenience. Flies, mosquitoes, a thousand insects are waiting to take possession of you during the night. Bathed in sweat, exhausted, you spend the hours devoted to rest itching and breaking out in boils. You rise in the morning . . . sick, bleary-eyed, queasy in the stomach, with a bad taste in your mouth, your body covered with pimples, or rather ulcers." "Egypt," another wrote, "is hell."

Still there were those who wouldn't have traded places with a king. Until 1798, the world knew little about Egypt; and what it did know came from inaccurate accounts by travelers over the centuries. Napoleon changed all that. Whenever he sent troops on a mission, scientists went along. The information they gathered laid the foundations for Egyptology, the study of ancient Egypt.

One unit marched south along the Nile in pursuit of Mameluke raiders. The further it marched, the more it seemed to be marching clear out of this world. To its right was the Libyan Desert, or Sand Sea, a wasteland stretching, for all they knew, to the ends of the earth. In the river itself, they saw their first crocodiles, twelve-footers resembling mud-covered logs. The animals lay motionless with open mouths, allowing birds to feed on bits of meat caught between their teeth. Soldiers discovered that they were quite harmless—if their bellies were full. Men bathed naked, near the gaping jaws, without ever being attacked.

They once rounded a bend and froze in amazement. Before them, on both sides of the Nile, was the ruined city of Thebes, Egypt's ancient capital. Gigantic temples, gateways, statues, tombs, and obelisks, stone needles sixty feet high, welcomed them in silence. The soldiers, moved by the same feeling of wonder, clapped their hands and cheered. Then, without waiting for orders, they formed ranks and presented arms. Such was their tribute to the genius of other men long gone.

Dominique Denon, the expedition's artist, began to sketch the ruins. Soldiers begged to let him use their knees for a drawing board, or stood in a circle to shield him from the sun. "I wish to give an idea of this scene to my readers," Denon wrote, "so as to make them share in the feelings I experienced in the presence of such majestic objects, and in the electrifying emotion of an army of soldiers whose refined sensibility made me . . . proud of being a Frenchman."

Thanks to these Frenchmen, modern Egyptians are aware of themselves as a people with a noble past. The French found monuments covered with hieroglyphics, or picture-writing. They copied so many of these that they ran out of pencils; only by melting lead bullets into reeds taken from the Nile could they make others. Still, they couldn't read a word they copied. The key to understanding hieroglyphics was found by an army engineer at Rosetta at the mouth of the Nile. The "Rosetta Stone" is a black rock with inscriptions carved into it. These are written in Greek letters, hieroglyphics, and a (then) unknown language called demotic. By comparing the

Greek, which scholars knew, to the hieroglyphics, they eventually learned to read the picture-writing. Four thousand years of Egyptian history became an open book.

Meantime, Napoleon had his hands full in Cairo. Early in September, he learned that Turkey had declared war on France. Already Turkish agents were urging Egyptians to destroy the "infidels," enemies of Islam. The French were said to be "atheists," men without God, and "sons of Satan." Any Muslim who died fighting them would go straight to heaven.

The people of Cairo needed little encouragement. Although Napoleon said they were free, they'd merely exchanged Mameluke for French tyranny. From sunup to sundown, they were regulated, insulted, and terrorized by the invaders. Every Egyptian had to wear the tricolor badge and every Nile boat fly the tricolor flag. No longer could holy men be buried in the streets, a public health measure deeply resented by the faithful. Egyptian girls appeared, unveiled, with their infidel lovers; a sin in the eyes of the faithful. Egyptians were taxed, forced to lend money, and pay fees for everything from selling a house to writing a will.

Those who protested lost their property or met Bartholomew the Greek, Napoleon's favorite policeman. A tall, dark fellow with blazing eyes and a temper to match, he went about town with an executioner's sword over his shoulder. Heads always rolled when Bartholomew appeared. He once gave French officers a sack full of heads while they were having dinner, and was surprised that they lost their appetites.

On October 10, Cairo rebelled. As crowds ran through the streets killing every Frenchman they met, the Mosque El Azhar, a Muslim house of worship, became rebel headquarters. Napoleon lost no time in sending for his "beautiful daughters." They pounded El Azhar without letup. The bombardment was so intense that the people of Cairo, who'd never seen such a thing, begged God to save them from the iron demons. French soldiers finally fought their way into El Azhar. Not only did they kill and loot, they urinated in the mosque and spat on the holy Koran. The rebellion ended in 24 hours with 300 Frenchmen and 2,000 to 3,000 Egyptians killed.

Napoleon wasn't satisfied. Egyptians needn't love him, but they must obey him. And since obedience came from fear, he'd teach them about terror. The decision to use terror was taken calmly, without any show of emotion. Terror seemed logical, and therefore necessary, like a bad-tasting medicine. He wrote General Berthier, his chief of staff: "You will have the goodness, Citizen General, to . . . have the heads of all prisoners captured with weapons in hand cut off. They will be taken to the bank of the Nile . . . after dark; their headless corpses will be thrown into the river." About thirty heads were chopped each night during the next few weeks. Those who saw the headless bodies floating in the river got the message and passed it on to their friends. Cairo settled into an uneasy quiet.

In February 1799, Napoleon learned that Turkish armies were massing to invade Egypt; one in Syria* under Ahmed Pasha Djezzar—"Ahmed the Butcher"—another on the island of Rhodes. If the Turks expected him to wait for their attack, they didn't know their man. "*Attaque! Toujours l'attaque!*" Rather than allow them to join forces, he attacked immediately.

The objective of Napoleon's "Syrian campaign" was actually

---

*Syria at this time was made up of today's Syria, in addition to Lebanon, Israel, and Jordan.

General Bonaparte speaks to his Egyptian subjects. Drawing based on a painting by Georges Bougain. Napoleon was as ruthless with the people he conquered, using systematic terror to gain their obedience, as he was on the battlefield. BELOW, the land battle of Abukir Bay, a stunning victory over the Turkish forces, and Napoleon's last battle in Egypt.

the Holy Land, a battleground for thousands of years. Hebrews and Romans, Crusaders and Muslims, had fought countless wars in the biblical "land of milk and honey." History was about to repeat itself.

After a grueling march across the desert, the French reached Jaffa in early March 1799. Located on the Mediterranean shore, Jaffa was a walled city defended by 5,000 Turks. Although in a strong position, they were outnumbered three to one. Napoleon, hoping to avoid a fight, sent an officer to point this out to the Turkish commander. Unfortunately, he wouldn't listen to any talk of surrender. Vowing to fight to the end, he had the officer beheaded and sent the head to Napoleon as a sign of his determination.

Napoleon, too, was determined. On March 7, his engineers blew a hole in Jaffa's wall and soldiers poured in. They were in a nasty mood and, once inside, went on a rampage. For a full day and night, they killed anyone who crossed their path. Men and women, young and old, were shot or stabbed; women were often raped, then murdered. But Jaffa was not Toulon, where Napoleon had to stand by while his superiors ordered a massacre. Now he was in charge, and duty-bound to protect civilians; by not doing so, he shared the killers' guilt. Indeed, he was about to earn an evil reputation that would stay with him for the rest of his life.

During the attack, 3,000 Turkish soldiers had fled to a fortress in the city's center. The next day, two of Napoleon's aides promised them good treatment if they gave up peacefully. But as soon as they did, Napoleon said he couldn't spare the food to feed them or the men to guard them. They must die.

Napoleon's excuses were a pack of lies. There was plenty of food in Jaffa—the Turks' own rations stored in warehouses and in the fortress. Two hundred Frenchmen armed with light

cannons and grapeshot could easily have kept them in line.
Napoleon's real purpose was to send a message to Ahmed the
Butcher. Ahmed, he knew, didn't scare easily. Well, then,
he'd show the Turk that he, too, could be ruthless and that
he'd better surrender before it was too late. If that meant
murdering prisoners, then so be it.

General Berthier was ordered to prepare a massacre. But
since massacres offended his soldierly honor, he appealed to
Napoleon's conscience. Napoleon bristled; when something
was necessary, he had no conscience. "I'll tell you what," he
said, pointing to a Christian monastery nearby. "Go on in
there. And if you know what's good for you, never come out
again!" Berthier obeyed.

The Turks were seated on the ground in front of Napoleon's
tent under heavy guard. Many had their children with them;
this was permitted so the children might help keep their fathers
calm. André Peyrusse, an army paymaster, wrote his mother
about what happened next:

The next morning, [prisoners] were taken to the sea-
shore and two battalions began to shoot them down.
Their only hope of saving their lives was to throw
themselves into the sea; they did not hesitate, and all
tried to escape by swimming. They were shot at leisure,
and in an instant the sea was red with blood and
covered with corpses. A few were lucky enough to
reach some rocks. Soldiers were ordered to follow them
in boats and to finish them off. . . . Once the execution was over, we fondly hoped that it would not
be repeated and that the other prisoners would be
spared. . . . Our hopes were soon disappointed when,
the next day, 1,200 Turkish artillerymen, who for two
days had been kept without food in front of General

Bonaparte's tent, were taken to be executed. The soldiers had been carefully instructed not to waste ammunition, and they were ferocious enough to stab
them with their bayonets. Among the victims we found
many children who, in the act of death, had clung
to their fathers. This example will teach our enemies
that they cannot count on French good faith, and
sooner or later, the blood of these 3,000 victims will
be upon us.

Vengeance came swiftly and in a horrible form—bubonic
plague. Known as the "Black Death," this disease had claimed
millions during the Middle Ages. Although no longer a problem in Europe, it still ravaged the Middle East. On the day
after the massacres (March 11), French soldiers began to de-
velop high fever and "buboes," swollen glands that burst when
filled with pus. Hundreds died in agony. Army morale sank
to an all-time low. Men, paralyzed with fear, demanded a
return to Cairo.

Napoleon wouldn't hear of the idea. Just as he'd coolly
ordered massacres to terrorize an enemy, he coolly faced
plague to calm his men. Accompanied by his staff, he visited
a hospital filled with plague victims, in itself an act of great
courage. No one came near that place of his own free will;
food was left a "safe" distance away, to be fetched by the
doctors' helpers. But he walked through the crowded wards,
spoke to those who could still hear him, and even helped carry
the body of a soldier whose uniform was sticky with pus. Word
of his visit raced through camp, as he knew it would. The
troops began to settle down. If their Little Corporal could go
among the sick so calmly, the plague couldn't be *that* bad.
They must be as brave as him.

Leaving its sick behind, the army set out for Acre and the

showdown with Ahmed the Butcher. Napoleon sent a message ahead, calling upon the city to surrender and trust in his mercy: "Since God gives me victory, I wish to follow His example and be merciful and compassionate." We don't know if he wrote this with a straight face. The Butcher, however, knew the value of the general's promises. He tore up the letter, calling upon God to destroy the infidels. After Jaffa, he and his men meant to sell their lives dearly.

Acre was built on a narrow peninsula jutting into the Mediterranean. Nearly surrounded by water, its land side protected by thick walls, it was the strongest fortress in Syria. In addition, a British naval squadron stood offshore, sending reinforcements as needed, among them Colonel Louis de Phélippeaux. He and Napoleon had been students together at the École Militaire in Paris, sharing a desk in class. They'd hated one another at first sight; their shins were always black and blue from the kicks they had given each other. When the Revolution began, Phélippeaux, a royalist, made his way to England. Now he'd settle scores with both the Revolution and his boyhood enemy.

Napoleon began the siege by digging trenches and placing cannons behind mounds of earth. The guns, concentrated on a small section of wall, would hammer it for days without letup. Phélippeaux, commanding the Turkish artillery, answered them shot for shot. The trenches filled with bodies, which were simply covered with a thin layer of dirt. During a bombardment, or even when the wind blew, soldiers were horrified to see a rotting hand, or head, emerge from the ground before their very eyes. When an opening was made in the wall, they'd dash forward, into a storm of grape and canister shot. Those who made it to the opening were met by Turks with bayonets and scimitars. The French learned to fear these turbaned warriors. Before an attack, it was often necessary to give them "liquid courage," extra wine to get them moving.

The Turks sent an army from Damascus to break the siege. Napoleon, warned of the attack, left part of his force at Acre and swept southward with the remainder. On April 16, he routed the enemy at Mount Tabor. That night the French slept in nearby Nazareth, once the home of Jesus. Soldiers, sightseeing at the Church of Nazareth, made coarse jokes; they'd lost their faith during the Revolution and saw no reason to respect the ancient building. Others, however, renewed their faith in the little church. A fellow who'd had a finger shot off buried it in the cemetery. "I don't know what will happen to the rest of my carcass," he said, "but at least I have a finger in the Holy Land."

The siege of Acre dragged on for another month. With no end in sight, and French losses mounting, Napoleon ordered a retreat. Not that he called it a retreat; far from it. During a stopover at Jaffa on May 27, he wrote the Directors to describe his "victory." He'd won every battle and was about to capture Acre, he said, when spies revealed that plague had broken out in the city. Rather than risk the army, he decided to end the siege. The report was a lie from start to finish. He hadn't come close to taking Acre. Of the 13,000 Frenchmen who'd invaded Syria, 1,200 were killed in battle and 1,000 died of disease; another 2,300 were sick or badly wounded.

That same day he revisited the Jaffa hospital, where fifty plague victims still clung to life. This time, however, there were no heroic gestures. He walked through the wards, striking the sides of his boots with his riding whip. Then, turning to a doctor, he said that the Turks would arrive in a few hours. Those strong enough to travel should be carried on army horses; the others must be poisoned with overdoses of opium.

They were given the drug, but for some reason survived to be taken prisoner. Still the fact remains: Napoleon ordered the murder of sick men who'd served him faithfully.

Returning to Cairo allowed the army to gather its strength for the next battle. A British squadron had landed the Turkish force from Rhodes at Abukir Bay. Taking the defenders by surprise, it captured a fort on the shore of the bay, wiped out its garrison and dug in, waiting to see what happened next. They learned that it was always a mistake to leave the next move up to Napoleon.

He rushed to the scene and, on July 25, attacked. Both armies had about 10,000 men, but except for that they were worlds apart. Napoleon was in top form that day. Using massed artillery, he blew a hole in the enemy line and sent his cavalry through it. The Turks panicked. Hundreds were cut down where they stood; many others jumped into the bay, where the French shot them like fish in a barrel. The water became filled with brightly colored turbans and sashes—and bodies. Napoleon called Abukir "one of the most beautiful battles I ever saw." It was also his last battle in Egypt.

Several days later, a packet of European newspapers arrived in the French camp. Napoleon hadn't seen a newspaper in a year, and these came as a shock. They told of one French disaster after another. Nelson's victory at Abukir Bay had brought about an alliance of Britain, Austria, Turkey, Russia, and the kingdom of Naples. A Russian-Austrian army under Field Marshal Alexandr Suvorov, a reckless officer described as "hero, buffoon, half-demon and half-dirt," had retaken northern Italy. Frenchmen were angry, frightened, and clamoring for leadership. The Directory seemed about to collapse. Here was the chance of a lifetime, and he had to be in Paris in time to pick up the pieces.

On August 24, 1799, he and twelve aides secretly boarded a ship at Alexandria. Luckily, the coast was clear for the moment and they got away safely. During the next six weeks, they dodged British warships, landing in France on October 9.

Things went from bad to worse for those left behind. In 1801, British and Turkish armies invaded Egypt, forcing them to surrender or face annihilation. The surrender terms, however, were most generous. In return for leaving Egypt, the French could keep their weapons and be sent home in British ships. Of the 50,000 men who'd sailed three years before, only 23,000 lived to tell the tale. Yet few of their countrymen cared to listen. For within a month of his landing, Napoleon had overthrown the Directory and become dictator of France.

The Napoleonic era had begun.

EMPEROR OF THE REPUBLIC

*"The government of the Republic
is entrusted to a hereditary Emperor."*
—FRENCH SENATE RESOLUTION, May 4, 1804

NAPOLEON RETURNED to a nation in turmoil. Not only were there military setbacks, living conditions hadn't been as bad since the start of the Revolution. The government, unable to pay its bills, issued money as fast as the printing presses could turn it out. Prices skyrocketed, until money wasn't worth the paper it was printed on. Unemployment spread, leaving millions desperate and without hope. The wealthy showed off in their fine clothes and carriages, while the poor seethed with resentment. "In Paris," a police report noted, "the newly rich—profiteers, suppliers, and speculators . . . flaunt their luxuries in the eyes of those who can eat only from time to time."

The government seemed unable to do anything right. According to the constitution, power was shared by two branches of government: the Councils and the Directory. A legislature consisting of two Councils—the Elders and the Five Hundred—made the laws that the five Directors were supposed to enforce. Unfortunately, the members of both branches were greedy and jealous of each other's power. Unable to work together, they bickered while the country went to the dogs. People had good reason to be disgusted with politicians. They wanted work and food and peace—peace at any price, even dictatorship.

Convinced that only a dictatorship could save the country,

some politicians were planning a *coup d'état*, a sudden overthrow of the government. The only problem was that they
needed a "sword," a general to do the job for them. He'd have
to be a simpleminded fellow, whom they could use and then
toss aside when he'd served his purpose.

Napoleon came along at just the right moment. Millions
of Frenchmen saw him as the only bright star in a dark sky.
His Italian victories had made him famous; his Egyptian defeats
were pushed into the background by his successes. The Battle
of the Pyramids made it easy to forget Acre. The land battle
of Abukir canceled the naval disaster of Abukir. People believed in him because they wanted to believe, *needed* to believe, in someone.

Once again Napoleon became an actor. He played two roles,
each suited to a particular audience. To the public, he presented the face of a solid citizen. He wore civilian clothes,
went to the theater, and lectured on Egypt. Power? No, power
didn't interest him; he only wanted to serve the nation in any
way he could. For the plotters, he played the plain soldier,
innocent in the ways of the world. Surely he was a willing
fool who'd gladly do their bidding. In the meantime, the man
behind the masks plotted against everyone.

The *coup d'état* began with rumors. On November 9, 1799,
the plotters let it be known that a conspiracy against the government had been uncovered. Urged on by Lucien Bonaparte,
a member of the Five Hundred, the Councils gave his elder
brother command of the Paris garrison and moved to a palace
outside the city for safety. Actually, they'd walked right into
a trap. Once outside Paris, whose people might interfere on
their behalf, they could be pressured into handing over power
to the plotters. If not, the troops would make them see
"reason."

The next day, Napoleon entered the Elders' meeting hall with a military escort. Traitors, he announced, were everywhere. Unless they put their trust in him, the Republic was doomed. When several Elders demanded the traitors' names, he began to shout. Traitors! Those who questioned him were traitors! Then, pointing to the soldiers, he warned: "Remember that the god of war and the god of luck are marching alongside me!" Anyone who resisted him would be crushed "by the thunderbolt of war." The Elders sat quietly for a moment, too stunned to reply. "Get out of here, General," an aide whispered, "you don't know what you are saying." But he ranted on for another few minutes before leaving the hall. The *coup d'état* was not going well.

The Council of Five Hundred knew about the general's threats when he strode into their meeting hall. As soon as he appeared, members pointed to him as the real traitor. "Death to the traitor!" they cried, shaking their fists in his face. "Dictator!" "Outlaw him!" One member, a giant of a man, grabbed him by the collar, practically lifting him off the ground. Someone else pushed him; another slapped him.

Napoleon was fearless in battle. Time and time again, he'd come close to death without batting an eyelash. But this was different. Ever since the Tuileries massacre in 1792, he'd been terrified of angry crowds. The anger he now faced opened the old wound. He lost his nerve. He became dizzy, the room spun, his legs turned to rubber. His hands reached up to his face, which was covered with large red pimples, souvenirs of Egypt. Without realizing it, he began to scratch them—hard. Blood was trickling down his cheeks when his men dragged him outside, to the palace courtyard.

The cool air brought him to his senses. Touching his face, he raised a bloodstained hand to the assembled troops. "I

wanted to speak to them [the Five Hundred]," he cried, "and
they met me with daggers!" In return for English gold, traitors
had tried to slay him as they hoped to slay the Republic.
"Soldiers! I led you to victory, can I count on you?"

He could. Cheers filled the courtyard: "*Vive Bonaparte!*"
("Long live Bonaparte!")

Soldiers with muskets and bayonets burst into the hall minutes later. There were no explanations, no legal make-believe.
Joachim Murat, their commander, snapped an order: "Throw
them out of the windows!" Without waiting for the bayonet,
the Five Hundred leaped from the windows on their own. It
was a short drop to the ground and, after landing, they ran
across the lawn, trailing their red robes behind them.

That night the Elders abolished the Directory and handed
over power to a committee of three "Consuls." Their action
was approved by the Five Hundred, some of whom had been
dragged back by the soldiers. All was well. The government
had been overthrown. The plotters were in power. There was
only one hitch: Consul Bonaparte became head of the committee.

Having wielded their sword, the plotters soon found that
they'd outsmarted themselves. Napoleon, backed by loyal
troops, took the lead in drafting France's new constitution.
Supreme power was given to the First Consul, himself; he
selected the Second and Third Consuls, advisers whose advice
he needn't follow. The First Consul appointed all officials
from small-town mayors to government ministers. He chose
the Council of State, which he guided in drafting bills for the
legislature. The legislature consisted of a Tribunate to discuss
each bill, a Legislative Body to vote on it, and a Senate to
decide if it was constitutional. Note: lawmakers could not
propose laws on their own, only deal with those presented to

them. They were, moreover, elected by a few thousand of the richest men, who had everything to gain from loyalty to the First Consul. In fact, if not in law, France was a dictatorship.

Napoleon didn't hide this from the people. He knew they'd had enough of the Revolution. On December 15, he announced: "Citizens . . . The Revolution is ended." He was so sure of himself that he allowed Frenchmen to vote on the constitution and his dictatorship. The vote was honest, as near as we can tell; 3,011,007 voted yes; 1,562 no. True, only men of property could vote. But they weren't bribed or bullied in any way. And there were few protests from nonvoters when the results were announced. If democracy means that people choose their form of government, then the First Consul ruled by the will of the people. That is more than can be said for the Terrorists or the Directors, who never put their actions to the vote. Or, for that matter, many of the governments in our world today.

In February 1800, Napoleon welcomed the new century by moving into the Tuileries with Josephine. Taking possession of the old royal palace was a milestone in his life. Eight years before, he'd watched the mob slaughter the Swiss Guards under their bedroom windows. That experience had changed him; and now he'd change France. He began with the Tuileries itself. Revolutionary slogans still covered its walls; liberty trees still grew in the courtyard. He ordered the walls whitewashed and the trees torn up by their roots. "Get rid of all that!" he ordered his staff. "I don't want that kind of crap!"

THE FIRST CONSUL's first problem was military. He'd taken power by force, but he needed peace (at least for the time being) to keep it. The war kept him from focusing his energies on the rebuilding of France, without which the Revolution might explode again. Things were already looking up. Russia had quit the war over disagreements with its allies. Once again Austria, overjoyed at its Italian victories, was the chief enemy. If he could defeat Austria quickly, Britain would probably end the costly struggle.

Napoleon's second Italian campaign took the enemy by surprise. This time he came through the Alps, over the Great St. Bernard Pass. Hannibal had crossed the Alps two thousand years earlier with his war elephants. But elephants, unlike cannons, can move on their own. Getting his beautiful daughters over the St. Bernard was a battle in itself. Nowadays, one can cross the pass on an all-weather highway. In 1800, however, it was rocky and snow covered, making it impossible to wheel cannons along. He solved the problem by taking them apart and placing them in tree trunks that had been hollowed out like troughs that men could pull uphill. Within five days (May 10 to 15, 1800), the army was through the pass and streaming toward the Lombard Plain *behind* the Austrian lines.

The showdown came at Marengo in southern Piedmont on June 14. Marengo was a fierce fight that Napoleon almost lost. Luckily, the arrival of fresh troops saved the day—and his reputation. Having broken the Austrian resistance, he left his aides to mop up and returned to Paris on July 2, after an absence of only fifty-seven days.

All of France had been awaiting the news from Italy. Now that it was better than anyone had expected, people could no longer contain themselves. The next morning, as cannons announced the First Consul's arrival at the Tuileries, thousands of Parisians gathered around the palace. Their cheers brought him to the balcony. He, too, was overjoyed. "Do you hear that?" he asked his secretary. "Those shouts are as sweet to me as Josephine's voice."

Napoleon faces the Council of Five Hundred, November 10, 1799. This drawing, after a painting by François Bouchot, is an example of Napoleonic propaganda. In reality, the Council's attack paralyzed Napoleon with fear and he had to be dragged from the room by his own troops. BELOW, Napoleon, standing at left, watches the Army of Italy crossing the Alps. Note how the cannon wheels are being carried on horseback, while soldiers drag the cannons themselves on sleds made from hollowed-out logs.

Napoleon seemed to have a magic touch: everything he did turned out right. Austria made peace early in 1801, confirming the Treaty of Campoformio. In the spring of 1802, Britain signed the Treaty of Amiens, giving France peace for the first time in a decade. The people showed their gratitude by voting 3,568,885 to 8,374 to make him First Consul for life. His powers, already large, were increased. He could name his successor, make treaties on his own, change the constitution, and appoint the lawmakers. Except for the title, he had become the king of France.

THE PERSON WHO SAID, "God made Bonaparte, and then He rested," had a point. Napoleon's four-and-a-half years as First Consul (November 1799 to May 1804) were the most productive in French history. Using his powers to the fullest, he pumped life into a country weary of revolution and war. In doing so, he proved that dictatorships are not all alike. A dictatorship may accomplish a great deal if the leader is intelligent and able. Napoleon was both. From the moment he took over, he made his influence felt in all areas of national life. Many of his reforms are still in effect, permanent parts of the national heritage. Having brought the Revolution to rest, he preserved and strengthened its achievements, carrying them to other lands, even across the seas. These accomplishments, not his battles, still endear him to the French people.

The Revolution had taught him that poverty is dangerous. He once said, "I fear a revolt caused by lack of bread more than a great battle." Battles kill thousands; revolts of the poor destroy entire societies. Napoleon was neither softhearted nor cruel toward the poor. He was practical. For their own good and the nation's, he decreed that they must work or be punished. Beggars were to be arrested, fed, and given jobs. If a beggar had no trade, he'd learn one in a government school. If he couldn't work, he'd go to a poor house to be cared for by the state. If he wouldn't work, he'd find laziness painful. He'd be whipped and made to work under armed guard.

The First Consul regulated workers in various ways. Workers, he insisted, couldn't be their own people; since they depended upon others for a living, they had to be obedient and quiet. Thus, in any dispute, only the employer's word was accepted. No one represented the workers or defended his rights. Trade unions were forbidden and it became a crime to organize or belong to one. Strikes were illegal. Every worker was issued a *livret*, or "labor book," to keep tabs on his movements. The *livret* told an employer, or a policeman, everything about him: date of birth, physical description, address, military service. Whenever he changed jobs, or traveled outside his home area, he had to show it to the authorities. Being found without one's *livret* brought six months at hard labor.

Napoleon created thousands of jobs within a short time. Factories were built and new industries begun with a stroke of a pen. Sugar, for example, had always come from the British or French West Indies. Since these sources were easily cut off in wartime, he ordered experiments in producing sugar from European-grown crops. The experiments paid off with the sugar beet, which is still Europe's main source of sugar.

Millions of francs were spent on public works projects, which were meant to do several things at once. Not only did they create jobs, they improved communications, making it easier to prepare for war. When Napoleon took over, France had 500 miles of canals; he built an additional 1,200 miles, linking all of the chief river systems. He also built harbors, docks, bridges, tunnels; over 40,000 miles of roads were built or repaired.

Under Napoleon, large towns "spoke" to each other by sem-
aphore telegraph, a device for sending and receiving messages
rapidly. France was covered by a network of T-shaped towers
with cross beams that could be set in various positions, each
having its own meaning. Since the towers were never more
than seven miles apart, messages traveled long distances within
minutes. For example, it took five minutes for a message to
go the 150 miles from Paris to Lille.

The First Consul found Paris a city of the Middle Ages,
dreary, dirty, and cramped. He changed it into a capital worthy
of a proud nation. For the first time in its thousand-year history, Paris had a full-time fire department and a system of
sewers; tourists now take boat tours through these underground
rivers. Stone bridges were built over the Seine, each named
for a Napoleonic battle. Old streets were widened and new
ones opened. Unlike most European streets, these were paved
to save pedestrians from walking in the mud; some even had
paved sidewalks. Lamps lit them at night, and houses were
numbered; it was Napoleon's idea to have even numbers on
one side of a street, odd numbers on the other. The Bank of
France, another of his creations, lent money at low interest
rates to pay for these improvements.

Napoleon had a keen interest in what the public thought
of him. Often he and an aide put on plain clothes and roamed
the streets of Paris at night. They'd visit the small shops in the
rue de l'Arbre Sec or the rue Saint-Honoré, where he'd ask
pointed questions. "Your shop seems to be very busy—do
many people come here? Tell me: What do they say about
that joker, Bonaparte?" Sometimes the shopkeepers glowered
but held their tongues. Sometimes they threw him out. Why,
the nerve of that young puppy! How dare he insult the savior
of France! He'd return to the Tuileries, laughing all the way.

Religion, however, was one subject he never laughed about. Like so many educated people of the time, he believed in God, but not in what any religion or church said about Him. During the voyage to Egypt, he had lengthy discussions on the subject with his scientists. Whenever anyone questioned God's existence, he'd point to the starry sky and say: "Very ingenious, Messieurs; but who made all *that?*" Only God, all-knowing and all-powerful, could have created the universe and set in motion the laws by which it operates. Yet he also claimed that man could know nothing about the creator. God is supernatural, beyond nature, and therefore beyond man's ability to learn about him.

Napoleon insisted that religion was a human invention and that priests were swindlers who used superstition to rob the people. But atheists, those who said there was no God, were even worse. They deserved the firing squad: "Men who do not believe in God—one does not govern them, one shoots them." Although religion was false, people needed faith; atheists, who destroyed their faith, were enemies of the state.

Given the realities of life, Napoleon believed that there'd always be rich and poor, happy and miserable, people. Religion dulled the pains of overwork and poverty with promises of happiness in the next world. Without it, there'd be no morality, no way for society to exist. "When a man is dying of hunger near another who stuffs himself, he cannot resign himself to the difference unless there is an authority that can say to him, 'God wills it so; there must be rich and poor in this world; but hereafter, and for all eternity, the division of things will take place differently.' " Thus, religion was at once a myth and a necessity.

Unlike the Terrorists, who persecuted religion, Napoleon wanted to use it to support his dictatorship. He was especially

keen on winning over the Roman Catholic Church. Making
peace with the Church meant ending the rebellion in the
Vendée, thus silencing his foreign critics and increasing his
influence in Catholic countries, especially Belgium and Italy.
He even planned on using Catholic missionaries as spies in
Asia, Africa, and Latin America.

In July 1801, the First Consul signed a Concordat—a treaty
between church and state—with Pope Pius VII. Although the
Concordat recognized Roman Catholicism as the religion of
the majority of Frenchmen, he refused to restore it as the
official state church. Nor did he return church properties
seized during the Revolution; instead, the government agreed
to pay priests' salaries. Best of all, Catholics gained the right
to worship as they pleased. As a sign of his good faith, Napoleon
reopened the churches. Church bells, silent during a decade
of revolution, rang out across the land, summoning the faithful
to prayer.

Grateful Catholics saw the First Consul as God's answer to
their prayers. Prayers for his health were said throughout the
land. Old women crossed themselves, blessing him "for giving
us back our Sunday." Despite bitter quarrels in the years ahead,
Pius VII always had a warm spot in his heart for Napoleon.
After his defeat at Waterloo, the Holy Father begged the allies
to have mercy upon the fallen dictator.

The Concordat was followed by Napoleon's finest achievement: the Civil Code, or Code Napoleon. When he took
power, there was no such thing as French law, only hundreds
of local codes inherited from the past. One area might be
guided by church law, another by feudal law, and yet another
by ancient customs. There were also the 14,400 laws passed
during the Revolution, which often contradicted each other
as well as earlier laws. The result was a confusing mishmash.

Right and wrong depended upon where you happened to live. Something that was legal in one town might be illegal a few miles away. A brilliant lawyer in one place might be an ignoramus elsewhere.

The First Consul ordered a committee of experts to write a set of laws for the whole of France. He encouraged the committee and, when it lagged, prodded it into action. He attended its meetings, often interrupting with probing questions and keen insights. Thanks to him, his work became law in March 1804.

The Civil Code is a masterpiece of logic and clarity, written in language anyone can understand. Its basic principles are *liberté* and *egalité*, the main ideas of the French Revolution. Liberty took many forms: freedom of religion, separation of church and state, freedom to choose one's occupation, the right to get a divorce. But equality was its crowning glory. Napoleon knew that people wanted equality most of all, which explains his motto: "A career open to all talents, without distinctions of birth." By ending hereditary privileges, the Code gave Frenchmen the opportunity to go as far as their talents and energies allowed. All professions were opened to every qualified person. All men, regardless of background, were equal before the law. All must pay taxes according to their means. Property was sacred: everyone could own property and use it as they wished, except as determined by law.

The Civil Code also had a less liberal side—at least by today's standards. It made men kings in their own homes; disobedient children could be imprisoned for six months at a time and wives had few rights. This was in keeping with Napoleon's belief that women were naturally inferior to men, that they were too emotional to think logically. "Women are our property," he insisted, they are "mere machines to make children." And the more children there were, the more soldiers there would be.

Nevertheless, these defects were outweighed by the Civil Code's benefits, felt far beyond France's borders. For nearly two centuries, it was the basis of legal systems throughout the world. Long after Napoleon's death, places as different as the state of Louisiana, Bolivia, Egypt, Rumania, Japan, and the Dominican Republic modeled their laws upon it. Even Communist Yugoslavia borrowed from it heavily. During his last years, Napoleon saw it as his finest achievement. He could rightly say: "My glory is not to have won forty battles, for Waterloo's defeat will destroy the memory of so many victories. But what nothing will destroy, what will live forever, is my Civil Code."

The Civil Code did not extend to politics and government. Napoleonic France was a dictatorship, and dictators always put themselves above the law. The First Consul followed the law when it suited his purposes. When it didn't, he brushed it aside. There was no *liberté* to challenge him, no *egalité* in sharing his powers. Where power was concerned, *nécessité* (necessity) ruled. And *nécessité* knew no law. He'd do anything to keep his power and increase it.

Napoleon believed that government was *for* the people, not *by* the people. Ordinary people were too ignorant to know what was good for them or how to bring it about. Just as sheep needed a shepherd, they needed to be ruled by a man of genius, like himself. He had no doubt about his own abilities. In his own eyes, he knew more than any of his subjects; indeed, he boasted, "I know more in my little finger than they do in all their heads put together."

This made sense when he recalled the dark days of the French Revolution. The Revolution had shown him humanity

at its worst. From that experience, he concluded that people—
all people—are despicable. "Bah!" became his favorite expression. His hatred of humanity is revealed in hundreds of sayings
that have come down to us. Some of these were written down
without his knowledge; others were told to aides with the full
knowledge that they'd become part of the historical record.
Napoleon didn't care. "Savage man is a dog," he'd snap. When
dealing with people, "I start out by believing the worst." He
defied anyone to trick him, since "Men would have to be
exceptional rascals to be as bad as I assume them to be."
Another time he said, "People certainly are worthy of the
contempt which they inspire in me!" But if he inspired contempt in others, it was because they were too foolish to know
better.

Napoleon's theory of government reflected his hatred of
humanity. It is summarized in two short sayings: "Men are
moved by two levers only: fear and self-interest," and "The
strong are good; only the weak are wicked." Fear kept people
in line, so that only the strong were fit to rule. Self-interest
meant that everyone had their price. A wise ruler bought his
servants' loyalty with titles and offices, money and praise. He
bought his people's loyalty with sound laws and strong government. But if these failed, he turned to his soldiers, policemen, and executioners.

The First Consul enforced his wishes by creating something
we've become familar with in the twentieth century: the police
state. A police state is a nation where the police, particularly
the secret police, stamp out all ideas and actions the leaders
consider dangerous. Other dictatorships—Nazi Germany and
Communist Russia—later took over and perfected police-state
methods. But the thing itself was invented by Napoleon.

His secret police were headed by Joseph Fouché, a former

Terrorist with plenty of blood on his hands. As Minister of
Police, Fouché made sure no one felt safe. Safety bred self-
confidence, and that led to opposition. Thus, political parties
were abolished and their leaders arrested. A network of spies
and paid informers blanketed the country. They were everywhere—in cafés, at the theater, in stage coaches—listening
to people's conversations. Citizens were followed, mail opened
at the post office, and priests encouraged to report anything
of interest told to them during confession.

Those who protested were put beyond the law's protection.
Nécessité made Napoleon revive the lettre de cachet and use
it as ruthlessly as any king. And it was necessary to do everything in secret. By arresting people secretly, the police chose
the moment to strike and to spread fear, which in turn discouraged opposition. The accused was held in a secret prison,
cut off from contact with the world. Search as they might,
loved ones could not learn their whereabouts until the police
were ready to tell. Sometimes they never told.

There was nobody to appeal to if you were wronged by the
government. Trials of political offenders were reserved for secret courts where the accused was not allowed to have a lawyer.
Napoleon had strong opinions about lawyers: he hated them.
Lawyers, he said, "stir up trouble and are the authors of crime
and treason. . . . I should like to cut out the tongues of [any]
who use them against the government." In effect he did, by
keeping them away from those who needed their help.

Napoleon was no mass murderer. When he used the death
penalty, it was for crimes like treason and murder, or to set a
harsh example. Still, those convicted of political crimes suffered frightfully. They'd be kept in prison, often with an iron
ball and chain clamped to a leg, for as long as he wished. Or
they'd be locked up in insane asylums, since anyone who

opposed him was obviously "crazy." Even release did not always mean freedom: many people were sent into "internal exile," told where to live and kept under police supervision for the rest of their lives.

Yet most Frenchmen were never touched by the dictatorship. If you kept quiet and minded your own business, you had nothing to fear. Some people, however, couldn't do either. For them, Napoleon was the devil himself. Revolutionaries accused him of betraying their sacred cause. Royalists would settle for nothing less than a restoration of the Bourbons, the old royal family. Both wanted him dead.

Killing Napoleon seemed easy, since he never worried about his personal safety. He carried no weapons, wore no armor, and had no bodyguards. When he appeared in public, there was no effort to keep the crowds away. Often he'd visit the public gardens in Paris, allowing people to stare at him, jostle him, even squeeze against him. Such openness made him popular, but also an easy target for assassins. He once listed thirty-one attempts on his life, some of them too close for comfort.

The first occurred on December 24, 1800. At that time, the war with Britain was still in full swing. The British government believed that getting rid of Napoleon was the only way to bring lasting peace to Europe. When royalists escaped across the English Channel, it hoped to use them for what we might call "state terrorism." They were given money and helped to form commando-type units to fight alongside the Vendée rebels. It also allowed them to have a training camp for assassins near the city of Southampton. That camp was run by a fanatical peasant named Georges Cadoudal. Known as Goliath to his friends, Cadoudal was a short, bull-necked man with red hair, a broken nose, and one eye larger than the other. He despised Napoleon and lived only to see him dead.

In the fall of 1800, Cadoudal sent three agents to give the First Consul a "Christmas present." A large wine barrel was to be filled with gunpowder, bullets, and jagged pieces of iron. The barrel would then be tied to a cart and left where Napoleon's coach was sure to pass. At the right moment, an agent would light the fuse and run. Six seconds later, the world would be rid of the "Corsican pest."

Napoleon was to attend a gala Christmas Eve performance at the Paris Opéra. The assassins, knowing he'd go by way of a narrow street near the Tuileries, placed the cart so that his coach would have to slow down as it came alongside. Unfortunately, someone had to stay with the horse to make sure it didn't wander off with the cart. Then, as now, terrorists were cowards who thought nothing of the innocent. Rather than risk their own skins, they gave a poor girl named Pensol a few coins to hold the horse's reins for them.

It was near curtain time when the clatter of two heavy coaches echoed off the cobblestones. Napoleon and three generals sat in the first coach, followed by the second with Josephine, her daughter Hortense, and Napoleon's sister Caroline. As soon as the first coach appeared, one of the men handed the reins to Pensol, ducked behind the cart to light the fuse, and made his getaway.

Caesar, the coachman, had been celebrating Christmas Eve with the wine bottle. The wine went to his head, making him very drunk and very careless. Noticing the cart, Caesar whipped the horses and raced through the narrow opening at top speed—just for the "fun" of it. Had he not gained those few seconds, the history of Europe would have been different. For once, at least, a drunken driver saved lives.

Meanwhile, Napoleon had dozed off and was having a bad dream. He dreamt of the Italian campaign, where he nearly drowned while crossing a swollen stream. Suddenly he awoke with a start.

The bomb exploded with a deafening *boom!* Pensol and the horse vanished in an orange flash. Twelve bystanders were killed instantly and twenty-eight wounded; forty-six houses were damaged, some so badly that they had to be torn down. Although no one in the first coach was hurt, those in the second had a close call. The coach shook and its windows shattered. Josephine fainted. Hortense's hand was cut by flying glass. Caroline, nine months pregnant, was badly shaken and gave birth to a child with epilepsy a few days later.

Police Minister Fouché went to work that same night. A born detective, he had the pieces of the horse collected and called in all the horse dealers in Paris. One recognized the horse as one he'd sold only a week ago. Yes, he knew the buyer's name and address. The would-be assassin was arrested and, under rough—*very* rough—questioning, revealed his accomplices. Two were sent to the guillotine; the third escaped to America, where he became a priest. Their chief, however, remained safely in England.

Things calmed down after the Treaty of Amiens. But when war broke out again in 1803, Cadoudal went back to his old game. He and four others landed from a British ship and made their way to Paris, where they hired a gang of sixty assassins. Money was no problem, since British officials had given them a million francs for the job.

The plan was for Cadoudal to wait for a Bourbon prince to arrive in Paris. Then, and only then, could he attack the First Consul. His men, dressed in soldier's uniforms, were to mingle with the troops at the weekly parade outside the Tuileries. As

Napoleon passed down the ranks, they'd pounce on him with daggers. In the confusion following his death, the prince would seize power and abolish the Republic. The Cadoudal plot did, indeed, end the Republic, but not in the way he imagined.

Fouché's police uncovered the plot and arrested everyone connected with it. When questioned, Cadoudal confessed and told of the expected prince. Prince? Who was this mysterious prince? Cadoudal went to the guillotine without saying.

Suspicion fell on the Duke d'Enghien, who was living in the Duchy of Baden, a German state just across the Rhine. Guilty or innocent, Napoleon wanted Enghien's blood. He was still a son of Corsica, land of the vendetta. And the rules of the vendetta entitled him to kill any member of an attacker's family. Besides being a just revenge, killing Enghien would send a message to the Bourbons. "I'll teach them to know what kind of man they are dealing with," he angrily told an aide.

On March 20, 1804, French cavalry crossed into Baden, with which they were at peace, to kidnap Enghien. There was no evidence that he was the expected prince, or that he'd planned to harm the First Consul in any way. That made no difference to his judges. They were army officers, and they had their orders. Early the next morning, after a mock trial, Enghien stood before a firing squad. Europe's kings condemned Napoleon's action, but the assassination plots became fewer and less serious.

These plots raised two questions in French minds. Though a dictator, Napoleon was the nation's "insurance policy," its guarantee of order and prosperity. But what if his luck ran out? The Republic would surely collapse. And who would pick up the pieces? The Bourbons, or the wildmen who still hoped to bring back the Terror?

There seemed only one way out. The First Consul must

become a hereditary emperor. If his enemies knew that a Bonaparte would always rule France, they'd stop trying to kill him; even if they did, his government would continue. This idea also suited Napoleon's own ambitions. But it didn't originate with him, nor could he have forced its acceptance. He really was emperor of the Republic, ruling with the consent of the majority of French people.

On May 4, 1804, the Senate formally declared him emperor. On November 6, for the third time, he asked the people's approval. Three and a half million voted to make him emperor, twenty-five hundred voted against him. On December 2, cries of *Vive l'Empereur Napoleon!* echoed in Notre Dame Cathedral. Next spring, in May 1805, he crowned himself king of Italy in a dazzling ceremony at Milan.

The emperor gave France a new nobility, complete with fancy titles and vast estates. During his reign, 2,830 nobles were created: 29 dukes, 44 counts, 1,468 barons, 1,289 knights. The Napoleonic nobility were nothing like the privileged, do-nothings of the old days. They were living examples of equality and the career open to talent. Titles were awarded not according to birth, but were earned by service to the nation. Yet some nobles never lost their rough edges. The wife of General François Lefebvre had been a washerwoman before the Revolution. Whenever she visited the Tuileries, she'd greet the usher by poking him in the ribs and saying, "That will impress you, my lad."

––––––––

NAPOLEON LIKED TO SAY that you could do anything with bayonets except sit on them. By that he meant that a ruler must not only control his people through force and fear, but through their minds. They must serve him willingly, gladly; indeed, they must be happy to lay down their lives for him.

As the pope looks on, Napoleon places the imperial crown on Josephine's head. Although Napoleon's mother did not attend the coronation, the artist painted her seated in the background. Detail from a painting by Jacques-Louis David.

And in order to reach their minds, he had to control the information they received and how they thought about it. He must be a master of propaganda.

Propaganda had existed since antiquity. All rulers had tried to shape public opinion at certain times. Napoleon, however, went further. He was the first to use the full power of government to "brainwash" a nation. By applying that power without letup, he became the creator of modern propaganda. For him, as for the twentieth-century dictators who perfected his methods, truth was unimportant. "It is not the truth that counts," he said, "but what people think is true." Truth, actually, was anything that served his purpose.

Napoleon's most valuable propaganda tool was the printed word. In 1800, Paris alone had seventy-three newspapers. Each had its own point of view, which led to endless squabbles among the papers themselves and their readers. To end this "disorder," he ordered sixty shut down. Those that survived became accountable to the General Direction of Printing and Bookselling—the official censors. Every newspaper, book, pamphlet, play, sermon, advertisement, and poster had to be approved in advance by these officials. Usually they changed only a few phrases, but sometimes an entire work was destroyed. Outspoken authors were visited by secret policemen and told to mend their ways. If they didn't, they went to prison.

Napoleon served as his own propaganda minister. Nothing escaped him. Police reports on new publications arrived at the Tuileries every morning. As his barber shaved him, his secretary read newspaper articles aloud. Sometimes he'd burst out impatiently, "Skip it, skip it. I know what's in them. They say only what I tell them to." That at least was the truth, for he alone decided how many articles would appear, where, and on what subjects. He even wrote articles for the *Moniteur*

(*Monitor*), a private newspaper that served as the government's mouthpiece. The *Moniteur* was all-important, since France's other newspapers had to copy their political and foreign news directly from its pages.

The arts, too, were made to serve the emperor. Hundreds of artists were kept on the imperial payroll. Napoleon's letters are filled with orders for works on special themes. Composers were to write songs such as "Let's All Protect the Empire"; the "Marseillaise" had gone out of style, since he couldn't stand anything that called for resistance to tyrants. Historians should contrast the weak monarchy with the powerful empire. Painters, poets, and playwrights must glorify France's heroes. Architects were to build monuments to the Revolution and the empire.

Naturally all artworks were censored. In the event that something escaped the censors, those responsible paid the price. Police agents, for example, always attended theater performances. In one play, a comedy, the following was thought insulting to soldiers, who might serve years without going on leave:

FIRST BUTLER: I have served.

SECOND BUTLER: And I, I am still serving.

The play was closed after its first performance, the censor fired, and the author jailed. The emperor had no sense of humor where his army was concerned.

The most important task of creative people, however, was to glorify Napoleon Bonaparte. Every day in every way his propaganda machine brainwashed Frenchmen into believing that he was the greatest person who'd ever lived. Whenever he was mentioned, it was in glowing terms. He was:

The conquering hero

Brave and intrepid

The nation's savior

Just, strong, liberal and wise
He who was sent by God
The Lord's chosen
L'Homme du destin—The Man of Destiny
The most active genius ever mentioned in the
history of peoples.

"Liberty, Equality, Fraternity" was replaced by another slogan: "Emperor, Country, and Honor." Note that the emperor came first. Only traitors and lunatics questioned his motives or doubted this "good," "generous," "wonderful" man.

Napoleon's name was always on Frenchmen's lips, his image constantly before them. The twenty-franc gold coin was known as the "napoleon," as was the pastry filled with custard and jelly. Everyday things like pocket watches, drinking mugs, tobacco pipes, snuffboxes, buttons, and playing cards carried his picture; "napoleon" was a card game named in his honor. Plaster statues of him were produced for schools and private homes. Schoolgirls embroidered his portrait on wall hangings. Furniture makers carved his profile into bedposts.

Paintings showed the emperor at his heroic best. Jacques-Louis David, his court artist, painted many huge canvases, all of them propaganda. David's *Napoleon Crossing the Alps* shows him on a rearing white horse, pointing his arm toward Italy. Actually, he crossed the St. Bernard on a sure-footed mule. Another favorite artist was Antoine Jean Gros. In Gros's *Napoleon at the Battle of Arcola*, he leads his men, flag in one hand, sword in the other, across a bullet-swept bridge. In fact, he did nothing of the sort. As he tried to rally the troops, they fled in panic, knocking him into a swamp. Had some soldiers not grabbed him by the arms and dragged him along, he would have been captured by the Austrians.

Every schoolchild learned its duty to the emperor. Schools

were not meant to produce independent people who could think for themselves, but the experts needed to run the empire. In the *lycées* (boys' high schools), students wore uniforms, lived in barracks, marched to classes, and pledged allegiance to the emperor. They learned to be good at what they did, but above all to be loyal, obedient subjects.

The church helped by drawing up a catechism, or set of religious questions and answers, to be memorized by young Catholics. One section of the catechism was written by the emperor himself:

QUESTION: What are the duties of Christians toward the princes who govern them, and what, in particular, are our duties toward Napoleon I, our Emperor?

ANSWER: Christians owe to the princes who govern them, and we, in particular, owe to Napoleon I, our Emperor, love, respect, obedience, loyalty, military service and the taxes ordered for the preservation of his Empire and his throne. . . .

QUESTION: Why do we have these duties toward our Emperor?

ANSWER: . . . Because God, who creates Empires . . . has set him up as our sovereign and made him the agent of His power, and his image on earth. So to honor and serve our Emperor is to honor and serve God himself. . . .

QUESTION: What must one think of those who may fail in their duty toward our Emperor?

ANSWER: According to the Apostle Paul, they would resist the established order of God Himself and would be worthy of eternal damnation.

In other words, God promised to send anyone who disobeyed Napoleon straight to hell. There was even a revival of the Feast of Saint Napoleon, one of the minor saints of the Middle Ages. The emperor, however, was no saint.

Napoleon enjoyed being emperor. Those days of poverty, when he'd eat cheap meals in shabby cafés, were behind him forever. Now servants surrounded him, catering to his every whim. An early riser, he began his day at six o'clock with a bath. He liked to stay in the tub for at least an hour, constantly turning on the hot water tap, so that the room filled with steam. Ever since Toulon, he'd suffered from "the itch," a skin rash that nearly drove him crazy at times. Hot baths relaxed him and relieved the discomfort.

His bath over, a servant, ordered to treat him "as he would a donkey," rubbed him with a hard brush and poured *eau de cologne* over his head. Then came the clothes. The emperor didn't dress himself but, like the kings of old France, had servants put on everything from his underpants to his overcoat. Since he hated tight shoes, a servant who took the same size broke in each new pair for three days. The famous Napoleonic pose—his right hand inside his coat—was typical of the time, since fine clothes had no pockets.

Never one to linger over meals, Napoleon allowed just five minutes for breakfast, eight minutes for lunch, and twenty minutes for dinner. If there were guests, he'd finish his meal and stalk out of the room, leaving them alone. He ate mostly meat, refusing all vegetables except bullet-hard lentils drowned in olive oil and vinegar. Desserts were simply gulped down without chewing them, and probably without tasting them, either. Small wonder that he always suffered from indigestion.

The emperor had a sharp mind and a curiosity about

everything. An avid reader, even on campaign, his coach was equipped with a traveling library of books elegantly bound in leather. He read as fast as he could turn the pages and, if a book displeased him, he'd fling it out the window. Gifted with a photographic memory, he remembered everything he saw in print. During the campaign of 1805, for example, he came across a small unit whose commander had lost his orders and couldn't locate his division. While aides searched their files, the emperor rattled off the division's location, where it would be for the next three nights, its strength, and gave a summary of the divisional commander's military record. There was never a problem with the flood of information that poured into head-quarters every day. His mind automatically sorted facts and filed them under the proper headings: "Different subjects and different affairs are arranged in my head as in a cupboard. When I wish to interrupt one train of thought, I shut that drawer and open another. Do I wish to sleep? I simply close all the drawers and there I am—asleep."

A bundle of nervous energy, Napoleon couldn't keep still for more than a few seconds at a time. He was always clipping his nails, glancing at his watch or taking snuff, sneezing, and dribbling the fine powder over his clothes. At council meetings, he'd carve the table with his pocketknife, slit the covering of his chair, and doodle on scraps of paper. In camp, he'd toss pebbles into the fire or kick the logs until his boots began to smoke. On the battlefield, he'd throw his hat on the ground; whenever an aide picked it up, he'd put it on for a moment, then throw it away again. Only Josephine could calm him down. During the painting of Gros's *Napoleon at the Battle of Arcola*, he'd leap up, stomp around the room, or shout for an aide. Josephine simply pulled him onto her lap; and there he sat, quietly, while the artist worked.

Few rulers have worked as hard as the emperor Napoleon. "Work is my element," he'd say proudly. "I was born and made for work. I have recognized the limits of my eyesight and of my legs, but never the limits of my working power." A normal workday lasted eighteen hours and began in his private office. He wrote about 80,000 letters during his reign— an average of fifteen a day. But since his handwriting was so bad that even he couldn't read it, letters were dictated, often to three secretaries at once. These covered everything from orders to generals to advice on women's fashions to warning Corporal Bernaudet of the Thirteenth Regiment "not to drink so much and to behave better."

The nerve center of government was the Council of State. Napoleon usually chaired its meetings, which might last from early evening until early the next morning. The Council was merely the emperor's sounding board; it discussed important questions and gave advice, but he alone decided. A glutton for information, he squeezed every fact and idea out of the councilors. He'd ask a minister for an opinion, then make him back it with facts. If he omitted something his master already knew, those gray eyes would flash and he'd shrink into his chair. Someone else might defend an idea, only to have its logic torn to shreds. Woe to him who was unprepared, or who grew drowsy around three o'clock in the morning. One fellow, accused of dozing off, replied: "What a hope! You torment us too much for that."

There was also a darker side to the emperor's character. No enemy could have described him in harsher, truer, words than he used to describe himself. Again and again, in letters and private conversations, he admitted to being selfish, greedy, ambitious, and power-hungry. Hundreds of examples have been collected by the historian J. Christopher Herold in his book, *The Mind of Napoleon: A Selection from His Written and Spoken Words.* Taken together, they form one of the ugliest word portraits ever made of a world leader.

As a "superior person," Napoleon believed he could do anything. If he could be a lieutenant, then he could be a general. The hero of Italy could also conquer the East and become First Consul. And the Emperor of France? He'd conquer Europe, then go on to rule the world. Make no mistake about it: world conquest was his final goal. He didn't speak of it often, and never in public, but he hoped to create a "world dictatorship." These are his words, not an enemy's. In 1815, shortly before the battle of Waterloo, he told a guest: "I wanted to rule the world, and in order to do this I needed unlimited power. . . . I wanted to rule the world—who wouldn't have in my place?"

Napoleon sacrificed everything to his ambition, even his own self-esteem. "When I need somebody," he boasted, "I am not squeamish: I'd kiss his arse." If he wanted to win someone over, he would turn on the charm, making him feel like a long-lost friend. He would smile lovingly, flatter, and plead. But if flattery was a device for getting his way, insults were as useful for keeping people in line. He'd wield words like daggers, calculated to wound. He'd turn on people, calling them "dolts," "blockheads," "idiots," "scoundrels," and "cowards who would spit on a corpse." The minister of the interior, a serious, softspoken man named Chaptel, was dubbed "Papa Enema." When Charles Maurice de Talleyrand, the foreign minister, displeased him, he sneered: "Do you know what you are? You're a turd in a silk stocking!" Talleyrand, deeply offended, bided his time until he could betray the emperor.

Selfish and self-centered, Napoleon only knew one use for people, as tools, to be used and tossed away when they'd outlived their usefulness. "I like only those people who are useful to me," he sneered, "and then only so long as they are useful." One thing he used people for was scapegoats, for Napoleon, convinced of his own perfection, believed he could do no wrong. Even when the fault was clearly his own, he couldn't admit his error. His motto was: "Never retreat, never retrace your steps, never admit a mistake." We see this even in his private life. During a hunting accident, he destroyed one of Marshal André Massena's eyes. Calmly, with everyone watching, he handed the gun to an officer and blamed him for the bad shot.

Napoleon also needed people to vent his rage. The emperor's temper tantrums were ferocious. Anything might set him off. When, for example, a bristle from his toothbrush got stuck between his teeth, he stamped his feet and cursed until a doctor removed it. The doctor was lucky to leave without a beating; others didn't get away so easily. He once kicked an official in the stomach, then rang for his butler to toss the writhing man out of the Tuileries. Not even General Berthier, his chief of staff, escaped his anger. One day he grabbed Berthier by the throat and battered his head against a stone wall. General Dominique Vandamme, as tough a fellow as ever wore a uniform, was terrified of his emperor: "So it is that I, who fear neither God nor Devil, am ready to tremble like a child when I approach him."

Even Josephine meant nothing alongside Napoleon's lust for power. He boasted that she could die and it wouldn't interfere for a quarter of an hour with his plans. But this insensitivity was due in part to Josephine herself. During the Egyptian campaign, he learned that she'd been unfaithful. Upon returning to France, he vowed to divorce her, but her tears and those of her children changed his mind. He forgave her and they became good companions. He liked her company and she, for her part, tried to make him happy. "I only win battles," he'd tell guests. "Josephine by her kindness wins people's hearts." But they were no longer lovers.

Josephine's betrayal made something snap inside of him. All his feelings, he confessed, "are dried up." From then on, he closed his heart, distrusting the very things that make life worth living, for most people. "I believe love to be harmful to society and to individual happiness," he said. Nor could he ever be a friend: "Friendship is only a word. I love no one. . . . I know I have no true friends." He loved only power. And power alone gave his life meaning.

At times Napoleon could show a gentler side and enjoy small pleasures. He liked games, especially chess, cheating to his heart's content. He cheated to add excitement to the game. If caught, he'd burst out laughing. If the game was for money, he'd confess at the end and return his winnings.

He was at his best with children. Nieces and nephews could count on a good time with "Nonon the soldier." When they were little, he'd bounce them on his knees and race them across the carpet on all fours. As they grew older, he'd scare them with ghost stories, then wipe away their tears. One morning he saw Napoléone, daughter of his sister Elisa. "Hey, Miss," he said, frowning. "I've just heard some fine news. You made pee pee in the bed last night." Napoléone, a proper lady of five, couldn't take a joke. "Uncle," she said, "if you can't say anything except stupidities, I shall leave." He laughed about the remark all day.

Such incidents were few and far between. For whatever Napoleon did, his two main concerns were never far from his thoughts: power and war.

In the end, they destroyed him.

ENGLAND'S
FLOATING FORTRESSES

"The Royal Navy of England hath ever
been its greatest defence and ornament;
it is its ancient and natural strength—
the floating bulwark of our island."

—Sir William Blackstone, Commentaries, 1765–1769

Englishmen learned of the Treaty of Amiens on April 1, 1802. When news of the signing reached London, it was as if King George III had declared a national holiday. Shopkeepers closed their doors. Workers laid down their tools. Even schoolmasters gave their pupils the afternoon off.

Crowds gathered in front of the Foreign Office throughout the day. They were friendly crowds, gay crowds, because peace had come at last. Not only did they cheer the peace, but the man they felt had done most to bring it about. In England, as in France, Napoleon was the man of the hour. "Long Live Bonaparte!" Englishmen shouted, "Long Live Bonaparte!" No one imagined that peace would last only fourteen months and be followed by the most desperate struggle in their nation's history.

The Treaty of Amiens was never given a chance to work. Its ink had hardly dried when Napoleon began to signal his true intentions. Holland, Piedmont, and the Mediterranean island of Elba were annexed to France; Switzerland was overrun and forced to accept a constitution drawn up in Paris. France made an alliance with Spain, for centuries one of Europe's leading naval powers. The English watched these developments with growing anxiety. Clearly, peace meant different things for different people. It meant, for them, an end to war and a return to normal life. For Napoleon, however, it merely provided a breathing space, a time to gather strength for the next war. Under the guise of "peace," he was tightening his hold on western Europe. Once he controlled the continent, he'd use its shipbuilding resources to challenge England's sea power, and thus her very existence.

His Majesty's government faced a hard decision. Should they continue to observe the treaty, knowing that Napoleon was preparing for their country's destruction? Or should they break the treaty, forcing his hand before he was ready? Rather than wait to be destroyed, they declared war on May 18, 1803. Britain would spare nothing in this struggle. She would encourage, with her friendship and her wealth, all nations to resist French domination. When her allies were defeated, she'd carry on alone. Her fight would last twelve years, ending only on the field of Waterloo.

Napoleon vowed to defeat "*la perfide Albion*" (treacherous Britain), that miserable "nation of shopkeepers." During the summer of 1803, the roads of France came alive with marching troops. Their destination was the northern coast, where several towns had been turned into bases for the upcoming invasion. Boulogne, the largest town, was the main base and Napoleon's headquarters. There he formed the *Grande Armée*, 149,000 strong, and began preparing it for its mission. Its troops were kept busy day and night, training, enlarging harbors, and building forts to keep enemy warships at a safe distance. Landing craft of various types were built in French and Dutch shipyards. Before long, there were 1,928 vessels to ferry the *Grand Armée* across the English Channel. The troops couldn't wait to be on their way.

Meanwhile, Britain waited, worried, and prepared. As always in war, people were unsure about what was actually happening. Rumors seemed to form out of thin air, hang about for a while, then disappear, only to be replaced by others. Most rumors had no basis in fact and were plainly ridiculous. It was said, for instance, that Napoleon had all kinds of secret weapons. People believed he was digging a tunnel under the English Channel that would surface behind the Houses of Parliament in London. He was also supposed to have troop-carrying balloons and gigantic rafts, each carrying 10,000 men and propelled by windmills 100 feet high. Then there was the porpoise brigade, troops trained to cross the Channel at top speed on the backs of porpoises. There were even stories about his plan to release criminals from English jails and turn them loose on the helpless population. This rumor was taken seriously by government officials, who ordered: "Prisoners are to be put into prison ships, in the most secure situations, so that they may be destroyed instantly, in cases necessary, for the defense of the country."

Newspapers began a campaign of hate propaganda against the French. People were reminded of the Reign of Terror and warned that it could happen again—in England. Napoleon was portrayed as a one-man Reign of Terror. Englishmen were told how he'd massacred Turkish prisoners at Jaffa and ordered his own wounded to be poisoned. "Little Boney," as he was now called, had an army and didn't play fair. He was the Enemy of the Human Race, the Fiend of the Bottomless Pit, the Serpent of Corsica, and the Vampire. This savage, said London's *Morning Post*, was "an unclassifiable being, half African, half-European, a Mediterranean mulatto." Cartoonists showed him as the "Corsican ogre," a giant with a red eye in the middle of his forehead and yellow teeth protruding from his mouth, with which he tore people apart and ate them. Josephine was shown as a fat witch stuffing her pimply face and grinning like a lunatic.

Tales of Boney the Beast terrified people, particularly the young. Mothers got rebellious youngsters to eat their porridge with promises that "Boney will come and get you" if they didn't. Nannies warned their charges that he'd swallow them, head first, if they misbehaved:

> Baby, baby, he's a giant,
> Tall and black as Rouen steeple,
> And he dines and sups, rely on it,
> Every day on naughty people.

Englishmen prepared to resist the invader as best they could. Their ancestors had been familiar with invasion threats. In 1588, Spain had sent its "Invincible Armada" against the island nation. Queen Elizabeth I replied by turning the country into an armed camp. If the Spaniards hadn't been defeated at sea, they would have met a united people determined to die rather than submit to foreign rule.

Queen Elizabeth's plans were taken from the Royal Archives and updated to meet the French threat. Hundreds of towers sprang up at key points along the coast from Scotland to the English Channel. Each tower was thirty feet high, had brick walls nine feet thick, and mounted from three to five cannons. These towers, called martellos, were meant to delay the invader while the country rallied. That was expected to take but a few hours, since every hilltop had its warning beacon of wood piled on top of barrels of tar. If the invader came at night, they'd be set on fire, alerting outposts on other hilltops, until the whole country was roused. By day, wet hay could produce tall columns of smoke that could be seen for miles in every direction.

British manpower was mobilized as never before. This was necessary because the regular army was small and stationed mainly in Ireland. The king asked every male between the ages of fifteen and sixty to join local militia units. Volunteers, 320,000 of them, answered the call. Yet they were soldiers in name only. Except for wearing a military uniform and drilling once a week, they went about their business as usual. Since there weren't enough guns to go around, most had only ancient spears and swords. Professional soldiers believed Napoleon's veterans would make mincemeat of them. If ever they landed, they'd be in London within two days. And once the capital fell, the whole country would fall.

Britain's admirals, however, were more optimistic. They believed the *Grande Armée* would be fishbait before it got halfway across the Channel. When they examined the facts, they saw that the odds were heavily in their favor. The French had many problems, not the least of which was Boney himself. Although a brilliant soldier, his ideas about fighting at sea were childish. Conferences with his admirals were like meetings with visitors from outer space. They saw things differently, spoke different languages. It seemed that they always found reasons for avoiding battle. The moment he offered a plan, they'd pounce on it like a school of sharks.

"Sire, this is impossible," they'd say.

"Why?" he'd ask.

"Sire, the winds don't allow it, and then the doldrums, the currents . . ."

Napoleon sputtered and fumed, while his admirals shook their heads and made long faces. Unfortunately, his arrogance was matched by his ignorance. He believed that he knew more than men who'd spent their lives at sea. On July 10, 1804, he killed as many French sailors as a full-scale naval battle.

That morning, he ordered a naval review of Boulogne. But Admiral Eustache Bruix, the area commander, saw signs of a coming storm and ordered it postponed. Napoleon flew into a rage. He rode to Bruix's headquarters, furious at the delay. Although the admiral assured him a storm was brewing, he insisted on holding the review no matter what happened. "The consequence is my affair, and mine alone," he roared. "Obey at once." When Bruix refused to obey, he raised his riding whip as if to strike him across the face. Bruix wouldn't back down. "Sire, beware," he said, placing his hand on his sword. Napoleon backed off, but dismissed him from the service. The review was held as scheduled. And the storm came as promised. Twenty transports were wrecked, and over 2,000 men drowned before Napoleon's eyes.

Weather was the least of Napoleon's problems. Originally, he'd planned to send his invasion ships across the English Channel and complete the landing within twenty-four hours. He quickly learned that this was impossible. His invasion ships were anchored close together inside their protected harbors. Getting them out to sea would take several days, during which time they'd be easy prey for British battle squadrons that scoured the Channel day and night. The invasion ships could not take care of themselves. Built only to carry men and supplies, they were helpless against warships bristling with heavy guns. These floating fortresses, though slow and clumsy, were unbeatable except by vessels of their own class.

Napoleon had to clear the Channel before launching his invasion. Yet his own battle fleet was nowhere near the invasion area. It was scattered in ports around the coasts of France and Spain—Toulon, Rochefort, Brest, Cadiz, Vigo, and Ferol. British squadrons also cruised outside these ports, daring the enemy to come out and fight. He seldom took the bait;

and when he did, he was sorry. The Royal Navy had an awesome reputation earned in hundreds of sea fights. Yet the emperor would challenge that reputation in the most famous naval battle of European history. To understand how this came about, we must first understand the basics of fighting in the Age of Sail.

BRITAIN'S NAVAL GLORY was built on the pain of thousands of horribly abused men. Life for the common seaman in the Royal Navy was dull, dirty, and deadly. For a few pence a day, he risked his life in loneliness far from home. Voyages often lasted three years, during which time he never set foot ashore. His ship was both a home and a prison. Although officers bunked in cabins with portholes, he slept in a hammock slung in dark, crowded compartments that stank of dampness, rot, and unwashed bodies. Seldom did he sleep soundly or through the night. Creaking timbers and rattling pumps woke him constantly. The lower decks swarmed with rats, who would climb into hammocks and nose through men's pockets in search of food.

There was never enough food, and what there was was usually awful. Meat came in salt-filled barrels. Sailors called it "salt horse" or "salt junk"; "junk" was slang for old rope and meat kept in salt so long that it became a mass of tough, ropelike fibers. Hardtack, a type of bread baked hard as rock, was alive with crawling, squirming creatures. A wise man tapped his hardtack before eating, to make sure that its largest tenants were shaken loose. Food was washed down with putrid water that made men hold their noses while drinking. Bernard Coleridge, an eleven-year-old cabin boy, wrote his parents:

Indeed we live on beef which has been ten or eleven years in corn [brine] and on biscuit which quite makes

your throat cold in eating owing to the maggots which
are very cold when you eat them, like calves-foot
jelly . . . being very fat indeed. . . . We drink water
of the color of the bark of a pear-tree with plenty of
little maggots and weevils in it and wine which is
exactly like bullock's [bull's] blood and sawdust mixed
together. I hope I shall not learn to swear, and by
God's assistance I hope I shall not. *

Dried peas and beans, oatmeal, butter, vinegar, cheese, and
sugar filled out the sailor's diet.

The most valued "foods" were beer and rum. Alcoholic
beverages were as necessary to the sailor's well-being as anything he ate. Alcohol warmed him in the cold dampness, gave
him energy for work, and dulled his aches and pains. Each
day he received a gallon of beer and a half-pint of grog,
watered-down rum mixed with sugar and lime juice; British
sailors are still called "limeys." If you saved your grog rations
and drank them at once, you'd become "groggy," drunk
enough to forget your troubles for a few hours. But if you were
caught—then God help you!

Royal Navy ships were ruled by terror. The captain, a sailor
explained, "is a kind of Sea-God, whom the poor tars worship
as the Indians do the Devil." There was no protesting his rules,
no appealing his decisions. His word was law, and he held the
power of life and death in his hands.

Many captains were decent men, whose sailors called them
"father." But there were also many brutes, who regularly used
the cat-o'-nine-tails, a whip made of nine strands of rope knot-
ted along their whole length. Ordinary offenses—drunkenness, gambling, lateness, spitting on the deck—brought sixty

*Bernard fell to his death from a mast at the age of fourteen.

lashes on the bare back. Captains might also invent their own "amusements" to pass the time at sea. Sir Peter Parker liked to hang an officer's coat on a broomstick and whip anyone who failed to salute it. Captain Hugh Pigot sent men up to the crows' nests at the tops of the masts. They were ordered to wait for a whistle, then race down as fast as they could, the last man on deck getting sixty lashes. Two men fell at Pigot's feet, breaking all the bones in their bodies. "Heave those lubbers overboard!" he sneered, turning to walk away.

Serious offenses—mutiny, desertion, striking an officer— were savagely punished. Hanging was a kindness, compared to "flogging through the fleet." The culprit was brought to a longboat, tied to a rack, and rowed to each ship in the fleet. Then, as drums rolled and everyone watched, he was whipped. Let Jack Nastyface, a veteran seaman, describe what happened next:

> The cat-o'-nine-tails is applied to the bare back, and at about every six lashes a fresh boatswain's mate is ordered to relieve the executioner of his duty, until the prisoner has received, perhaps, twenty-five lashes. . . . [He is] conveyed from ship to ship, receiving alongside each a similar number of stripes with the cat until his sentence is completed. . . . His back resembles so much putrefied liver, and every stroke of the cat brings away the congealed blood: and the boatswain's mates are looked at with the eye of a hawk to see they do their duty, and clear the cat's tails after every stroke, the blood at the time streaming through their fingers: and in this manner are men in the navy punished for different offenses. . . .

Those whipped around the fleet normally received six hundred lashes. Many died during the ordeal, but the whipping continued until the sentence was completed. Survivors were generally crippled for life or went insane from the pain.

Life in the Royal Navy was so harsh that deserters always outnumbered volunteers. Ships' crews had to be filled by impressment, a form of legalized kidnapping. Impressment, or "pressing," could take place anywhere, anytime. A warship's captain might stop a British merchantman in midocean and take sailors to fill vacancies in his crew. We have accounts of men who cut off their fingers rather than go to a warship. Ashore, criminals were offered the hangman's noose or service aboard a warship; some chose the noose, calling warships "gallows afloat." The worst sentence a court martial could impose on a soldier was not the firing squad, but "removal to the navy." At least fifty percent of warship crews were forced into the service against their will.

"Press gangs" roamed British coastal towns, searching for men to drag aboard their ships. Although they preferred experienced seamen, no one was immune. Press gangs broke up wedding parties, leaving the bride and female guests in tears. They took men after church on Sundays. Homes were raided at night and husbands dragged away as wives and children pleaded for mercy. People resisted in various ways. In some towns, they banded together to ambush the gangs with rocks and knives, even muskets. Others resorted to trickery, like the fellow who pretended to be dead. He lay in a coffin, stiff as a board, while his womenfolk wailed and moaned. But the press gang's lieutenant demanded a closer look, and the "corpse" was brought back to life with clubs. Another fellow, John Teed by name, denied being a seaman. The press gang stripped him and found his body tattooed with emblems of love and the sea. "You and I will lovers die, eh?" said the grinning lieutenant as his men clamped poor Teed in irons.

Conditions in the French navy were mild in comparison, thanks to Napoleon. Although he knew little about fighting at sea, he knew a lot about building morale among fighting men. His sailors had better food, and more of it. Cruel punishments were abolished. No one was whipped, although he might have a rope tied around his waist and be dropped from a mast into the sea. Impressment was unknown in France, since all seamen were liable to serve for a set period of time at a fair wage.

The backbone of any navy was the ship of the line, ancestor of the modern battleship. To get a clear picture of this vessel, let's look at His Majesty's Ship *Victory*, the most famous of her kind. *Victory* took six years to build and was launched in 1765. She was 226 feet long, 52 feet in beam (width), weighed in at 2,162 tons, and had a crew of 850 officers and men. Built of oak and elm, her sides were 2 feet thick and her masts rose 200 feet above the waterline. She was held together not by nails that would rust, but long oak pins and copper bolts 6 feet long and 2 inches thick. Known as a "three-decker," because of her three gun decks, she carried 104 cannons of various sizes. "Two-deckers," smaller ships of the line, carried either sixty-four or seventy-four cannons. Two-deckers were faster and easier to handle than their bigger sisters.

Ships and sailors existed for one purpose only: to provide a stable platform for the guns. Naval guns were larger than army artillery, which had to be pulled to its destination by horses and men. Warship guns were either of the long or short type. Long guns had long barrels (nine to ten feet) for sending shot long distances. Such weapons usually fired iron balls (shot) weighing eighteen, twenty-four, and thirty-two pounds apiece. A thirty-two-pounder long gun could hit a vessel two miles away. But since these balls traveled at high speed, the holes they made were round, neat, and easy to mend.

Holes made by the carronade, or short gun, were different. The carronade was a British specialty. Named for its manufacturer, the Carron Iron Works of Scotland, sailors called it the "smasher" and "devil gun." Just five feet long, its range less than half a mile, the carronade fired a forty-two- or sixty-eight-pound ball, together with a keg of 500 musket balls. The effect was shattering. Since the heavy balls traveled slowly, they made huge, jagged holes and sent clouds of wooden splinters speeding through the air. Ranging in size from a few inches to several feet, splinters always killed and wounded more men than solid shot. The musket balls could sweep an enemy's deck, mowing down everyone in their path.

Each gun had a five- to nine-man crew, depending on its size. The gun and its needs came first. Crews spent endless hours tying and retying the ropes that kept it in place; if it broke loose and began to roll, it could smash through the ship's side. Its barrel was cleaned until it sparkled; a poorly cleaned gun might misfire or, worse, explode when fired, showering the deck with chunks of iron. Gunners constantly practiced loading their "pieces," since quick firing meant more damage to the enemy. At night, they slept above them in hammocks slung from the ceiling.

Naval guns fired special types of shot for special purposes. As with land guns, solid shot put holes in targets or smashed them to bits. Gunners also aimed at enemy sails and rigging, the ropes that held them in place; once its rigging was torn away, a ship became unmanageable. *Chain shot*, two balls attached by a chain, whipped through the air, cutting riggings. *Spider shot*, two-foot blades fastened to an iron ring, slashed sails to ribbons. *Bar shot*, a smaller version of the weightlifter's barbells, brought down masts and yards, the crosspieces that support the sails. *Langridge*, leather tubes filled with nails, scrap metal, and broken glass, scattered death over large areas. *Hot shot* was solid shot heated in a furnace. When it became red-hot, it was lifted with tongs and placed in the gun barrel on top of a pad of wet junk. Passing through the hull of an enemy vessel, hot shot started internal fires. Fire was the sailing ship's worst enemy. Mighty warships were sometimes burnt to the waterline by a tipped-over candle, or a sailor's pipe ashes. If hot shot reached the paint stores or gunpowder room, the vessel exploded.

Tactics in the Age of Sail were like an elaborate dance— to the music of roaring guns, crashing timbers, and screaming men. When rival fleets met, the ships of the line formed two parallel lines—"lines of battle"—with each vessel several dozen feet behind the other. Moving ahead as quickly as possible, they fired their broadsides, all the guns on one side of a vessel, as the distance between the lines closed. The object was for one line to pass the other at right angles. This "crossing the T" allowed the guns of the faster fleet to blast the enemy's line without his being able to bring more than a few guns to bear at one time. Once they'd crossed the T, the ships broke formation to meet the enemy one-on-one. Each captain tried to put his vessel at right angles to the enemy's bow or stern (rear) in order to "rake," fire broadsides down his full length. Nearly every shot hit something during a raking. Masts toppled, crushing those beneath them. Internal compartments blew apart. The dead and dying lay everywhere. Once a broadside had been fired, the captain wheeled his ship around to fire another from the opposite side, giving the first gun crews time to reload.

Naval actions were seldom won by cannons alone. The nature of wood is to float, so that no matter how many holes were made in a ship, it stayed afloat. Only fire or lucky shots below the waterline could sink a wooden vessel. The gun's real job was to weaken the enemy, setting him up for the main blow. That came when the ships were deliberately run into one another and the marines swung into action.

Every warship had its detachment of marines. These "soldiers of the sea" normally served as ship's police and guards for the supply rooms, especially the rum stores. During battle, marine marksmen manned the fighting tops, platforms high in the masts. Their job was to clear the enemy's fighting tops and pick off men on his decks, preferably officers.

Other marines waited below for their orders. At the right moment, officers shouted "boarders away," sending them swarming onto the enemy's deck. What followed was a wild free-for-all with every man for himself. Armed with pistols, swords, and short spears called boarding pikes, they fought until they were driven off or the enemy surrendered. A vessel surrendered when its commander "struck his colors," took down his flag. If a captured vessel was in good condition, it was sold as a prize of war and the money divided among the victorious crew. Vessels that couldn't be salvaged were burned. Captured seamen were usually put ashore and paroled, freed after promising not to fight for the rest of the war. Anyone who broke his parole was hanged if recaptured.

———

EARLY IN 1805, Napoleon made plans to clear the English Channel of enemy warships. Admiral Pierre Villeneuve's squadron was to escape from Toulon and head for the West Indies. British blockaders, not knowing his whereabouts, would go in search, allowing other vessels to break out of their ports. The French ships would join forces within forty days, then make a dash for the Channel. The outnumbered British would scatter, allowing the invasion fleet to cross in safety.

All went well—at the beginning. Villeneuve slipped out of Toulon and avoided the British Mediterranean squadron, commanded by Admiral Nelson in the *Victory*. When Nelson realized that he'd been tricked, he crowded on every inch of sail his masts could hold and set course for the New World. We've already met Nelson at Abukir Bay, and must now get to know him better.

Horatio Nelson was born in 1759. Since his father was a poor country parson with a large family, it was difficult to pay for their education. He was therefore relieved when Horatio decided to go to sea. He immediately wrote his brother-in-law, a Royal Navy captain, asking his help. The captain was surprised at the request, for his nephew was sickly and seemed unsuited to the hard life of a seaman. "What has poor Horatio done," he wrote, "who is so weak, that . . . he should be sent to rough it out at sea? But let him come; and the first time we go into action a cannonball may knock off his head and so provide for him." And so he became a midshipman, an officer-in-training, at the age of twelve.

Children were no strangers to the navy. Life was shorter in Nelson's time, and boys took on adult responsibilities sooner than nowadays. We know of boys as young as eight who sailed aboard warships. They grew up fast. One eleven-year-old midshipman strode the gundeck, a pistol at his side, sucking his thumb; he lost a leg in battle the next year. Another lad was spanked by his father, an admiral, in front of the ship's crew. The spanking must have done him good, since he went on to earn commendations for bravery.

Nelson blossomed in the navy. He recovered his health, grew stronger, and learned all there was to know about sailing and fighting. He did plenty of both during the American Revolution, when he became captain of a frigate, a small, fast

warship. But his real chance came during the French Revolution. Nelson disliked all foreigners, calling them "a dirty set
of fellows." But he despised the French. He hated everything
about them: their country, their ways, their language. Most
of all, he hated Napoleon, whom he called an "animal."

In any action, however deadly, Nelson could be counted
on to lead the way. He was fearless; indeed, he often told
friends of his wish to die fighting for his country. Several times,
he nearly had his wish. During a raid on Corsica in 1793, a
cannonball hit the ground and threw some pebbles into his
face, blinding him in the right eye. Four years later, a bullet
smashed his right elbow, making it necessary to amputate the
arm. "Tell the surgeon to get his instruments ready," he
snapped, "for I know that I must lose my arm, and the sooner
it is off the better." During the battle of the Nile, a piece of
langridge tore open his forehead, causing the skin to drop over
the tip of his nose. It healed, leaving a long red scar.

Nelson's promotions kept pace with his wounds. By the time
he'd lost his arm, he was an admiral and the idol of the fleet.
His men loved him, because they knew that he loved them.
Unlike other officers, he spared the whip, even dug into his
own pockets to buy decent food for his crew. "Men adored
him," a sailor recalled, "and in fighting under him, every man
thought himself sure of success." His presence, they felt, was
a guarantee of victory.

Men gladly sacrificed themselves for Nelson. During a raid
on a Spanish port, his barge was boarded by enemy sailors.
The swordplay was fast and furious. Men were dropping all
around when seaman John Sykes saw a Spaniard swing his
blade at the admiral's head. There was no time to parry it with
his own sword, so he grabbed it with his hand. Most of the
hand fell at his feet, but Nelson got off without a scratch.

Sykes's shipmates envied him the "honor" of losing a hand for their beloved chief.

Nelson arrived in the West Indies in June 1805, only to find the enemy gone. Villeneuve had waited the forty days, but since no other ships joined him, he sailed in time to give Nelson the slip. The next month, after a rough voyage, he slipped into Cadiz harbor, the Spanish navy's home port. Nelson, unable to locate him, sent his squadron to patrol the Spanish coast and returned home after two years at sea. While *Victory* went for repairs, he took a much-needed rest.

This was to be the happiest three weeks of Nelson's life. Lady Emma Hamilton, his lover, welcomed him with their child, Horatia, whom he was seeing for the first time. Wherever he went, crowds followed, eager to have a glimpse of their hero. During a visit to the War Office in London, he met a lanky army officer, Sir Arthur Wellesley, the future Duke of Wellington. Soon afterward, word came that Villeneuve was in Cadiz. *Victory* was ready and waiting. There was nothing to do but rejoin the fleet and make ready for the big battle.

Nelson hoped to leave England quietly on September 14. But when it was learned that *Victory* was about to sail, thousands lined the way to Portsmouth harbor. Many had tears in their eyes. Many others knelt in the road, blessing him as he passed. As his longboat pushed away from the dock, he returned their cheers by waving his hat. Afterward, they stood silent and sad, gazing out to sea as if they knew he'd gone on his last voyage.

Exactly two weeks later, *Victory* appeared off Cadiz. She flew the white ensign of the Royal Navy, along with the admiral's personal flag. Morale was low. Officers and men were not looking forward to winter in those stormy waters. Suddenly the mood changed. "Lord Nelson is arrived!" a captain wrote his wife. "A sort of general joy has been the consequence." A feeling of pride spread through the fleet; men were even eager for battle. But no one knew if the enemy would fight. There was no way to go into Cadiz after him, as the harbor entrance bristled with heavy cannons. Villeneuve was safe as long as he remained in port.

The disaster that followed need not have happened, and would not have happened, but for Napoleon's arrogance and stupidity. During the spring of 1805, the British had made an alliance with Russia and Austria. The emperor had no choice: he must call off his invasion plans or risk a massive land attack on France. By late August, the camp at Boulogne was broken up and the *Grande Armée* began its march toward Central Europe. Let's leave it there for the time being.

Villeneuve, meanwhile, was ordered to return to the Mediterranean. When navy men pointed out the danger of this move, Napoleon lost his temper. The navy had failed him! Were it not for that pack of fools, he'd be dictating peace from London. The fleet could rot, for all he cared. It was almost as if he wanted to be rid of it—wanted it destroyed. "His Majesty counts for nothing the loss of his ships," his order said, "provided they are lost with glory." They *would* be lost, not gloriously, but in France's worst naval disaster: Trafalgar.

———

DAWN, MONDAY, OCTOBER 21, 1805. The British crews were awakened by loud cheering. Barefoot, struggling to put on their breeches as they ran, sailors came topside to see the sight. There, twelve miles to the east, sails had begun to emerge from the gloom. The enemy had come out! He was moving slowly southward, toward the entrance to the Mediterranean.

The fleets were about evenly matched. Nelson had twenty-seven ships on the line to Villeneuve's thirty-three: eighteen

French and fifteen Spaniards. If Nelson's ships fired all their guns at once, the shot would weigh 29,000 pounds, compared to 30,000 pounds for Villeneuve's ships. Several of these vessels were especially interesting. *Victory*, Nelson's heaviest hitter, was dwarfed by Spain's *Santissima Trinidad*, or *Holy Trinity*, a four-decker with 136 guns and the largest warship afloat. *Britannia* was nicknamed "Old Ironsides," because shot was said to bounce harmlessly off her sides; the Americans' *Constitution* would earn that same nickname fighting Britain in the War of 1812. Then there was *Bellerophon*, known to her crew as "Billy Ruffian." She was a bad-luck ship for Napoleon. A veteran of Abukir Bay, she was destined to take him away from France for the last time in 1815.

As soon as there was enough light to see signal flags, Nelson ordered the fleet into battle formation. That formation was a revolution in the art of sea warfare. The Englishman meant to do with ships what Napoleon had done with infantry columns: break the line. His fleet formed two columns. The main, or northern, column had the heavy hitters—*Victory, Neptune, Téméraire*—with a total of 300 guns, followed by nine two-deckers. The second, or southern, column was commanded by Admiral Cuthbert Collingwood in the *Royal Sovereign*, a 100-gun ship. The plan was to break the enemy line, then have a free-for-all in which each captain chose a foe and fought him at close range. Naturally this would allow the enemy to cross his "T" during the approach, causing frightful damage. But Nelson was prepared to pay the price if that meant success. Whereas other admirals would have been satisfied to capture a few vessels, Nelson wanted a battle of annihilation. Enemy seapower must be destroyed for a whole generation. He had such confidence in his plan that he led the way in *Victory*.

Horatio Nelson, England's greatest fighting admiral. From an oil sketch, done about 1801, by Sir William Beechey in the National Portrait Gallery, London.
BELOW, the French-Spanish line of battle opens fire on the British at Trafalgar. The British ships, with Nelson leading the column on the left and Admiral Collingwood leading the right, would break the enemy line in two places, then crush her in a free-for-all battle. An engraving based on a painting by Thomas Whitcombe, 1817.

Having given his orders, Nelson went to his cabin for some quiet moments alone. A deeply religious man, he knelt at a table and wrote what was in his heart. The result was one of the most beautiful prayers in the English language:

May the Great God, whom I worship, grant to my Country, and for the benefit of Europe in general, a great and glorious Victory; and may no misconduct in any one tarnish it; and may humanity after Victory be the predominant feature of the British Fleet. For myself, I commit my life to Him who made me, and may His blessing light upon my endeavours for serving my Country faithfully. To Him I resign myself and the just cause which is entrusted to me to defend. Amen. Amen. Amen.

Meanwhile, drummers rapped out long, urgent rolls to call the crews to battle stations. Instantly the sound of bare feet slapping on wood came from every direction. The long hours of training began to pay off as sailors readied their ships for action. Everyone knew what he had to do, and did it automatically. Topmen went aloft on rope ladders to take in or let out sail as needed. Marines manned the fighting tops and stacked pistols, swords, and pikes to repel boarders. Deckhands hung rope netting under the masts to catch any wreckage, or men, falling from above. Their most important task, however, was fire control. Buckets of water were hoisted aloft and poured over the sails. Fire hoses were connected and played on the upper deck, rigging, and anything else that could burn. Wet blankets were hung around hatchways to keep fire from passing downward, into the heart of the ship

Below decks was a beehive of activity. Carpenters readied shot-plugs, giant wooden "ice cream cones" to hammer into holes in the ship's sides; really large holes were covered with sheets of lead. The surgeon and his assistants prepared for the wounded. Their preparations would give a modern surgeon goosebumps, but they were the best available at the time. Saws and knives, scissors and needles, were laid out on a table, along with a small stove for boiling water; the water was not to sterilize instruments, but to heat them, since cold metal cutting into raw flesh causes unbearable pain. Operating tables were rough wooden planks set on barrels and covered with layers of old sails. One's rank, or the seriousness of one's wound, had no effect on the surgeons, whose rule was "first come, first served." Not all wounded, however, would see a surgeon. Those hurt so badly that they couldn't live were thrown overboard to end their agonies and prevent their screams from upsetting their comrades. The dead went overboard as soon as they fell so as not to clutter the narrow decks.

The gun decks were busiest of all. As the drums beat, gun crews sent their kit bags below or tossed them overboard if time was short. Powder monkeys—ammunition carriers—brought cartridges from the gunpowder room. Boys spread wet sand on the decks, for blood is slippery and plenty of it flowed during battle; the ship's sides were painted red to hide any blood that spattered on them. Gunners stripped to the waist and tied kerchiefs around their heads so that the blast of the guns wouldn't deafen them for life. After loading their pieces, they opened the gun ports and rolled them into place. The guns' mouths were also painted red, like those of fire-breathing dragons. Finally, midshipmen with drawn pistols took their places behind the gunners. They were to shoot anyone who left his post without orders.

Both fleets were cleared for action within ten minutes. Action, however, was long in coming. There was only a slight breeze and a calm sea that day, meaning that it would take several hours before the enemy came within range. Officers used the time to inspect their ships and deliver pep talks. Captain Mansfield's speech to the crew of the *Minotaur* was typical. "I shall say nothing to you of courage. Our country never produced a coward," he told his crew. "For my own part I pledge myself to the officers and ship's company never to quit the ship I get alongside of, till either she strikes or sinks, or I sink. . . . Be careful to take good aim, for it is to no purpose to throw away shot. . . . God Save the King!" Enemy captains were just as encouraging. The French paraded the Eagle banner, symbol of Napoleon, and shouted "*Vive l'Empereur!*" The Spaniards hoisted crosses into their ships' rigging and begged God's favor.

By late morning, the fleets were closing for battle. They moved slowly, rolling with the low swells slap, slap, slapping against their bows. In the distance, outlined against the horizon, was a long, low sliver of land jutting from the Spanish coast. Veterans pointed it out to the newcomers. A famous landmark, it was only a few miles from the Mediterranean. They called it Cape Trafalgar.

Nearly all British vessels had bands, and now they began to play. They played stirring tunes, tunes that had sent their countrymen into battle for generations. Strains of "Britons Strike Home" mingled with "Hearts of Oak." Most of all they played "Rule, Britannia:"

> Rule, Britannia,
> Britannia rules the waves;
> Britons never, never, never will be slaves.

Outwardly, the men were brash. "A glorious day for old England!" they shouted to ships nearby. Others chalked *Death or Victory* on polished gun barrels. They spoke of glory and the joys of home. They peered out of gun ports, wondering how much prize money the enemy ships would fetch.

Yet there were long silences, when men watched and listened and thought their private thoughts. Everyone knew what to expect if things went wrong, and was afraid. They made their wills, not in writing, but man to man. Jack Nastyface recalled how two of his friends "were making a sort of mutual verbal will, such as, if one of Johnny Crapaud's [the Frenchman's] shots knocks my head off, you will take all my effects; and if you're killed and I'm not, why, I'll have yours." They were also afraid of being afraid. Each man made a silent pact with himself that, no matter what happened, he would not lose his self-respect by letting his shipmates down.

Toward noon, thirty-one flags appeared atop *Victory's* mainmast. They were Nelson's final signal and would inspire Englishmen from that day forward: "ENGLAND EXPECTS THAT EVERY MAN WILL DO HIS DUTY." Cheering erupted as the signal was decoded and passed from ship to ship. Suddenly a burst of smoke came from the French line and the thunder of guns echoed across the sea. The Battle of Trafalgar had begun.

Admiral Collingwood was first to engage the enemy. The *Royal Sovereign* was making way steadily when the first shots struck. Her mizzen topmast, the top section of her third mast, came crashing down. Paul Nicholas, sixteen, a marine officer, became speechless at the sight of a sailor struck in the chest by a cannonball: it splattered him across the deck. But *Royal Sovereign* kept coming, followed by her sister ships. Collingwood was thrilled, for he had the "pleasure" of being first to break the line. "What would Nelson give to be here!" he told an aide, smiling.

Victory was under fire for forty minutes without being able to strike back. *Bucentaure,* Villeneuve's flagship, *Santissima Trinidad,* and several two-deckers pounded her mercilessly. Nelson and Thomas Hardy, *Victory's* captain and his close friend, paced the quarter-deck, the small raised deck at the rear of the vessel. Both wore full-dress uniforms, complete with silk stockings and tall hats. In addition, Nelson's chest was covered with medals, indicating his rank as supreme commander. They were perfect targets, but it would have been unmanly for them to take cover. Commanders were supposed to inspire their men by showing contempt for the enemy. If the crew saw them take cover, they might lose faith in themselves.

They were walking side by side when Mr. Scott, Nelson's secretary, was killed by a cannonball. "Poor fellow!" said Nelson, as marines tossed the body overboard. It had barely hit the water when a bar shot struck eight marines standing at attention nearby, killing them all. Puddles of blood lay on the quarter-deck, but Nelson and Hardy kept walking without missing a step. Another ball passed between them, tearing up splinters, one of which sliced the buckle off Hardy's left shoe. The captain's face showed no emotion. Nelson just smiled and said: "This is too warm work, Hardy, to last long." It must have seemed to many that it had already lasted too long. But it was just the beginning.

The enemy vessels grew larger each minute. Looming ahead of *Victory* were *Bucentaure* and, following closely behind, *Redoubtable,* one of France's finest warships. It was impossible to pass between them without crashing into one or the other, exactly what Nelson wanted. Slowly *Victory* swung toward *Redoubtable.* At one o'clock that afternoon she, too, broke the line.

All the punishment she'd been taking now seemed worthwhile. *Victory*, turning, passed *Bucentaure*'s stern. The broad, high stern contained the admiral's cabin and was decorated with colorful designs and beautiful carvings. *Victory* changed that in a flash. As she turned, her port (left) carronade fired pointblank through the windows of Villeneuve's cabin, hurling two 68-pound balls and 500 musket balls along the whole length of the ship. They were followed by a full broadside of fifty double-shotted cannons. The English gunners could hear the crunch of splitting wood and the shrieks of wounded men. It was music to their ears.

Just then their comrades fired a full starboard (right) broadside into *Redoubtable*. A moment later there was a sickening *crunch* followed by a jolt that sent men sprawling. The ships crashed and swung about until their sides came together. Crewmen threw small, sharp-pointed anchors called grapnels across the enemy's deck rails to bind the vessels together. Boarders stood by, awaiting the command to leap across. Cannons, their muzzles practically touching, banged away. Iron balls broke through hulls and kept going, passing out the other side. High above, in the fighting tops, snipers took aim.

A French sniper scored the most important hit of the day. Nelson and Hardy were walking the quarter-deck when the admiral suddenly collapsed. His friend, seeing him fall, said he hoped the wound was not serious. Nelson knew better.

"They have done for me at last, Hardy," he groaned.

"I hope not."

"Yes, my backbone is shot through."

A marine sergeant and some sailors took him below, where the surgeon was at work. Even as they carried him, Nelson thought of his duty. He covered his face with a handkerchief, so that the men wouldn't see their helpless commander.

One look told the surgeon that Nelson was right. A musket

ball, plunging downward, had struck his left shoulder, gone through his chest, and lodged in his spine. He was dying. Nothing could be done, except to make him as comfortable as possible. The battle raged, while aides fanned him and gave him lime juice and water to drink.

Nelson had said he wanted a free-for-all, and that's what he got. There had never been anything like it before. With Villeneuve's line broken in two places, sixty vessels were moving on their own in a square mile of sea. Each had several enemies in range at once, while always being in range of several enemies. Survival became a matter of luck and skill. Each moved no more than a mile an hour, and turning took many minutes. Still death came swiftly—and horribly—at Trafalgar.

The scene was much the same aboard each vessel. Upper decks were a shambles. Torn sails hung in tatters. Cut chains and cables whipped about. Masts toppled in a tangle of wood and rope. Smashed lifeboats dangled over the sides at crazy angles. The sea was filled with wreckage, bodies, and pieces of bodies.

There was pandemonium on the gun decks. Each gun captain held a "match," a slow-burning rope attached to a forked stick. Whenever he brought it down, the powder in the touchhole gave a loud *huff* and squirted a jet of flame that scorched the timbers above. The cannon roared and leaped back in recoil; anyone caught in the way had his legs broken like dry twigs. The concussion set off shock waves that struck the ears like a hard fist and left them ringing.

The gunners lost track of time once they took up the rhythm of their work. Each piece became a living being and they existed only to force "food" into its gaping mouth. A large vessel, firing one broadside at a time, burned as much as 1,100 pounds of gunpowder a minute. Smoke built up faster than it could escape through the gun ports, filling the decks with a thick, gray haze. Men saw each other as moving shadows; they loaded their weapons by touch. They coughed and sneezed; their eyes stung and tears flowed. Particles of unburned gunpowder clung to their sweaty bodies, turning them black as coal. They stank like cattle, but everyone stank alike and was too busy to notice.

The noise was hellish. Gunners shouted "Hurrah! Hurrah! Hurrah!" if one of their shots found its mark. Often, though, the *boom* of their guns was followed by the *crunch* of a ball bursting through their ship's side; one sailor likened it to "the smashing of a door with crowbars." There was a long *hissss* as the ball passed, or the *wheee* of razor-sharp splinters twisting through the air. And there were screams—lots of screams.

Gun decks were so crowded that it was hard for an enemy shot *not* to hit someone. Blood, a sailor recalled, "flowed like bilge water." It sloshed from side to side with the rolling of the ship, tracing odd patterns on the deck. Wounded men were carried below, to the sound of drops of blood falling *pat, pat, pat* on the deck. The dead were simply pushed out through the nearest gun port.

Not all the "dead" went willingly. In the *Revenge*, the ship's cobbler, a jolly fellow and quite a dancer, was helping with a gun when a shot knocked him cold. Crewmen were pushing him through a port when he came to and began kicking. "A good thing I showed you some dance steps," he said as they hauled him back, "otherwise I would have been snug in Davy Jones's locker."

Excitement often dulled pain, so that some men took the most awful wounds in stride. In the *Bellerophon*, an officer met a friend waiting for the surgeon, and said he was sorry to see him there. " 'Tis only a mere scratch," he replied, "and

I shall have to apologize to you by and by for leaving the deck on so trifling an occasion." Later, it turned out, he was waiting to have an arm amputated. Thomas Main, a sailor aboard the Leviathan, sang the whole of "Rule Britannia" while the surgeon cut off his arm.

There were even those who didn't realize they'd been hit until after the battle. A seaman aboard the Royal Sovereign wrote home about his experience:

But to tell you the truth of it, when the game [Trafalgar] began, I wished myself [home] with my plough again: but when they had given us one duster and I found myself snug and tight, I bid Fear kiss my bottom and set to in good earnest, and thought no more of being killed than if I were at the [country fair]. . . . How my three fingers got knocked overboard I don't know, but off they are, and I never missed 'em till I wanted 'em. You see by my writing it was my left hand, so I can write to you and fight for my King yet. . . .

Enemy vessels began to strike their colors one by one. Redoubtable's marines were about to board Victory when Téméraire hove into view. Though badly damaged herself, her guns were still intact, and she used them well. A broadside raked the Frenchman, hitting 200 men, including the captain. Nearby, Santissima Trinidad, her masts shot away, became a rolling wreck. Achille, a seventy-four-gun beauty, exploded in an orange ball of fire.

Among Achille's survivors was a black pig and a naked woman. Both were rescued. The pig was roasted and eaten with salt junk and grog. Jeanette, the woman, was a sailor's wife who'd come aboard as a stowaway: she'd taken off her clothes when they caught fire. Her rescuers gave her men's clothes, fed her, and later reunited her with her husband. They were not surprised to see a woman in the midst of the battle. Nearly all British vessels had female stowaways who couldn't bear to be away from husbands or lovers. They weren't supposed to be aboard, but officers pretended not to notice them if they behaved. During combat, however, they, too, did their duty. There were several women aboard *Victory*, who brought the gun crews water, served as powder monkeys, and even helped load the guns when men were put out of action.

Nelson lived long enough to learn of his greatest triumph. Shortly before *Achille* exploded, Captain Hardy told him that fourteen or fifteen enemy ships had been captured thus far, and that more were expected to surrender by evening. But by then the admiral was going fast. Taking his friend's hand, he told him that he had little time, adding, "Don't throw me overboard, Hardy."

"Oh, no, certainly not," the captain replied.

"Kiss me, Hardy," he said, asking for the comfort of a friend's touch in his last moments.

Hardy knelt down and kissed his cheek.

"Now I am pleased. Thank God, I have done my duty," he moaned. At half past four in the afternoon, Horatio Nelson died in the surgeon's arms.

Trafalgar was a magnificent triumph. By sunset, eighteen enemy ships had been captured or destroyed; another seven were taken or wrecked after the battle. Although the British ships were badly damaged, not one was lost.

The battle's human cost was staggering. British losses were 449 killed and 1,241 wounded, for a total of 1,690. French and Spanish losses were 4,408 dead, 2,545 wounded, and about 7,000 prisoners, for a total loss of 13,953. Most prisoners were put ashore and released on parole.

British sailors were horrified when they came aboard their prizes. Captured ships were filled with dead and dying. Casualties had been so heavy that few remained to throw them overboard. Midshipman William Badcock described the *Santissima Trinidad* in a letter to his father; he was sixteen and not very good at punctuation:

> I was on board our prize the Trinidad getting the prisoners out of her, she had between 3 and 400 killed and wounded, her Beams were covered with Blood, and pieces of Flesh, and the after part of her Decks with wounded, some without Legs and some without an Arm; what calamities War brings on, and what a number of Lives were put an end to on the 21st. . . . This Action is a famous thing for me [and] it will get me a Commission . . . as I have a claim on the Service, and my country.

That evening word of Nelson's death spread throughout the fleet. The joy of victory suddenly turned to sadness. Strong men, who'd accepted the horrors of war without flinching, suddenly gave in to their emotions. "Our dear Admiral Nelson is killed," a sailor wrote his father; "chaps that fought like the devil sit down and cry like a wench." A young lieutenant wrote that they'd lost a parent, "the seaman's friend and the father of the fleet." It broke their hearts to write about "our beloved Admiral," "our dear Admiral Nelson," "a friend I loved." Love is not a word one expects to hear after a bloody battle. But it was never more appropriate than after Trafalgar.

At the news of Nelson's death, Britain went into mourning. Friends, even strangers, stopped in the streets to cry, "We have lost Nelson!" His body, preserved in a barrel of brandy, was brought home and buried in St. Paul's Cathedral in London. The coffin was made from the mainmast of *L'Orient*, the

French flagship destroyed at the Battle of the Nile. Admiral Villeneuve took part in the funeral procession out of respect for a brave foe. The admiral was allowed to return to France, where Napoleon blamed him for the disaster. Disgraced, he committed suicide shortly afterward.

Several years later, the hero's statue was put atop the Nelson Column in Trafalgar Square in central London. *Victory*, when she was no longer of use to the fleet, was brought to Portsmouth. There she remains, a monument to her commander and his triumph. Painted black, with three broad yellow bands painted around her hull, she is much as Nelson left her. Thousands of visitors go each year to see the spot where he fell and relive his triumph. Nor has the Royal Navy forgotten their hero. To this day a seaman's daily rum ration is known as "Nelson's blood."

There is no French monument to Trafalgar. The French people were never officially told of the disaster. It remained a nonevent, something they learned of from foreign newspapers and by word of mouth.

Trafalgar did not "save" Britain: the danger vanished when Napoleon broke up the camp at Boulogne. Nor did it end the sea war. The emperor rebuilt his fleet to 71 ships of the line, but these were no match for Britain's 235 warships. Britannia still ruled the waves. The blockade continued to deprive France of overseas supplies and markets. The Royal Navy continued to score victories. Throughout the Napoleonic Wars, it sank or captured 115 enemy warships. Yet not a single one of its ships was sunk or burnt by enemy action; five were captured, of which three were later retaken. More English seamen (97,120) died of disease, shipwreck, and accident than were killed (6,540) by the enemy—a sad commentary on how Britain treated her defenders.

Napoleon disliked seamen more than ever. Yet there was one he could not help but admire. In the years after Trafalgar, he ordered a motto to be painted on all his warships: *"La France Compte Que Chacun Fera Son Devour"* ("France Expects Each One To Do His Duty"). He also kept a bust of Nelson in his study, which he'd stare at for hours on end. That was the highest honor he ever gave an enemy commander.

It was well-earned.

MASTER OF EUROPE

*"Power tends to corrupt, and
absolute power corrupts absolutely."*
—LORD JOHN ACTON, 1887

ADMIRAL VILLENEUVE's fleet was still anchored at Cadiz when his master set out for Central Europe. His objective was still Britain, only he was approaching it in a roundabout way. So long as Britain could find allies on the Continent, his empire would be insecure. His plan was to defeat her allies—Austria and Russia—bringing Europe under his control and leaving her isolated. Later, at his leisure, he'd prepare another invasion. This time he'd surely succeed, and then the future would be his to shape. Nothing would stand between him and world domination.

Napoleon had reason to be confident. Unlike other generals, who took orders from their governments, he *was* the government. As both supreme commander and ruler, he could do anything he pleased. And it pleased him to create the *Grande Armée*. It was his chosen weapon, designed by him for his personal use. He shaped it as a sculptor shapes marble, slowly, carefully, attending to every detail. The result was the deadliest war machine Europe had known since the Roman legions.

By the summer of 1805, the *Grande Armée* numbered a quarter of a million men. These were the flower of French manhood. Every male between the ages of twenty and sixty was required to sign up for the draft and serve as long as necessary. Napoleon, however, didn't take everyone of military age. Only those between twenty and twenty-five were put into combat units; the others went into the reserves, to be called up only in an emergency. He also realized that certain men were needed more at home than on the battlefield. These men—a husband with children, a widow's only son, a son with a father aged seventy-one or older—were excused from the service altogether.

Soldiering wasn't a bad life, especially if you were poor, illiterate, and knew nothing of the world beyond your dingy village or city slum. From this squalid existence you passed into a world of color and pageantry, of comradeship and pride. Joining the army was the first step in an adventure in which anything seemed possible. For some, it led to fame and wealth. For many others, however, it led to unmarked graves scattered the length and breadth of Europe.

Draftees joined their units in training camps, where they lived in crude wooden barracks with windows of greased paper rather than glass. Each unit initiated rookies in its own way. The most common method was tossing in a blanket; veterans often put pistols or other hard objects into the blanket with them, causing painful cuts and bruises. Newcomers took pain in stride, or earned their comrades' contempt as mama's boys, which hurt even more.

During the early weeks, you learned the ABCs of soldiering. You learned that rank must have its due; you must salute sergeants, as well as higher officers, or scrub latrines on your hands and knees. Countless hours were spent in mastering the musket and bayonet. And you marched. From sunup to sunset, you marched across fields, over hills, and through mud. Marching was good for both body and mind. It tightened your muscles and made you feel part of the group. You were no longer an individual with your own thoughts, but a member

ATLANTIC

OCEAN

Nort

Sea

SCOTLAND

Edinburgh

IRELAND

KINGDOM OF
GREAT BRITAIN
AND IRELAND

WALES   ENGLAND

Bristol   London   Amster...
Plymouth Portsmouth   Dover

English Channel   Boulogne   Antwerp

BELG...

Brest

Paris

FRENCH
EMPIRE

	FRENCH EMPIRE ABOUT 1811
	STATES CONTROLED BY FRANCE
	NEUTRAL STATES
✕	SELECTED MAJOR BATTLES
→	MAIN FRENCH CAMPAIGNS

Loire R.   *Seine R.*

Ge...
Lyons

La Coruña

Bayonne   Toulouse

Marseilles

Porto   Valladolid   Burgos

Pyrenees Mts.

KINGDOM OF
PORTUGAL

Torres
Vedras
✕
Lisbon

KINGDOM OF
SPAIN

Tagus R.   Madrid

Saragossa   *Ebro R.*   CATALONIA

Barcelona
Tortosa

Rhone R.

Badajoz

Sierra Morena

Guadalquivir R.   Bailén   ✕

Valencia

*BALEARIC
ISLANDS*

Seville

Cadiz   Malaga

Trafalgar ✕
Gibraltar

MEDIT...

of a fighting team. The team came first. You took pleasure in
its successes, felt shame at its failures.

The uniform also played a key role in shaping the soldier.
Infantrymen wore blue uniforms of thick, scratchy wool that
fit tight as a straightjacket. These were designed not only to
clothe you, but to make you feel bigger and tougher than you
really were. Bearskin hats gave an impression of height; padded
coats of strength. Unlike modern uniforms, whose dull colors
make poor targets, uniforms in Napoleon's day were meant to
attract attention. Loud colors enhanced pride, and thus courage. Coats were trimmed with all the colors of the rainbow.
They dripped with yellow, red, or gold braid. Cuffs and lapels
ranged from white to pink to green. Hats had sixteen-inch
plumes of scarlet, green, and yellow. Regimental badges were
embossed with the Eagle, the imperial coat of arms. God help
you if the sergeant caught you with unpolished buttons!

Rations were better than most men had known in civilian
life. Bread was the basic item in the soldier's diet. Known as
"munition bread," loaves were shaped like rings; you simply
strung them on a cord, tied the ends together, and slung it
over your shoulder. In addition to bread, you received a pound
of meat each day, plus vegetables, dried or fresh, depending
on the season. Soldiers, like sailors, disliked water. Besides
being unhealthy, water was a beggar's drink. Their basic drink
was a daily pot of beer, a bottle of red wine, and a glass of
brandy. Brandy, or *eau de vie* (water of life), was the French
soldier's painkiller and cheerer-upper. Wise generals issued a
double brandy ration before each battle. If brandy was in short
supply, soldiers received a mixture of pure alcohol and water,
colored with tea and spiked with pepper to give it zing. Men,
their spirits stiffened with "liquid courage," often went into
battle tipsy.

Whether drunk or sober, soldiers had to obey the rules. Napoleon believed that the punishment should fit the crime. Crimes like desertion, murder, and striking an officer meant the firing squad. Lesser offenses—stealing, absence without leave, drunkenness—brought a week in the guardhouse on a diet of bread and water. One's comrades, however, had their own ideas of justice. Barrack-room law made the guardhouse seem like kindergarten. A thief, for example, might have to "run the gauntlet." His unit would form two lines and, as he ran between them, whack him with their heavy shoes. No one was above the law. When General Gouvion Saint-Cyr left his post without permission, the emperor calmly told him: "If, in two hours, you are not on the road [back], you will be shot before noon."

A soldier could hope, in time, to become a member of the Imperial Guard. Not only did the Guard protect the emperor, it was his last word on the battlefield. Ordinarily, it stood on the sidelines during a battle. Men might be dying by the thousands, but he kept it in reserve. Only in the most desperate actions, with disaster staring him in the face, did he send it into action. Then, without fail, it rolled over the enemy like a tidal wave at sea.

The Guard was an army within an army. Divided into two branches—Young Guard and Old Guard—it consisted of 45,000 handpicked men. Guardsmen had to be at least five feet ten inches tall; ordinary draftees need be only five feet one inch. The Young Guard were the best of the draftees. Members of the Old Guard had at least five years of service, had fought in two campaigns, and had a spotless record. Guardsmen wore fancier uniforms, lived in better quarters, and earned twice the pay of others of the same rank.

The Old Guard were fearsome in appearance. Tall, bony

The most feared forces of Napoleon's army. AT RIGHT, a grenadier of the Imperial Guard, whose members were picked from the toughest veterans of the *Grande Armée*. From a drawing based on a painting by Nicolas-Toussaint Charlet. BELOW, Joachim Murat, probably the finest cavalry commander in Europe at the time, leads the French cavalry at the Battle of Jena. From a painting by Henri Chartier.

fellows with gold earrings and quick tempers, they strutted about as if they owned the world. A visitor to their camp described a typical Guardsman: "Shako [tall cap] over the ear; sabre trailing; face disfigured and divided into two by an immense scar; upturned moustaches half a foot long, stiffened with wax, and losing themselves at the ears; two great plaited tresses of hair hanging from the temples, which appeared from under the shako and fell on the chest; and with all this what an air!—the air of a swaggering ruffian." He and his comrades were men after Napoleon's heart. They were his *grognards* (grumblers)—those who'd never let him down.

The emperor was one of the best military psychologists of all time. He knew about soldiers, what made them tick and how to get the most out of them. "In war," he said, "morale and opinion are more than half the battle." By this he meant that tactics and weapons and overwhelming numbers cannot bring victory by themselves. Nor can bravery be bought with money. The key to victory lay within the human spirit, in the soldier's eagerness to serve beyond the call of duty. To achieve that, a commander had to light the *Feu Sacre* (Sacred Fire), in each of his men. He must make them want to fight and win, or die trying.

Napoleon knew how to light the *Feu Sacre* so that nothing could put it out. During campaigns, his tent was pitched in the center of the camp, surrounded by his trusty *grognards*. He'd wander around the campfires alone, freely mixing with the men. At one fire he'd help himself to a bowl of soup from the bubbling pot; at another he'd pass around his snuffbox with the golden letter "N" on the lid. Soldiers never addressed him as "Sire" or "Your Majesty." He was simply *"Mon Empereur!"* ("My Emperor!") They could just as easily have called him *"Mon Ami!"* ("My Friend!")

Napoleon always made it a point to recognize the old-timers. Once he saw a soldier who'd risked his life to recover his hat during the siege of Acre. He wanted to know why he was still a private. When the man replied that he drank too much, the emperor shook his head in disapproval but smiled and patted his cheek. "You were with me in Egypt," he'd say to another. "How many campaigns? How many wounds?" The man stood before him, ramrod-straight, chin in, chest out, smiling from ear to ear. His favorite compliment was to grab a man's earlobe and give it a hard pinch. Anyone pinched by the emperor felt himself grow ten feet tall in front of his envious comrades.

Napoleon listened to soldiers' complaints—and saw that they were taken care of promptly. A soldier once stepped from the ranks during a review. His mother was sick and he needed a few weeks' leave. The emperor instantly produced a fistful of gold coins and told him to get going. Then there was the time he found an exhausted sentry asleep at his post. Another general would have had him shot; he stood guard in his place.

Napoleon even shared his quarters with common soldiers. A thunderstorm once forced him to spend the night in a one-room farmhouse. Upon entering, he found a drummer dozing beside the stove. His aides ordered the fellow out, but he was in a feisty mood. "There's room enough for everybody!" he shouted. "I'm cold. I'm wounded. I like it here, and I'm going to stay." The aides were outraged. The nerve of the fellow! How dare he talk that way in front of the emperor! Napoleon merely laughed and waved *them* out the door. The next morning, they found the two sitting, and snoring, on either side of the stove. For days afterward, soldiers spoke of nothing but their emperor's concern for their well-being.

The emperor was forever holding parades, giving stirring

speeches, and distributing rewards. Brave men received pensions and honors. The bravest of the brave entered the Legion of Honor, an organization founded by Napoleon to recognize those who'd served France beyond the call of duty. The Legion included civilians and soldiers, privates and generals. Unlike the old nobility of birth, legionnaires were a nobility of merit, and thus the best of all.

The army embodied the Revolution's ideal of equality. Every draftee, according to the saying, "had a marshal's baton in his knapsack." Education and connections didn't matter in the *Grande Armée*. Whatever your background, you could rise through the ranks on ability alone. It happened all the time. After a battle, Napoleon would ask for the names of the bravest soldiers. Officers sent their most deserving sergeants, even privates, to the emperor's tent. He'd ask each a few questions about his record and wounds. If he liked what he heard, he'd say: "I make you an officer!" When the new officer, usually a lieutenant, returned to his unit, the privates would shoot his pack to pieces, for he'd no longer have to carry it. The army's highest officers, the marshals, had all proven themselves in battle. Marshal Murat, regarded as the best cavalry officer in Europe, was the son of an innkeeper. Other marshals were the sons of barrel makers, millers, stonemasons, and stable boys.

The bonds between emperor and army were so strong that not even defeat could break them. Soldiers so loved Napoleon that they gladly gave their lives for him. His own life, however, was so precious that they'd do anything to keep him from harm. Even disobey. During one battle, for example, the Guard refused to charge unless he moved to a less exposed position. His presence alone seemed to work miracles. The

Duke of Wellington used to say that his presence on a battlefield was worth 40,000 troops. Even enemy enlisted men admired "Boney."

Napoleon, however, cared little for his soldiers' lives. If he
was kind to them, it was for the same reason that a farmer
cares for his oxen: to make them serve him better. But he
didn't love them. Like anyone else in his empire, soldiers were
merely tools to be used—and used up—in achieving his aims.
"Troops," he explained, "are made to let themselves be killed."
He used to refer to draftees as "income," of which he "spent"
a certain number each month.

FROM BOULOGNE to the Rhine River, France's eastern border,
is over 300 miles. The *Grande Armée* covered the distance in
quick-time, or 120 steps per minute. It was an exhausting pace,
especially since each soldier wore a pack weighing at least sixty
pounds. Everything he needed was on his back: musket and
bayonet, sixty rounds of ammunition, a spare pair of pants,
shovel, water canteen, wine bottle, full-dress uniform, two
pair of shoes, two extra shirts, food, and personal things such
as a pipe, tobacco, writing materials, and letters from home.
Units marched day and night with only ten-minute breaks
every two hours. Many collapsed along the way; many others
marched while asleep.

Soldiers sang to set the pace and keep awake. Then, as now,
soldiers' songs were much the same. There were sentimental
songs like "Where Could One Better Be Than in the Bosom
of His Family?" and food songs like "I Love Onions Fried in
Oil." There was also no end to humorous songs. A special
favorite boasted of what they'd do to the enemy: "We Are
Going to Jab Their Ass." Another made fun of torn pants:

My britches have been torn in half.
Boy, that makes me want to laugh!
Most of all, they sang of courage and glory. Strains of "The
Victory is Ours" mingled with the "Song of Departure":
The trumpet of war sounds
The hour of battle nears.
Tremble, enemies of France!

The Austrians were first to tremble. No sooner did the
Grande Armée cross the Rhine than Napoleon hurled it toward
their base at Ulm in eastern Germany. It moved so swiftly that
on October 20, 1805, the enemy was surrounded before it
realized its danger. Since a battle would have meant certain
annihilation, General Karl Mack, the Austrian commander,
gave up without striking a blow. Austria's loss of 27,000 troops,
18 generals, and 65 cannons offset the defeat at Trafalgar the
following day.

Emperor Francis II, however, refused to ask for peace terms.
Vienna was abandoned to the invader, while his remaining
forces linked up with the Russians under Czar Alexander I.
The allies planned to do to Napoleon what he'd done to them
at Ulm: slip behind him to cut his line of retreat and trap him
far from home.

A glance at his maps told the emperor what they were up
to. Rather than walk into their trap, he decided to bait a trap
of his own. Toward the end of November, the *Grande Armée*
took positions along the Goldbach, a shallow creek sixty miles
north of Vienna. Across the creek, and overlooking it, was a
low plateau with a tiny village called Austerlitz. Napoleon
would let the allies take the high ground. While his main force
stood along the creek, opposite the plateau, he'd deliberately
extend his right flank, or right wing of his army. It would be

like dangling a wriggling worm before a hungry fish. The allies, tempted by an "easy" victory, would snap at the bait, weakening their own main force in front of Austerlitz. At that moment French columns would storm the plateau, split their force in two, and attack each half from the sides and rear. It was a beautiful plan and it worked like a charm.

Toward evening of December 1, the Austro-Russian forces occupied the plateau. The *Grande Armée* saw their campfires above, thousands of pinpoints of light flickering against the black sky. A cold wind blew as the French huddled around their own fires, chewing their hard crusts of bread and waiting for the dawn.

Napoleon decided to visit the campsites alone. He'd just set out when his horse stumbled over a log. A soldier was lighting a torch to show the way when he realized who the visitor was. "*L'Empereur!*" he shouted.

"Silence!" Napoleon scolded. "All you should be thinking of right now is sharpening your bayonets!"

This time his words fell on deaf ears. Once the soldiers knew he was among them, they ran from their campsites, lit more torches, and waved them as he passed. Enemy sentries could see the swaying torches on the plain below. They were also happy, for they believed the French were preparing to run away.

When Napoleon returned to his tent, he was happiest of all. "This is the finest day of my life!" he murmured again and again. Victory was in the air. He could feel it in his bones.

December 2, the first anniversary of his coronation, was a fine autumn day. The sun burned off the morning mist, revealing 35,000 Russians moving to attack the French right. Tall men in fur hats, they advanced behind a glinting wall of bayonets. Nearing the stream, they gave their battle cry: "Urrah! Urrah! Urrah!"

Suddenly 10,000 Frenchmen cut loose with cannons and muskets. Spouts of earth leaped skyward, shooting bodies aloft. Soldiers fell in rows, only to have others take their places. The defenders refused to yield while the attackers refused to quit. Russian commanders, convinced that a breakthrough was near, poured in their reserves, further thinning their line on the plateau.

Napoleon smiled as he followed the action with his spyglass. "Now, gentlemen," said he, snapping it shut, "let us begin a great day."

His staff knew what had to be done. Orders were shouted. Drummers beat the *pas de charge* (signal to charge). It was a strange, ominous sound that sent chills up men's spines:

The rum dum. The rum dum.

The rummadum dummadum, dum, dum, dum

The rum dum. The rum dum.

The rummadum dummadum, dum, dum, dum

Massed infantry columns were already attacking when a terrific pounding rose above the din of battle. The French cavalry were on the move.

The old armies used cavalry as modern armies use tanks. During an advance, cavalry scouted ahead of the main force to gain information and keep enemy scouts at a safe distance. Once the enemy was located, cavalry probed his defenses, searching for weak spots. On the day of battle, the cavalry, armed with long swords and a pair of pistols, were held in reserve until the critical moment. The most important cavalrymen were known as cuirassiers. Big men on big horses, each wore a steel helmet and a cuirass, a steel vest that protected the chest and back.

Napoleon's cuirassiers waited "boot to boot" in solid ranks, ready to charge as one and strike the enemy line together.

Marshal Louis Davout, their commander, was a veteran of countless battles. His order was brutally simple: "Let no one escape!"

Davout's bugler gave the signal, which was taken up by each squadron's bugler in turn. Soon the entire plain echoed to the metallic calls. The attack began with a trot that changed to a slow gallop as the squadrons advanced. The solid mass rolled onward like a force of nature. Faster, faster, it moved, until fifty yards from the enemy line.

The bugle sounded again.

"Charge!"

Troopers spurred their mounts into a full gallop. "*Vive l'Empereur!*" they shouted and drew their swords.

The allies broke under the combined weight of French infantry and cavalry. Thousands threw down their muskets and ran for their lives. It was now every man for himself.

Cuirassiers galloped after them at top speed. Their heavy swords rose and fell as they came up behind the fugitives. Men dropped, screaming, their backs torn open from shoulder to waist. The most horrible scenes were on the French right, where whole regiments tried to escape across a frozen pond. Napoleon had his guns bombard the ice, breaking it and sending thousands to a watery grave.

Czar Alexander joined the fleeing mob. Hours later, safe at last, he reined in his horse and sat down beside the road. "We are babies in the hands of a giant," he moaned. Then the Lord's Servant, Czar of All the Russias, buried his face in his hands and burst into tears. He was twenty-eight and an amateur soldier who loved to watch parades and hear the boom of artillery salutes. Austerlitz was his first real battle, and it turned his stomach.

Austerlitz was Napoleon's masterpiece and one of the most

"perfect" battles ever fought. By nightfall the enemy had ceased to exist as a military force. Over 11,000 Russians and 4,000 Austrians lay dead on the field; another 12,000 had been captured, along with 185 heavy guns. French losses were light by comparison: 1,305 killed and 6,940 wounded.

The next day Napoleon congratulated his victorious troops: *Soldats! Je suis content de vous!* (Soldiers! I am pleased with you!) On the day of Austerlitz, you justified everything that I had expected of your boldness. . . . When I lead you back to France you will be the object of my most tender care. My people will greet you with joy and it will be enough for you to say, "I was at Austerlitz," to hear them reply, "There stands a hero!"

The emperor was as good as his word—this time. Even before their return, construction began in Paris on the Arc de Triomphe (Arch of Triumph), his monument to the *Grande Armée*. Captured allied guns were melted down and cast into a huge statue of himself dressed as a Roman Caesar. He honored the dead by adopting their children as his own and allowing them to add "Napoleon" to their names. All orphans of Austerlitz received the best education at government expense.

One of the wounded was singled out for special praise. In 1792, while still a teenager, Mary Shellench had disguised herself as a man and enlisted as a private. She'd fought bravely in many battles, keeping her secret until wounded at Austerlitz. The surgeons were shocked when they stripped the young "fellow" to dress the wound. Napoleon was delighted. He made Mary a member of the Legion of Honor and discharged her with the rank and pay of a lieutenant.

Meanwhile, the allies begged for a truce. In exchange for a ceasefire, the Russians agreed to leave Austrian territory, while the Austrians began peace talks. By the Treaty of Pressburg (December 26), they handed over forty million francs in gold and gave up Venetia in Italy, the Tyrol in western Austria, plus several smaller districts in Germany—a total of three million subjects.

Napoleon had won a battle but not the war. As the Russians retreated eastward, Prussia joined the struggle. Prussia had once been a great military power. Although its army was still large, its training and tactics were outdated. King Frederick William III knew little about the changes in warfare since the French Revolution. All he knew was that Napoleon had to be destroyed, and that he was the man to do it. He'd defeat that "robber" with his whip—no need to waste gunpowder on such a small job. His soldiers agreed. The Prussian army, to them, was still second to none. Officers sharpened their swords on the steps of the French embassy in Berlin as a sign of contempt. One old colonel, a red-faced braggart with a drooping mustache, didn't see what the fuss was all about. "We don't need swords," he snorted. "Clubs will suffice for those French dogs!"

The "French dogs" showed their teeth the following year. Napoleon invaded Prussia and made a dash for Berlin. On October 14, 1806, he fought two battles at the same time— Jena and Auerstädt. The Prussians wore splendid uniforms and marched to perfection. The French formed their columns, unlimbered their guns, and chewed up the enemy divisions one after another. Two weeks later, Berliners watched in stunned silence as the *Grande Armée* paraded through the Brandenburg Gate, a monument to Prussia's past triumphs.

Prussia was defeated, but Russia seemed stronger than ever. Already Russian troops were flooding into East Prussia, along the border with Poland. To block their advance, Napoleon marched into Poland with 80,000 men. The Poles, who hated the Russians, welcomed him as a liberator. Thousands of their young men joined the *Grande Armée*, serving loyally in the wars that followed. Napoleon also fell in love with Countess Marie Walewska, an eighteen-year-old beauty from Warsaw. Known as "The Emperor's Polish Wife," she was to bear his first child, a son named Alexander.

On February 8, 1807, Napoleon caught the Russians at Eylau. This time, however, things didn't go according to plan. For seven hours, during a howling blizzard, 150,000 men stabbed, shot, and blew each other to bits on the frozen plain. The Russians finally withdrew, allowing the emperor to claim victory. But he knew it to be a hollow claim. He wandered the battlefield, head bowed, hands clenched behind his back, brooding. The dead lay around him, stiff and blue, in piles five deep. Everywhere blood had turned snowdrifts into pools of red slush. "What a massacre!" he told an aide. "And to no purpose!" The Russians were far from beaten; they'd be back, stronger than ever.

Both armies went into winter quarters to rebuild and wait for the next round. That came in the spring, on June 14, at Friedland a few miles north of Eylau. This time there was no doubt about the winner. After losing 25,000 men and all his artillery, Czar Alexander asked for peace.

The two emperors met at Tilsit on the Russo-Polish border. They liked each other—or *said* they did—from the very beginning. Napoleon admired the czar's education and sense of humor. Alexander praised the emperor's charm and intelligence. After lengthy discussions, they made peace at others' expense. Prussia was crippled as a major power. Not only did she lose her western provinces, she was fined 311 million francs and forced to accept a French army of occupation. Russia was given a "free hand" in Sweden, Finland, and Turkey. Translation: she could take them over if she wished. Finally, Alexander offered to make peace between Britain and France. If Britain refused, he promised to declare war and join a Continental blockade against British manufactured goods.

Here was the key to the Treaty of Tilsit. By 1807, Europe was at the dictator's mercy. But Britain, safe behind her floating fortresses, continued to defy him. His only weapon against her was an economic blockade—the "Continental System." Napoleon believed that cutting her trade with the European continent would bring her to her knees. A bankrupt Britain couldn't help her allies with money and weapons. Unemployment would spread, causing riots in the crowded factory towns. There might even be a revolution in which the rebels asked for French aid.

The only problem was that the Continental System couldn't work. British products were better and cheaper than those made on the Continent. Keeping them out was like keeping a sieve from leaking. The goods poured in through every opening. They entered in ships flying Portuguese and Spanish flags; the certificates declaring these as their countries of manufacture were fakes printed in London. Often tradesmen didn't even bother with such formalities. Every deserted stretch of coast, every tiny cove, became a smugglers' den. People saw the smuggler not as an outlaw, but as a helper who brought what they needed at fair prices. Even the *Grande Armée* dealt with smugglers. Troops based in Poland, for example, wore British-made overcoats and shoes.

The true meaning of Trafalgar now became clear. Britain's command of the sea enabled her to send her products anywhere, anytime. Napoleon, unable to control the sea, was forced to dominate the Continent. The Continental System had to be made airtight. It became an obsession with him, a kind of madness driving him on and on. Every opening into Europe had to be sealed, plugged, nailed shut. It was this effort that triggered the Peninsular War and the Russian invasion, the most disastrous of the Napoleonic Wars. Within four years, they tore the heart out of his empire.

After Tilsit, only Portugal stood outside the Continental System. In November 1807, Napoleon demanded that she close her ports to British trade. She refused and a French army marched across Spain to seize Lisbon, her capital and chief seaport. The Spaniards had allowed the French to pass in return for a secret promise of one-third of their neighbor's territory. It seemed like a good deal: France would do the fighting, while Spain reaped the profit.

Napoleon's generosity, however, had a hidden purpose. Months earlier, he'd decided to conquer the entire Iberian Peninsula—Spain and Portugal. The capture of Lisbon, though necessary in itself, was an excuse to slip his troops inside Spain without a fight. Once there, they'd quietly occupy the main cities, ports, and fortresses. It would all be over before the Spaniards realized what their "friends" had done.

The plan seemed foolproof, if only because Napoleon had fooled himself. People tend to underestimate those they despise. And he despised the Spaniards. Their king, Charles IV, really was a silly do-nothing; Queen Maria Luisa was vicious and, some said, had a face that could stop a clock. The Spaniards took after their rulers; or so they did in Napoleon's mind. "The Spanish people," he wrote in a private letter, "is vile and cowardly, about the same as I found the Arabs to be." They'd be a pushover for brave, clever Frenchmen.

Napoleon made his move in April 1808. The Spanish royal family was invited to visit France as the emperor's honored guests. But as soon as they arrived, they were arrested and the king forced to abdicate in favor of Joseph Bonaparte. Thus, with a stroke of the pen, the emperor carried out a "bloodless conquest." Or so he thought.

Spaniards were outraged. On May 2 (*El Dos de Mayo*), Madrid, the capital, rose against its foreign "friends." The revolt, unorganized and unplanned, was like an idea that clicks in many people's minds at the same moment. Suddenly *madrileños* grabbed whatever weapons were handy and swarmed into the streets. Scores of Frenchmen, taken by surprise, were massacred. Battle-hardened cuirassiers found themselves fleeing before surging crowds. Women attacked a cavalry squadron, plunging knives into the horses' bellies and into the riders' throats as they fell. Bricks and tiles, pieces of furniture and boiling water, poured from windows. A flowerpot dropped from a balcony cracked a French lieutenant's skull, killing him instantly.

Yet people could do no more than sacrifice their lives. As *El Dos de Mayo* wore on, French discipline and firepower began to tell. The worst outrages of the Reign of Terror were now reenacted in Madrid. People were arrested, tied in batches, and bayoneted. Hundreds of others died before firing squads. The innocent fell with the guilty, for the executioners wanted to set an example. They did, only it wasn't the example they expected.

El Dos de Mayo was a torch flung into a barrel of gunpowder. As the sound of musketry echoed through the night, frightened, dazed people fled Madrid. Their cry, carried from village to village, echoed across the land:

Vengeance and war!

Vengeance and war!

War to the knife!

Spain exploded in hatred and rage. There had never been

anything like it in European history. A whole nation rose as
one person. *Juntas* (patriotic councils) sprang up everywhere
to lead the uprising. Spaniards of all classes—nobles, priests,
soldiers, peasants, workers—joined in a national holy war.
The French, they said, weren't ordinary enemies, like the
English. They were not human beings at all, but devils risen
from hell. And their devil-in-chief, Napoleon, was the enemy
of God and humanity. Despite his Concordat with the pope,
he was the "Great Satan," the "Antichrist," lord of evil and
darkness. Religious people made the sign of the cross over their
mouths after mentioning his or the devil's name. King Joseph
was "king by the grace of the devil." Once the uprising began,
it became impossible to put down. Napoleon had reason to
call it the "Spanish ulcer."

The first test of Spanish determination came at Saragossa,
a walled city on the Ebro River. The arrival of a 15,000-man
French army in June stirred up a hornet's nest. Saragossans
rushed to their city's defense. Volunteers, among them women
and children, dug trenches. Barricades were raised in the narrow streets and each house turned into a fortress. Olive groves
outside the city gates were burned by their owners to deprive
the enemy of cover.

French artillery blasted the defenders day and night. Guns
roared, the earth shook, buildings collapsed in clouds of dust.
French infantry units often broke into the city's outskirts, where
their troubles really began. Every open space became a killing
ground, claiming hundreds of lives. If they entered a house,
the Spaniards fought from room to room, floor to floor, setting
it on fire rather than see it taken.

Agostina Domenech, twenty-two, outdid everyone in saving
her city at a critical moment. One day French infantry attacked
the main gate. They were drawing near when shells wiped out

a gun battery covering the gate. Fortunately Agostina, whose job it was to bring water to the fighting men, saw the French coming. She dropped her bucket and ran among the dead gunners, sprawled near their weapons. One still clutched a rope match in his hand. Shouting *"Viva España"* ("Long Live Spain"), she grabbed the match and went from gun to gun, firing them as she passed. A storm of grapeshot stopped the French in their tracks. Spanish soldiers, inspired by her courage, then hurled them back with a bayonet charge. Agostina fought in all the battles that followed. Known as "the Maid of Saragossa," she is still considered Spain's most heroic woman.

In the meantime, General Pierre Dupont had been sent to conquer southern Spain. Dupont had a fine record, but his troops were raw recruits who often got out of hand. Wherever they appeared, they stole whatever they could carry; everything else was left in ashes.

Their crimes roused Spanish fury, as 30,000 soldiers and volunteers gathered along their line of march. On July 20, they trapped them at Bailén in the Sierra Morenas. Dupont surrendered his entire force of 17,242 men. The Spaniards quickly moved to threaten Madrid, forcing King Joseph to abandon his capital at the end of July. Finally, on August 10, he gave up the siege of Saragossa.

Napoleon was furious. It was all Dupont's fault, he shouted, his face flushed and the veins bulging in his throat. Here he'd worked out such a beautiful plan, and that nitwit had failed. Not that he cared about the captives' lives; they meant nothing to him. But the emperor's pride had been wounded, his "good name" dragged in the mud. Better death—other people's deaths—than dishonor! "I would have preferred being told that they are dead . . . to knowing that they have dishonored themselves . . . without fighting."

Bailén was a disaster, although no "Austerlitz in reverse," as Napoleon's enemies claimed. That didn't matter. As he himself liked to say, it is not the truth that counts, but what people believe is the truth. Until Bailén, his armies seemed invincible, having never been defeated in battle. Bailén showed that they could not only be defeated but forced to surrender. All of a sudden Europe's captive peoples began to hope that they could break the dictator's power.

Yet even now Napoleon couldn't imagine the dangers lurking in Spain. He continued to think of it as an ordinary war that could be ended by a few crushing victories. Late in October, he took 100,000 of his finest veterans across the Pyrenees Mountains into Spain. This time he pulled no punches. He smashed Spain's poorly led army, scattering it like dry leaves in a windstorm. On December 4, he entered Madrid, where he tried to smooth things over by abolishing the Spanish Inquisition, which had persecuted those with "false" religious beliefs since the Middle Ages. But the people wouldn't take anything from his "devil's" hands. After a brief stay in the capital, he defeated the remaining Spanish forces and a small British army that had been sent to help them.

Saragossa fell on February 20, 1809, after a second siege lasting sixty days. Marshal Jean Lannes, one of the *Grande Armée*'s most brilliant officers, attacked with 50,000 troops and scores of heavy guns. Lannes' gunners blew the defenders from street to street, house to house, until there was nothing to do but surrender. The city was a mass of charred rubble and decaying bodies. A German officer serving with the French army never forgot the hellish scene. Years later, he wrote:

Under the arcades could be seen pell-mell, children,
old people, the sick, the dying, corpses, household
articles. . . . On the square itself there were countless
corpses, many completely naked . . . lying around in
heaps. Among the living one saw awfully sad figures.
Especially pitiful were the skeleton-like children. Although we stayed only a short time in Saragossa, a sort
of terror grips me even today when I think of what
took place there.

The battle for Saragossa was still raging when Napoleon
hurriedly left the country. The Austrians, encouraged by Bailén, were preparing for another war when the news reached
him in Spain. From April to July 1809, he met them in three
battles. At Eckmühl (April 29), he routed a large army and
went on to capture Vienna after a thunderous bombardment;
it was so noisy that Beethoven held pillows over his aching
ears. A month later, on May 21 and 22, Napoleon lost the
battle of Aspern-Essling near Vienna. It wasn't a serious defeat,
but it was his first ever and it raised enemy hopes. Perhaps,
people wondered, he'd lost his touch. They learned better at
Wagram, where, on July 5 and 6, he killed or captured 45,000
enemy soldiers. It was all over with Austria. Once again Francis
II sued for peace. This time Napoleon's demands were crushing. Austria lost 32,000 square miles of territory, mostly along
the eastern shore of the Adriatic Sea, which he wanted as a
base for future conquests in Turkey.

Spain fought on. Her armies broken, she began guerrilla
warfare soon after Napoleon's departure. *Guerrilla* is Spanish
for "little war"; that is, war fought by roving bands of civilians
operating behind enemy lines. Spain's "little war," however,
was little only in name. Spain was the first civilized nation to
fight a guerrilla war on a large scale. Guerrilla warfare showed

Napoleon watches his cavalry ride into action at the Battle of Wagram, which brought Austria under his control once again. From a drawing based on a painting by Émile-Jean-Horace Vernet. While Napoleon's empire grew, only Spain continued to resist his forces. BELOW, a scene from Francisco Goya's "The Disasters of War" series depicts one of the countless atrocities commited by French troops in their war against the Spanish guerillas.

that it could cut a more powerful enemy down to size. Better
still, it showed *how* this could be done. The lessons learned
in Spain were applied in the twentieth century by Mao Tse-
tung in China and by the Vietnamese communists, or Viet
Cong.

Guerrillas came from all walks of life. They were nobles,
peasants, merchants, students, shepherds, and former soldiers.
Women served in many capacities: cooks, nurses, spies, fighters. Some of the fiercest fighters were Roman Catholic priests
who saw the French as enemies of God. Among them was
Fray Lucas Rafael, a monk who claimed to have killed 600
French "devil worshipers" with his own hands—a claim no
one has ever disputed.

Patriots formed bands of 50 to 150 under leaders chosen by
themselves. Being small, these bands could hide easily, move
swiftly, and strike without warning. Spain, a land of rugged
mountains, deep gorges, and gloomy forests, is well-suited to
this kind of warfare. Guerrillas would spring out of nowhere,
kill, and vanish like wisps of smoke. If they met strong resist
ance, they broke contact, fleeing to their hideouts until ready
to strike elsewhere. Traveling lightly, they lived off whatever
they could take from the enemy and gifts from friendly villagers. It was essential to stay on good terms with the locals,
who provided valuable information and hid their wounded
until they were well enough to travel.

No Frenchman was safe. Guerrillas might ambush a patrol
here, raid an outpost there, and make nuisances of themselves
everywhere. Individual soldiers were sniped at, clubbed, and
stabbed; Spanish girlfriends slit their lovers' throats while they
slept. These actions, small as they were, hurt the enemy more
than Spain's armies had ever done. During the five years 1808
to 1813, guerrillas killed over 180,000 Frenchmen, or about

100 per day. The wounded were at least three times that number.

This was a new kind of war for the French. Elsewhere in Europe, after winning a few big battles the war ended and the soldiers could relax; civilians wouldn't dream of angering their conquerors. In Spain, there was no such thing as winning a battle against guerrillas. The French controlled only the ground they stood upon—usually a walled town or a fortified monastery. Everything else belonged to the guerrillas. If a local commander tried to retaliate, he was beaten even before he started. It was impossible to keep secrets, since the occupied areas swarmed with spies. As soon as they saw troops preparing to leave, they sent word to their friends in the countryside.

Guerrillas could never be taken by surprise. If troops came too close for comfort, they simply went elsewhere. Villages loyal to them were unpleasant places for outsiders. The moment the French entered, they felt the people's hatred. This took different forms. People became sullen, refused to speak, or looked away when spoken to. Often there were problems with the food they demanded. A *señorita* would spit (or worse) into wine before serving her unwelcome guests. Or soldiers noticed strange brown objects floating in their soup kettle—mice. Bread might be smeared with "butter" made from the fat of executed criminals. Some soldiers, not knowing the truth, said their bread tasted unusually good.

Fear and frustration deepened the soldiers' hatred of Spaniards. Hatred gave rise to atrocities, horrible crimes against civilians. Villages giving shelter to guerrillas were looted and then burned to the ground. No effort was made to separate the innocent from the guilty: all villagers suffered. Men were shot, women raped, and children tossed into burning churches. The village of Arenas de San Pedro was typical. In

February 1809, it was raided by Germans serving with the French army. "Sharpshooters," an officer recalled, "amused themselves by running after fleeing Spaniards and shooting them down like hares at the hunt. I have seen men burst out laughing when their victims fell into the grass."

The Spaniards replied with atrocities of their own. Soldiers who fell into their hands were shown no mercy. Captives might be placed between two boards and sawed in half, or buried up to the shoulders and their heads used as pins in bowling matches. Still others were torn to pieces, boiled in oil, crucified upside down, and hung up by the feet in fireplaces. Guerrillas raided hospitals, burning the patients alive in their beds. The French retaliated in kind, taking ten lives for one. And so it went, an eye for an eye, a life for a life, until it seemed that no one would remain but the blind and the dead.

Yet it was the war's very horror that began to wear down French morale. It all seemed so hopeless, so useless—so endless. "Dear Mother," a private wrote on May 18, 1810, "I don't think that since the day I became a soldier I have ever been so badly off as now. For the past month and a half we have been in the mountains chasing brigands [i.e. guerrillas]. . . . All these mountains have been pillaged in such a manner that there is not one soul that is not against us." "Dear Mother and Sister," wrote another, "the war is still playing its game and we still don't know when it will end. . . . The peasants here are all brigands. Every day they murder some of our men. We burn their villages. But it is all in vain. They are incorrigible people."

The guerrillas might tie down Napoleon's forces for years, but they could never defeat them on their own. Only Britain could provide the help they needed. Protestant England and

Roman Catholic Spain had been enemies since the days of the Invincible Armada. Yet each country remembered the old adage: "The enemy of my enemy is my friend." Since they now hated Napoleon more than each other, they became allies. Britain had already helped on a small scale in 1808. Early the next year, the vanguard of a 100,000-man army landed in Portugal.

The army's leader was Sir Arthur Wellesley, one of England's greatest soldiers. Born the same year as Napoleon into an aristocratic family, he'd also entered the army in 1786 at the age of seventeen. After serving in India, he returned to Europe to fight the French. Wellesley was five feet ten inches tall, slim and muscular, with broad shoulders and a pale face with a large nose and clear blue eyes. Although a general, he dressed as a civilian. His favorite outfit was a blue coat, a short cape, and a small cocked hat; except for a few medals, there was nothing to show his rank. Identification wasn't necessary, since everyone knew "Old Nosey" on sight. A shy, tense man, he felt most comfortable around children. Whenever there was time, he'd take walks with Spanish children, telling them stories and buying them sweets in the local marketplace.

Wellesley was a no-nonsense soldier. Like Napoleon, he had a quick temper. Although soft-spoken, his words stung like hornets' stings. He once made a British general burst into tears; another time he left a Spanish general shivering in his boots. A stickler for military form, he insisted that soldiers look the part. The British Guards, for example, were forbidden to carry umbrellas in the pouring rain; umbrellas, he growled, were "not only ridiculous but unmilitary."

Wellesley called his troops "the scum of the earth," "a pack of rascals," "a crowd who only enlist for drink, and can only be managed by the whip." There was truth in his description. Respectable families would sooner see a son dead than "gone for a soldier." Soldiering was a low, mean profession. No one joined the ranks unless he had to. Britain's tramps, no-goods, and dropouts enlisted as a last resort to fill empty bellies. Enlistment was for life, or until one was too old or too ill to serve. It took a firm hand to keep such men in line. And Wellesley's hand was *very* firm. During the Peninsular War, he had hundreds whipped, hanged, and shot for breaking the rules. His Redcoats respected him, but they had no love for him.

Nor did they have any love for their allies. Private William Wheeler could find nothing good to say about the Iberian peoples. Wheeler was unusual for a common soldier: he could write. *The Letters of Private Wheeler, 1809–1828* is the best account of the Peninsular War as seen from the ranks. Britain's allies were:

> . . . an ignorant, superstitious, priest-ridden, dirty, lousy set of poor Devils. . . . Without seeing them it is impossible to conceive there exist a people in Europe so debased. The filthiest pigs' sty is a palace to the filthy houses in this dirty stinking City [Lisbon], where all the dirt made in the houses is thrown into the streets, where it remains baking for months until a storm of rain washes it away. The streets are crowded with starving dogs, fat Priests and lousy people. . . . In the middle of the day the sunny sides of the streets swarm with men and women picking vermine from their bodies, and it is no uncommon sight to see two respectably dressed persons meet to do a friendly office for each other by picking the crawlers from each others

persons. . . . Half of their religion consists in ringing
of bells. Such a confounded clatter is kept up all day
and half the night, that it is enough to drive one mad.
Woe to any poor soul that has got an headache.

Wellesley gave the French plenty of headaches. In the summer of 1809, he chased them out of Portugal and invaded
Spain. After fighting two French armies to a standstill, he was
forced to return to Portugal. There he took up defensive positions at Torres Vedras (Old Towers)—a line of hilltop forts
he'd secretly built to protect Lisbon. Before entering the lines,
however, he turned the surrounding country into an artificial
desert. Everything that could not be taken away, and that might
be useful to the enemy, was destroyed. The French under
Marshal Massena suffered terribly, losing 25,000 men within
six months. Battle deaths amounted to only 1,500; the rest
were victims of disease, starvation, and guerrillas. Wherever
they fought, the British were aided by guerrillas, who constantly attacked the enemy rear, pinning down units needed
at the front.

While at Torres Vedras, Wellesley devised a system for
dealing with French attack columns. His system required
"steady troops"; that is, disciplined men who would not be
cowed by the enemy's numbers. The Redcoats had always done
their duty. Rugged and well-trained, they'd proven themselves
on battlefields from India to America.

These men, however, mustn't be exposed to enemy gunfire
until the right moment. Only Wellesley seems to have realized
that placing them just behind the crest of a hill could save
lives. There they'd sit out a bombardment while the cannonballs passed harmlessly overhead. Once the guns stopped, allowing the French columns to move forward, they'd come

over the crest. There they'd stand, two-deep, silent, motionless—and waiting. These were the terrible "thin red lines" no Frenchman ever forgot.

The columns drew closer, closer, gaining speed by the minute. Cries of *"Vive l'Empereur!"* rose from the ranks. *"À la baionette!"* ("Let them have the bayonet!") others replied.

As the columns came within range, redcoated sergeants shouted "Ready!" Instantly thousands of muskets came up into firing position.

"Fire!"

Hell broke loose. A hail of lead balls struck the advancing columns, tearing them wide open. Wounded men thrashed and screamed on the ground. Their comrades stepped over them and kept moving, until the next volley. Two or three volleys were usually enough to stop the most determined columns.

Frenchmen came to respect *"Monsieur Goddam,"* a nickname based on the Redcoat's favorite expression. They would see a lot of him in the years ahead. The Spanish ulcer continued to bleed, draining away French lives and resources.

―――――

MEANWHILE, Napoleon's empire grew steadily. At the beginning of 1809, almost the entire European continent lay at his feet. His empire stretched from the Atlantic Ocean to the Russian border, from the icy Baltic to the warm Mediterranean. Its population, including that of France, was over eighty million. Not since the Roman Empire had so many Europeans been ruled by one person.

The emperor ruled three kinds of territories. First came France and the lands annexed to it: Belgium, Piedmont, Genoa, Tuscany, Rome, Istria, and Dalmatia. Second, there was the Kingdom of Italy, the old Cisalpine republic plus

Venetia and several of the papal states; that is, territories around Rome that had belonged to the church since the Middle Ages. Third, there were the "allies": Spain, Holland, and Naples. The allies also included most of Poland, freed from Russian domination and called the Grand Duchy of Warsaw, and the Confederation of the Rhine, German kingdoms such as Bavaria, Württemberg, Westphalia, and Saxony. Although not part of the empire, the allies were actually French puppets.

Napoleon turned the empire into a Bonaparte family business. Joseph was not his only relative to wear a crown. Brother Louis became king of Holland; Jerome was king of Westphalia. Lucien received no crown, because he refused to divorce his wife, whom Napoleon disliked. Sister Caroline married Joachim Murat, who'd been promoted to king of Naples; Elisa and Pauline were made duchesses. Stepson Eugène Beauharnais took over as viceroy of Italy. Mother Letizia received a palace and an income of a million francs a year. A wise woman, she feared for the future, saying: "It's all very well while it lasts." She did her best to save money in case her children's luck changed.

Napoleon's empire was "reformed," as France had been, whether its peoples wanted reform or not. Laws were modernized, ancient privileges abolished, careers opened to talent, and individuals made equal before the law. Still, equality had nothing to do with self-government.

The emperor regarded his subjects merely as pawns in his vendetta against Britain—the one nation that had never given in to him. Their rulers, lacking any power of their own, served his interests, then the interests of France; their peoples' own interests counted for nothing. Napoleon despised his subjects and spoke of them with contempt. Germans were "clowns" and "drunkards"; there was nothing to fear from the likes of them. "The Italian people is ill-suited for freedom," a race of slaves unfit to rule a pigpen.

Napoleon exploited his subjects in countless ways. Their art treasures were stolen and sent to beautify his capital. Their taxes were kept high, as in Italy, where half the money collected found its way to Paris. Taxation also took the form of "quartering"; that is, forcing civilians to feed French troops and give them rooms in their own homes. These measures allowed the emperor to keep most of his troops outside France, thereby lowering the bill for the French taxpayer. Finally, taxes were paid in flesh and blood. Nations under French control had to send their young men to the *Grande Armée*.

Napoleon ruled his empire with an iron hand. All protests were to be crushed; all insults erased with blood. His written orders left no doubt about his intentions. At the first sign of resistance, every tenth villager in southern Germany must be shot and the village burned down. In 1807, two Prussian actors were hissed at when they appeared on stage in French uniforms. The emperor wrote the king, "requesting" that the guilty parties be executed. Two years later, he learned that the Italian bishop of Udine had said kind things about the enemy. "If this is true," he informed Viceroy Eugène, "have him shot."

Not even the pope was safe. Napoleon demanded that Pope Pius VII join the Continental System and break diplomatic relations with Britain. When the Holy Father refused, he arrested several cardinals and seized the remaining papal states. On July 6, 1809, troops kidnapped the pope himself and brought him to France, where he remained a prisoner until Napoleon's downfall. People's outrage at such high-handedness made no impression on the dictator. They could choke on their anger, for all he cared. He'd do as he pleased, no matter what others thought.

Napoleon was at the height of his power in 1809. He was master of Europe, king of kings, ruler of rulers. Everything he touched (except Spain) turned out right. Power and success, however, were not good for him. They corrupted him, twisting his judgment until he became a menace to himself and everyone else. He began to believe his own propaganda. Once he'd questioned everything; now he shaped the facts to suit his desires. If anyone disagreed, he had a temper tantrum. How dare such imperfect beings question him! He knew everything. He had always been right, and would always be right.

The emperor's selfishness grew along with his power. He became the center of the universe, leaving the rest of humanity in cold and darkness. It was always "I" and "my," never "we" or "us": "I order," "I insist," "I want," "my crown," my "empire," "my army."

Except for his faithful *grognards*, Napoleon lost the common touch. He became cold and distant, surrounding himself with yes-men. They'd smile, nod their approval, and agree with everything he said, however ridiculous. But the one thing they'd never do was tell him the truth.

Yet the more he gained, the more he wanted. His sharpest advisers began to sense danger. Talleyrand resigned as foreign minister after Tilsit; he wouldn't risk his neck for such a man. The cautious Fouché was dismissed in 1810; he'd asked too many difficult questions. Loyal soldiers came to doubt their master's sanity. Marshal Lannes, having lost both legs to a cannonball, shouted at him from the stretcher. "Your ambition is insatiable, and it will be the end of you. Unsparingly and unnecessarily, you sacrifice the men who serve you best; and when they die, you feel no sense of loss." It was the truth, and Lannes felt better once he'd gotten it off his chest. He died in pain three days later.

Napoleon went on his own way. He'd built an empire, only it seemed so fragile. *He* seemed so fragile. On October 12, 1809, a young German named Frederick Staps was arrested with a butcher knife a few feet away from him.

"Why did you want to kill me?" he asked.

"To kill you is no crime. On the contrary, it is the duty of every good German. I wanted to kill you because you are the oppressor of Germany."

"But if I pardon you, will you be thankful for it?"

"I will try to kill you again."

The emperor had him shot at sunrise.

Staps's knife made Napoleon aware of his mortality. Even he could die suddenly and without warning. Then what? His empire would perish along with him. The only way to save it was to have a son, an heir. Unfortunately, Josephine could no longer bear children.

Shortly before Christmas, 1809, Napoleon divorced his wife of thirteen years.* Four months later, he married the Archduchess Marie-Louise of Austria. He was quite blunt about the reason: "I want to marry a womb!" She seemed to fit the bill: her grandmother had had eighteen children, her mother thirteen.

Marie-Louise, nineteen, was Emperor Francis's second daughter. A heavyset blonde, she had a long nose, a large mouth, and light blue eyes. She'd been brought up to believe that Napoleon was the *Krampus*, a horned devil who devoured little girls; she used to burn her dolls, saying she was "roasting

---

*Napoleon did not abandon Josephine. He gave her a palace, a large income, visited her sometimes, and wrote her often. She died in May 1814, after a brief illness. His last word on his deathbed was "Josephine!"

the Corsican." And now she became his wife. She married not for love, but because her father believed she could influence him in Austria's favor. Marie-Louise was a *very* devoted daughter.

As things turned out, Napoleon was not the monster she'd imagined. The terrible *Krampus* could be gentle, kindly, even playful, with his bride. He'd ask her whether she understood this or that and, if she said no, pinched her nose. Soon she couldn't bear to be away from her dear "Napo." She loved him. On March 20, 1811, she gave him a son, Napoleon II, also known as the king of Rome. The emperor was overjoyed. As the guns announced the glad tidings, he began to plan further conquests. Conquests in the East.

In Russia.

RUSSIA, 1812

*"It is the devil's own country,
for it is hell all through."*

—Sergeant François Bourgogne

During the Christmas season of 1811, nuns from a Moscow convent ran to their mother superior in a panic. The sky was falling, they cried, pointing upward. God's fire was about to engulf the earth, bringing the world to an end. The old woman rushed outside to see what was the matter. There, trailing its flaming tail across the night sky, was a comet. Comets, she explained, were signs sent by God before any great calamity. They announced floods, wars, and the fall of empires. That night, and every night the comet blazed overhead, the nuns asked one another: "What misfortunes will it bring upon us?" Although sophisticated Muscovites laughed at this superstition, they were to learn that it wasn't so silly after all. For as they laughed, Napoleon was planning to invade their homeland.

The emperor had been annoyed with Russia for quite a while. Although the czar had joined the Continental System at Tilsit, he had second thoughts when it began to threaten national prosperity, not to mention his own crown. The Russian nobility once had a profitable trade with Britain. Each year they'd sold their wheat and timber, using the profits to buy British manufactured goods. Losing that trade not only cost them money, it hurt their pride. Why, they asked, should foreigners dictate to their country? Why should their czar give in to a "Corsican bandit?" Perhaps he wasn't God's beloved after all? Perhaps he was a fraud?

These questions troubled Alexander I. He remembered how his father, Czar Paul I, had also displeased the nobles. One fine day they knocked him over the head and strangled him as he lay helpless. Determined not to let this happen to him, Alexander left the Continental System early in 1810. Russian ports were opened to British ships and a tariff placed on goods imported from France.

Here was a challenge Napoleon couldn't ignore. He'd built his empire on force and fear. The czar's actions now threatened everything. If Alexander could defy him and get away with it, others would be encouraged to do the same. Thus, he reasoned, the only way to preserve the empire was to push Alexander back into line. And the way to do that was with a super-Austerlitz, a knockout blow aimed at the Russian army. If the czar continued to defy him, he'd conquer the entire country.

Responsible Frenchmen—diplomats, soldiers, government ministers—warned against such a war. Attacking Russia was inviting trouble, they said. With the Peninsular War going so badly, it made no sense to fight at the other end of Europe. Russia would not be a pushover. The czar had made no secret of his intentions. He'd boasted that Napoleon might defeat all his generals, but not "General Winter." General Winter fought not with weapons of iron, but with the forces of nature: cold, wind, fog, sleet, snow, and ice. Alexander planned to trade space for time. He'd lure the invader into the interior, avoiding battle whenever possible, then wait for General Winter to do his work.

Napoleon wouldn't listen to advice. "Bah!" he growled whenever objections were raised. Those who disagreed with him were timid softies. Russian "slaves" and "barbarians" were no match for his genius. His vendetta with Britain must be played out to the end. One big battle—that's all he needed to

crush his enemies forever. "A single blow delivered at the heart
of the Russian Empire, at Moscow the Great, Moscow the
Holy, will in a single instant put that whole blind and apathetic
mass at my mercy. . . . Let destiny be accomplished and let
Russia be crushed under my hatred of England!"

Orders went out from Paris in every direction. Slowly at
first, then with the speed of a river in flood, the invaders
assembled in eastern Poland. The "Grand Army of Russia,"
as Napoleon called it, was the largest force ever seen in Europe.
By June 1812, it numbered 614,000 troops, plus 150,000
horses to pull its 1,422 cannons and 25,000 vehicles. There
were also tens of thousands of noncombatants, without whom
the army couldn't exist: barbers, bakers, blacksmiths, book-
keepers, cobblers, clerks, cooks, millers, tailors, and teamsters.
Finally, there were uncounted women and children, soldiers'
families unwilling to be separated from their loved ones. Wherever the army went, they followed in rickety wagons or on
foot.

The Grand Army of Russia was built around the *Grande
Armée*. Except for the Imperial Guard, however, this was no
longer the splendid war machine of Austerlitz and Wagram.
With some 200,000 veterans tied down in Spain, its ranks
were filled with half-trained recruits. Moreover, the French
were outnumbered in the army as a whole. More than half
its fighting men were foreigners: Italians, Poles, Swiss, Saxons,
Bavarians, Belgians, Westphalians, Württembergers, Prussians, Austrians, Dutchmen, and Spaniards.

This was an army divided against itself. Not only did its
nationalities often dislike one another, they felt that they'd
been dragged into a war that was none of their business. Despite
the fact that Napoleon had married their emperor's daughter,
Austrians resented the haughty French. Prussians would gladly

have turned their guns on the French *schweinhund* ("dirty dogs"). A Spanish unit, kindly lent by King Joseph, did just that. When it began sniping at French officers, Napoleon had every second man shot. That did not win him friends among the survivors.

Supplies were also a problem. It is five hundred miles from the Niemen River, the Polish-Russian border, to Moscow. That is a long way even for a mechanized army, as Adolf Hitler's tank divisions found in 1941. It was even longer in Napoleon's day. Everything the invaders needed had to be hauled over narrow roads filled with potholes. Worse, the army brought along too many of certain things and too little of others. Wanting the comforts of home, officers had carpets for their tents, chinaware for their tables, and wardrobes full of dress uniforms. Colonel de Rouget of the Old Guard was typical: "I had a carriage, two wagons, books, a great many maps, twelve horses, [and] six servants." Yet there wasn't enough food or medical supplies. Nor was there any warm clothing, since no one but the Russians expected a winter campaign.

The invasion plan was in the best Napoleonic style. He'd cross the Niemen and slip between Russia's two defending armies, preventing them from linking up and defeating each in turn. Alexander would then have to choose between a dictated peace or losing Holy Moscow. Either way, Napoleon would be the winner. A dictated peace would cripple Russian power and seal Britain's doom. The loss of Moscow would shatter Russian morale and force peace on his terms. The whole campaign would be over in six weeks, he thought.

————

THE NIEMEN RIVER, opposite the city of Kovno, Wednesday, June 24, 1812. The river was a silvery ribbon under the summer sun. Fields shimmering with yellow flowers stretched as far as the eye could see.

The emperor's tent stood on the highest hill overlooking the river. Around it, every hillside and valley was covered with men and horses, cannons and wagons. At his command, bugle calls shattered the stillness, setting the mass in motion. The army formed three columns, each heading for its own bridge over the Niemen. So eager were they for the "glory" of crossing first, that two divisions would have opened fire on each other had their officers not intervened.

The French were in high spirits. With Napoleon leading them, they felt capable of anything. They were so confident, in fact, that they thought this was to be the last campaign. After Russia, he'd rule the world. There'd be an end to war and mankind would live forever in peace—and boredom. "What a pity," wrote a lieutenant of the Young Guard. "What a pity that we are arriving so late, after so many splendid victories, at the end of everything!" Little did they know that, for most of them, Russia literally would be the end of everything.

What follows is based on eyewitness accounts. The Russian campaign was well-described by those who lived through it. A few were ordinary soldiers; most were officers. Their writings tell of superhuman courage, hardship, and stupidity. On the French side, our best source is *The Memoirs of Sergeant Bourgogne, 1812–1813*. François Bourgogne of the Old Guard has given us the most vivid war story ever told by a common soldier. Count Philippe de Ségur left a book entitled *Napoleon's Russian Campaign*. Ségur, one of Napoleon's aides, saw him daily and painted an unflattering picture of his master. So did General Armand de Caulaincourt in his *With Napoleon in Russia*. A former ambassador to Russia, Caulaincourt tried to talk his

Alexander I, Czar of All the Russias, as pictured in a contemporary print. In withdrawing from the Continental System, Czar Alexander invited war with Napoleon, a struggle that would prove the end of Napoleon's war machine.

master out of war. Hitler's generals had Caulaincourt's book
with them during their invasion of Russia 129 years later. They
knew the fate of Napoleon's army, and they feared (rightly)
that history would repeat itself. For the Russian side, there is
General Wilson's Journal, 1812–1814. Sir Robert Wilson was
a British officer who'd volunteered to serve the czar. Although
written by a cool-headed soldier, the book has the impact of
a bomb blast; it is not for the squeamish.

   Trouble began the moment Napoleon set foot on Russian
soil. After crossing the Niemen, he noticed that the bridge
over a nearby stream had been burned. Angry at the delay,
he ordered a cavalry squadron to cross immediately. The troopers forged ahead, ignoring the swift current. They'd gone only
halfway, when they were swept off their mounts. Swimming
was impossible. Their strength was failing. Death was certain.
But they were dying under their emperor's eyes and for his
glory. As the water closed over them, they turned to him,
saluted, and shouted *"Vive l'Empereur!"* The army was
stunned, but this was just the beginning.

   Napoleon's line of march led eastward from the Niemen to
Vilna in Russian Lithuania, then to Vitebsk in White Russia.
The month-long march (June 24 to July 27) became a living
nightmare. Some of the horrors were manmade. Except for
the invaders themselves, the countryside was deserted. Peasants
and farm animals had vanished as if swallowed by the earth.
The very sky seemed lifeless, empty even of birds. Distant
plumes of smoke rose thousands of feet into the air. Veterans
of the Peninsula War knew what that meant. They'd seen it
all before, at Torres Vedras.

   Russians called it the "scorched earth." Everything that
might be useful to the enemy had been removed or destroyed.
Villages were burned to deny him shelter. Bridges were torn

down to slow his advance. Signposts were removed to confuse him. Wells were filled in or polluted with the bodies of dead horses. Sergeant Joseph Schrafel's squad made a grisly discovery at the bottom of a well: "We found a man's leg which had been amputated at the thigh. . . . This explained the sweetish taste of the water." Yet thirst finally triumphed. Water was so scarce, another wrote, "that I saw men lying on their bellies to drink horses' urine in the gutter!"

Nature, however, was the worst enemy. Russian summers can be as awful as Russian winters. Clouds would suddenly roll in, turning day into night and sending lightning bolts streaking across the sky. Rain fell in torrents, often for six or seven hours without letup. Roads became seas of mud—thick, sticky mud that bogged down wagons and sucked the boots off men's feet. Each step took all their energy, leaving them breathless and panting. The rain was followed by scorching heat. Temperatures soared to 102 degrees Fahrenheit, exhausting even veterans of Egypt and Spain. Napoleon couldn't stand his uniform; he'd undress, lie on his bed, and receive officers in his underwear. The heat also dried the roads, turning mud into clouds of yellow-brown dust. It was so thick, so blinding and suffocating, that drummers had to be posted at the head of each unit to signal the direction. Swarms of buzzing, biting insects tormented the marchers day and night. Horseflies turned men's faces into masses of red welts. If a unit was able to bed down in a ruined hut or barn, it was overrun by cockroaches.

The march claimed thousands of lives. Horses fell in droves, overcome by heat, overwork, and hunger. Ten thousand horses died during one stormy night; 75,000 horses, half the total, were gone within a month. The army itself began to fade away. By the time Napoleon reached Vitebsk, he'd lost 150,000 men without ever seeing the enemy forces, let alone fighting them. Diseases such as diphtheria and typhus took a frightful toll. So did dysentery, uncontrollable diarrhea caused by drinking polluted water; it was so bad that camps stank like sewers. Men lost hope. A lieutenant reported, "Hundreds killed themselves, feeling unable to endure such hardship. Every day we heard isolated shots ring out in the woods near the road. Patrols were sent to investigate, and they always came back and reported: 'It's a cuirassier . . . an infantryman, a Frenchman, or an ally, who just committed suicide.' "

Napoleon was surprised at the orderliness of the Russian retreat. There was no sign of panic or haste. Not a wagon had been abandoned, not a soldier left behind who might provide information. He'd hoped for a battle at Vitebsk—the "one big battle"—only to find the enemy gone.

The six weeks allowed for victory were nearly over. What then? He couldn't decide. At first, he said he'd go into winter quarters, regroup, and capture Moscow next spring. But it was only July, which meant eight months stuck in the middle of nowhere. No, he couldn't stand that. He needed action. When some generals advised him to stay, he lost his temper. "I've made my generals too rich," he snarled. "All they dream of now is following the hunt and flaunting their elegant carriages in Paris. I suppose they have lost their taste for war!" Their honor questioned, the generals hung their heads without replying. Onward to Smolensk!

Only two hundred miles from Moscow, Smolensk is an ancient city built on high bluffs on both sides of the Dnieper River and joined by a bridge. Its southern section lay behind a red brick wall thirty feet high reinforced by thirty stone towers. Russian soldiers guarded the walls and had dug lines of trenches outside. They were spoiling for a fight. When Napoleon arrived on August 16, he was thrilled. At last he'd have his battle!

The battle raged throughout the following day. It soon became clear, however, that the Russians were not pushovers. They fought bravely, doggedly, making the invaders pay dearly for every gain. Although the fighting died down at sunset, French artillery kept firing, turning Smolensk into a sea of flame.

The emperor and his staff watched the blaze from their camp. It was awesome, like a volcano bursting from the earth. "An eruption of Vesuvius!" he shouted, slapping Caulaincourt on the back. "Isn't it a fine sight?"

"Horrible, Sire!"

"Bah!" he said with a smirk. "Gentlemen, remember the words of a Roman emperor: 'A dead enemy always smells sweet.' "

Napoleon was mistaken if he thought the Russians would allow themselves to be trapped. They crossed the Dnieper during the night, leaving him to occupy the ruins on the morning of August 18. Smolensk was more like a cemetery than a city. The bodies of 10,000 Frenchmen and over 15,000 Russians lay thick on the ground. The odor of charred flesh hung in the air. In the hospitals, the surgeons ran out of bandages and had to dress wounds with shirts torn from the backs of the dead. Some used paper from the city records office; parchment was made into splints.

The French commanders were shaken by their costly "victory." It would be foolish to go further, they muttered among themselves. Only Murat dared speak out. He fell on his knees before his brother-in-law and begged him to halt while there

was still time. No one could accuse Murat of being soft. A
man of reckless courage, he never *sent* his cavalry into action;
but always *led* them himself.

But Napoleon couldn't see anything but Moscow. "I must
have a great victory!" he said, turning away. "A battle in front
of Moscow! I must capture Moscow and amaze the world!"

In the meantime, Russia was gearing up for total war. Czar
Alexander called his people to arms: "Let us drive this plague
of locusts out! Let us carry the Cross in our hearts, and steel
in our hands!" Priests read his appeal in their churches, adding
their own brand of fuel to the fire. God, they cried, was the
people's Father in Heaven. Alexander was their "Little Father"
upon earth. And their country was "Holy Mother Russia." By
invading Russia, Napoleon menaced heaven itself. Let everyone join the crusade to send him back to hell! God wills it!

After Smolensk, the Russian armies were put under a unified
command. Field Marshal Prince Mikhail Kutuzov became
their supreme commander. Kutuzov, sixty-seven, hardly
looked the part. Thick-lipped, with a puffy face and drooping
eyelids, he was too fat to ride a horse; jokers said he could
only get around by resting his belly in a wheelbarrow and
rolling it ahead of him. Yet looks were deceiving. He'd served
in the army since boyhood, had been wounded several times,
and had lost his right eye to a Turkish bullet. Cautious and
sly, he never took unnecessary risks. Like a poisonous snake,
he'd bide his time, then strike when the enemy least expected.

Kutuzov's men could hold their own against any foe.
Vanka—"Little Ivan"—the Russian footsoldier, was a peasant
drafted into the army for life. Superstitious, used to hard work
and little food, he made a tough enemy. Someone once said
that it wasn't enough to kill him—you had to push him over
afterward. His stubbornness came from pride and from fighting

the Turks, who seldom took prisoners. Little Ivan would rather
die than surrender.

The Russian cavalry had no equal. Its finest units, the cossacks, were the Mamelukes of the North. Fierce warriors born
to the saddle, each carried a sword, a pair of pistols, and an
eight-foot lance; boys learned to use the lance soon after they
learned to walk. Unlike cuirassiers, who charged in tight formations, cossacks came as a swarm. They struck suddenly,
seeming to be everywhere at once. Their object was to isolate
small enemy units, cut them to pieces, and be off before help
arrived. They were often joined by tribesmen from the plains
of Central Asia—Mongols, Bashkirs, and Kalmuks. Known as
"Cupids," because of their bows and arrows, they rode like
the wind and fought like the devil.

Vanka had his chance when Kutuzov decided to fight outside Borodino, a village seventy miles west of Moscow. Kutuzov had taken up a strong position on a field ringed by low
hills. His forward troops were placed behind earthworks,
mounds of earth protected by cannons and backed by lines of
infantry and cavalry.

Napoleon's advance guard found Borodino screened by
squadrons of cossacks. The French cavalry didn't charge. They
stopped in their tracks and a lone horseman came forward. It
was Murat. He looked like the prince in a fairy tale, riding to
slay a dragon. His uniform and sword belt were covered with
gold braid. His breeches, edged with gold, were pink and his
boots bright yellow. His hat was topped by white ostrich plumes
and egret feathers. The cossacks watched this sparkling, glittering creature draw near. Halting only a few yards from them,
he drew his sword and ordered them away with such arrogance
that they left in amazement. There would be no battle—yet.

The Russians used Sunday, September 6, to prepare themselves spiritually. At midday scores of bearded priests in gorgeous robes came through the camp. They moved in a solemn procession, chanting prayers and holding up the Black Madonna, a holy statue rescued from the flames of Smolensk. The soldiers knelt, crossing themselves as the priests sprinkled holy water on their shaved heads. The French had no chaplains and no religious services.

Napoleon was restless that night. He'd get up every few minutes to watch the Russian campfires and send scouts to make sure that they hadn't slipped away. "I need a great battle!" he'd mumble repeatedly. "I need a great battle!" He got just that—and plenty more.

Dawn of September 7 found the armies at their battle stations. Both sides were evenly matched. Kutuzov had 120,000 men. Napoleon counted 133,000 men; the rest were either dead, sick, or guarding the supply lines that stretched back to Poland.

At half past five in the morning, the emperor arrived at his observation post on a hill one mile west of Borodino. As he took his place, the sun rose, shining through the mist as it had done on another day seven years before. "It is the sun of Austerlitz," he declared, an omen of victory. His staff smiled hopefully. Moments later 587 French guns opened fire and were promptly answered by 640 Russian guns.

The battle of Borodino began with the greatest artillery duel in history. Not until World War I would so many guns be in action at once. Suddenly the plain came alive with tongues of flame, followed by explosions and the whistling of cannonballs. The fury of the guns was such that many soldiers had trouble finding words to describe it. The shots came so thick and fast that it was impossible to tell one gun from another. All one heard was a continuous roar that masked even the crackle of thousands of muskets. Men became so deafened that they couldn't clear their ears for hours on end.

Borodino was an old-fashioned slugging match. It involved no skill, no maneuvering, just head-on assaults. Attacks and counter-attacks followed one upon the other, turning the field into a vast open-air slaughterhouse. Men fought with guns, bayonets, and swords; they rolled on the ground, biting, clawing, punching one another. After nine hours of confusion and horror, the Russians abandoned their earthworks and began to pull back a few hundred yards. This was Napoleon's big chance.

The emperor, however, wasn't himself today. He'd caught a bad cold and could hardly speak. He just sat on a stool, his feet propped on a drum, shaking with fever and unable to concentrate. Sometimes he'd get up and pace back and forth, trying to decide what to do next. Russian cannonballs passed overhead. Several came rolling up to his feet, and he kicked them aside like so many large pebbles. The Imperial Guard stood around him in a vast hollow square, while their bands played stirring marches. Guardsmen stood at attention, in full-dress uniform, waiting for orders.

Marshal Michel Ney, leading the main assault, scribbled a message calling for the Guard. It was now or never. The Russians, weakened by heavy losses, seemed about to break. If the Guard charged while they were still forming up, it might finish them off with a single blow. Napoleon denied the request. His staff was stunned. Ney was furious. "What's he doing *behind* his army," he shouted when the news came. "He's not a general anymore. he's an emperor. Let him return to the Tuileries and leave the fighting to us!"

Napoleon missed his chance for a knockout blow. Kutuzov reformed, held out until sunset, and then resumed the retreat.

He retreated in good order, claiming victory. That was an exaggeration, but only a small one. He hadn't defeated the French; nor had they defeated him, in itself a victory of sorts.

That night the French campsites were quiet. There was no singing, no joking, no swapping of stories; only hunger, thirst, and worry. Already the leaves were turning red, and the night air had a cold edge. Old-timers knew that Borodino hadn't been another Austerlitz. True, they held the battlefield, and the road to Moscow was open. But they'd expected more from their emperor. A real victory meant captured battleflags, pleas for a truce, even surrender. It meant thousands of prisoners, not the 800 exhausted men sleeping on the ground nearby. The Russian army was still intact, able to fight another day.

Napoleon inspected the battlefield the next morning. Philippe de Ségur, who rode with him, had never seen anything like it. The ground, plowed up by cannonballs, was littered with broken weapons, smashed helmets, bloodstained flags, shreds of uniforms—and 74,000 corpses. Borodino had claimed the lives of 44,000 Russians and 30,000 Frenchmen, 37 French generals had been killed or wounded, plus hundreds of junior officers. The wounded were everywhere, screaming in agony; one surgeon amputated 200 limbs, giving his patients a stick to bite on and a swig of brandy before his knife cut. Staff officers exchanged glances; words weren't needed. They knew that another "victory" like this would mean the end of their army.

Napoleon knew only that he must reach Moscow.

———

ON SEPTEMBER 14, about noon, French scouts emerged from thick woods and climbed a steep hill. Reaching the crest, they halted in stunned amazement. A city was spread out before them, less than a mile away. It was breathtaking, a magical city out of *Arabian Nights*. Golden towers, their roofs painted red and black, shimmered in the sunshine. Church spires, topped with sparkling silver crosses, soared heavenward. Wooden houses painted in bright yellows, greens, and reds dotted the ground like so many Christmas ornaments.

"Moscow! Moscow!" they began to shout.

Other troops, coming upon the scene, broke ranks, clapped their hands, jumped up and down, kissed their comrades' cheeks and shouted themselves hoarse. "Moscow! Moscow!" At last, after 82 days and 500 miles, they'd reached the promised city. Instantly trouble, danger, and hunger were forgotten. Now they'd have good quarters for the winter and loot—plenty of loot. When they returned home, they'd be rich. Pretty girls would run after them and they'd be set for life.

Although the capital had been moved to St. Petersburg a century before, Moscow was still the holiest place in Russia. Known as "the City of Golden Domes," it was a jumble of some 295 churches and 1,500 palaces. At the city's center, bordering the Moskva River, stood the ancient fortress, or *Kremlin*, a city within a city of palaces, churches, and government buildings. Outside the Kremlin wall was Krasnaya Ploshchad (Red Square)—meaning "beautiful square"—and the Place of the Head, the stone execution block to which the czars once sent their victims. Nearby stood the Kitai-Gorod, or "Cathay Town," where caravans from China unloaded their wares.

Napoleon halted at the western gate to receive Moscow's surrender. It had always been so—in Vienna, Berlin, Madrid, Milan, and Warsaw. The city fathers would greet the conqueror, give him the keys to their city, and say how glad they were to see him.

The emperor waited an hour. Two hours. No one appeared.

His impatience turned to anger, and he sent some officers to find the cause of the delay. The officers returned with startling news: "Moscow is empty!" Its 250,000 inhabitants were nowhere to be seen. They'd met a few stay-behinds, who explained that people had begun to flee the city soon after Borodino; even now hundreds were leaving through the eastern gate. Most went on foot, poor people taking whatever they could carry. Rather than see Moscow in unclean hands, they'd chosen to abandon their homes.

The Old Guard began picking its way through the deserted streets. It was on full alert, for news had come of a plot to kill Napoleon with an "infernal machine." The plot was real. A German "pyrotechnician"—explosives expert—had been hired to build a gigantic balloon and fill it with gunpowder. He was to fly over the French army, single out the emperor, and pour down a rain of fire. Napoleon didn't know that the balloon had never gotten off the ground. But rather than take unnecessary risks, he decided to spend the night at an inn outside the city walls. It was a nasty place. The beds swarmed with fleas, and it stank to high heaven. He stayed up half the night, complaining that this was no way to greet an emperor.

Nevertheless, the French did get a warm reception—warmer than they expected or wanted.

That night, as Napoleon fought fleas, fires broke out in Moscow. The Old Guard, having reached the Kremlin, noticed them right away. Sergeant Bourgogne believed that careless soldiers had upset lanterns in buildings they'd broken into. That sort of thing happened all the time. Nothing to get excited about. Little did he know, then, that the fires had been set deliberately.

It has been said that the Russians burned Moscow as part

of their scorched earth policy. That is a myth. The "Russians" did not burn the city; its governor did, without permission and on his own authority. Governor Theodore Rostopchin was an important nobleman. Nicknamed "Crazy Theo," he was also hotheaded, impulsive, and fanatical. He strongly disagreed with Kutuzov's plan to abandon Moscow. It was unthinkable that the French should take the holy city intact and without a fight. Rostopchin decided that burning it would rob Napoleon of his prize, deprive him of winter quarters, and force him to retreat. It would also force the czar to fight to the end. There must be no negotiations with the "French beasts."

Rostopchin made his plans carefully. Shortly after Borodino, he opened the prisons, releasing nearly a thousand criminals, both men and women. Police officials then explained that it was their duty to burn Moscow. They had everything to gain and nothing to lose by doing so. Those who survived would win pardon for their crimes; those who didn't would surely go to heaven. The police organized them into arson teams, each with it own targets; some policemen disguised themselves as beggars and stayed to help with the burning. Grenades were issued from the Kremlin arsenal. Fire engines were wrecked, fire hoses cut, and fire boats sunk in the river.

The first fires were scattered, allowing the French to control them or let them burn out safely. Things really got going on September 15, after Napoleon moved into the Kremlin. Early the next morning, he was awakened by a flickering of light on the ceiling above his bed. Followed by his aides, he climbed the Tower of Ivan the Great, the highest point in the capital. What he saw was at once horrible and fascinating. A sea of flame surrounded the Kremlin on three sides; only the riverside was clear. The emperor was stunned, hardly able to believe his eyes. "This is unbelievable!" he said between clenched teeth. "Those barbarians! Those savages! To burn down their own city! What worse could an enemy do?"

A north wind carried hot cinders over the Kremlin wall, sending Guardsmen rushing to the roofs to put them out. Four hundred gunpowder wagons were parked below, turning the Kremlin into an immense bomb ready to explode at any moment. The emperor must escape. After ordering all arsonists to be killed on sight, he left through a gate at the riverside.

Not all arsonists were killed, however. Luckily, the emperor's party met one, a policeman, whom they promised to save if he guided them through the maze of streets around the Kremlin. It was an offer he couldn't refuse.

They set out on horseback along a narrow, winding street with houses ablaze on either side. The fires, lashed by gale-force winds, hissed and crackled and roared. Sheets of flame arched and swayed over their heads. Roofs collapsed, throwing clouds of sparks into the air. It was like entering the mouth of hell. Heat burned the fugitives' eyes, but they had to keep them open at all costs. Smoke made them breathe in short, painful gasps. Their hands were scorched as they tried to shield their faces from the heat, or brush away embers that landed on their clothes. "We were walking on a floor of fire, under a sky of fire, between walls of fire," is how Philippe de Ségur described the journey.

Just as the fire rose to its full fury, Napoleon reached a palace several miles beyond the city walls. It was the evening of September 16—a night to remember. He stood in the palace garden, hypnotized by the scene. Flames shot thousands of feet into the sky; he could read by the glare even in the garden. They cast a glow upon the countryside for miles around. It could be seen from Tula, a hundred miles south of Moscow. Groups of refugees paused and turned toward the glow. "Mother Moscow is burning," they whispered, then continued their sad march. A soldier named Sergei Glinka was overcome by grief. He threw himself on the ground and cried tears of sadness—and hatred.

The fire was finally quenched by a thunderstorm on the morning of September 18, and Napoleon returned that afternoon. What he saw was a scene from hell. On both sides of the road into Moscow troops sat around bonfires fed by mahogany furniture and gilt doors torn from their hinges. Philippe de Ségur recalled:

> Around these fires, on litters of damp straw . . .
> soldiers and their officers, mud-stained and smoke-
> blackened, were seated in splendid armchairs or lying
> on silk sofas. At their feet were heaped or spread out
> cashmere shawls, the rarest of Siberian furs, cloth of
> gold from Persia, and silver dishes in which they were
> eating coarse black bread bakèd in the ashes, and half-
> cooked, bloody horseflesh—[a] strange combination
> of abundance and famine, wealth and filth, luxury
> and poverty!

The City of Domes was no more. In its place Napoleon found miles of smoldering rubble whose foul odor made him nauseous. Chimneys rose, towerlike, over heaps of charred beams. The corpses of hundreds of arsonists hung from half-burnt trees. Most of the churches, islands in the center of cobblestoned squares, had survived to become stables for French horses. The squares were piled with stolen goods, or goods taken from burning buildings. Everything was for sale or trade. Flour was offered wrapped in linen curtains, sugar loaves in ballroom gowns, and liquor in washbasins and chamber pots. Drunken soldiers stumbled about in priests' robes; their women wore army boots and mink-lined capes.

Napoleon made his headquarters in the Kremlin, spared when the wind shifted during the fire. In the days that followed, he discussed the situation with his aides. They advised him to leave while he could. Autumn had come, and winter was close behind. A winter in these ruins would also ruin the army—what remained of it. Food supplies were low. Soldiers wanted to go home with their loot. And the Russians were getting stronger. Spies told of troops flocking to Kutuzov's army. Peasant guerrillas were growing bolder. During the next four weeks, over 15,000 soldiers were lost in clashes with Russian army patrols, cossacks, and armed peasants.

Napoleon wouldn't listen. Moscow, he insisted, was a political, not a military, position. Even the word "retreat" made him cringe. Retreat would be a sign of weakness, triggering rebellions throughout his empire. An emperor must never back down, never admit an error. If he makes a mistake, he must stick to it regardless of cost—"that makes it right!" The only solution was a negotiated peace. He'd offer the czar generous terms, appeal to his humanity—anything to avoid losing face.

Alexander thought differently. "Peace?" he said to his nobles. "But we haven't had war yet! My campaign has only just started!" He knew that the longer the French remained in Moscow, the harder it would be for them later. Rather than reject Napoleon's offers outright, he strung him along from week to week.

The emperor waited for a reply. Surely, he kept telling himself, Alexander would "see reason." It was only a matter of time, and patience. To pass the time, he held spectacular parades, dictated letters, and read novels. Hours were spent

dozing in an overstuffed chair. He had a servant place two
candles in his window every evening, to make the soldiers
think he worked day and night.

Napoleon lived in his own little world—a world of day-
dreams. He made ridiculous plans, like marching to St. Petersburg, only to discard them; they wouldn't work, he
explained, because his generals didn't understand their gran-
deur. Warnings about winter were brushed aside with contempt. "Bah!" he'd growl, pointing to the clear sky. "See how
fine it is." General Winter was only a fairy tale to frighten
children. As a result, he made few cold-weather preparations.
Had it not been for General Caulaincourt, not even the emperor's own horses would have been roughshod for ice and
snow. The Russians, however, were fitting their mounts with
shoes studded with small nails and exchanging wheeled vehicles for horse-drawn sleds; even cannons were being
mounted on wide skis.

The first snow flurries came in mid-October and melted
quickly. With them also melted the emperor's illusions. At
last he saw the danger. After wasting a full month, he gave
the order to evacuate Moscow.

On October 19, about 107,000 troops, plus other thousands
of camp followers, began passing through Moscow's western
gate. They were in a race against time, a race against General
Winter.

Despite the danger, speed had been sacrificed to greed. The
Grand Army of Russia resembled a pirate nation on the march.
Lines of vehicles, of all types and sizes, stretched to the horizon
and beyond: ambulances, buggies, carriages, carts, coaches,
ammunition, and supply wagons. Each was piled high, not
with necessary gear, but with expensive and useless items. To
make room for loot, tons of food had been left behind or

destroyed. Soldiers' packs were dangerously overloaded. Sergeant Bourgogne, for example, carried a half-bottle of liquor, a Chinese silk dress, a woman's riding cloak, several gold and silver ornaments, several lockets, a Russian prince's spittoon, a crucifix of gold and silver, a porcelain vase, and two silver picture frames each a foot long and eight inches wide. To lighten the load, he threw away an extra pair of trousers, "feeling pretty certain I should not want them again just yet." Some of his friends took so much that they had to move it in wheelbarrows. It was backbreaking work, but worth the effort, they felt.

Napoleon planned to move southward, then turn west, avoiding his old invasion route, now a wasteland of burned-out villages and fields. He intended to spend the winter at Smolensk, regroup, and capture St. Petersburg in the spring. Surely *that* would bring the Russians to their knees.

Kutuzov, however, had other plans. The moment he heard that the emperor had left Moscow, he moved to catch him at the town of Malo-Yaroslavets. During the battle that followed, the Russians lost about 7,000 men, the French and their allies 4,000. Although the French won the field, the Russians kept a strong position on the heights above. Napoleon became desperate. Seeing his route blocked, he had to order the army northward, onto the old Smolensk road.

There would be no more battles after Malo-Yaroslavets. From then on, Kutuzov would follow at a safe distance, jabbing the enemy constantly, but relying mainly on General Winter. "Let winter do the job," he told an impatient aide. Thus began the death march of the *Grande Armée*. One of the epics of human suffering, when it ended no one could ever again speak of the "glorious" Napoleonic Wars. Indeed, it is a reminder of how ghastly war really is.

The army's route led across the battlefield of Borodino. It was a sight to shock even the most hardened veteran. Most of the dead had been left unburied. For seven weeks, they'd lain out there rotting in the wind and rain. Heads and limbs, trunks and skeletons, lay helter-skelter amid rusting equipment and smashed gun carriages. Ravens, nicknamed "cemetery birds," fed on bloated corpses barely recognizable as human. At least one poor fellow was still alive—a Frenchman who'd lost both legs but survived on putrid horseflesh and muddy water from a stream full of bodies. They put him in a wagon with the other wounded, but it is unlikely that he lived through the next few days. Napoleon ignored the scene; he had other things on his mind. The army passed in silence.

On November 6, two days' march from Smolensk, General Winter struck with a vengeance. Temperatures plummeted to minus twenty-two degrees Fahrenheit. Winds from the North Pole howled at thirty miles an hour, making it feel like fifty-two degrees below zero. Cold sliced through thin summer uniforms. Men's lips turned blue and their teeth chattered. Icicles hung from their nostrils; their breath froze on their beards. Anyone who touched metal with his bare hands left behind strips of his own flesh when he pulled away. It was the worst cold Sergeant Bourgogne had ever known. "Our lips were frozen, our brains too; the whole atmosphere was icy."

Snow accompanied the cold. There was a total whiteout as the big flakes fell silently to earth. Men lost sight not only of the sky, but of comrades walking in front and to the sides. Snow blanketed the ground, burying landmarks under mountainous drifts. Windblown snowflakes struck exposed skin like pebbles flung from slingshots. Each step became an ordeal. The loot accumulated at such risk and hauled so far had to be abandoned. The roadside was lined with carts buried up to

The burning of Moscow. Napoleon watched the fire from the highest tower in the Kremlin, which can be seen in the background between the banks of smoke. BELOW, Marshal Ney (at center in a cocked hat) leads his men on the retreat from Moscow. Note the women and children, the families of the French soldiers, in the background; very few would survive the long journey home. From a drawing based on a painting by Adolphe Yvon.

their axles in snow. Valuables were strewn on the ground, marking the path of the infantry. Fine paintings, religious statues, and books bound in leather lay about for the taking— only there were no takers.

Men trudged on, drawn to Smolensk as if to the Promised Land. There, the emperor said, they'd find food and rest and warmth. Instead they found a burned-out shell and barely enough food for a few units. True, supplies had been moved up from Poland and Germany, but most had been consumed by the troops who brought them. That was the last straw! Discipline collapsed as mobs broke into the warehouses. Men stuffed themselves before bringing their comrades what remained. They cared nothing for the thousands who wandered the streets hungry. Many of these simply gave up and found a quiet place to die amid the ruins.

It was no army, but a mob of famished paupers, that stumbled out of Smolensk on November 12. Only the highest officers still wore complete uniforms. The others were in rags, or in anything they'd managed to bring from Moscow. They wore a motley combination of Siberian furs and strips of carpet, Chinese silks, and shabby overcoats. One might see a soldier in a woman's coat of blue or pink satin, trimmed with blue fox. Soldiers' heads were wrapped in brightly colored scarves. When their boots rotted, they wrapped their feet in bits of straw, cloth, and paper. Unwashed men stank and crawled with lice, gray crablike creatures that drove them crazy with itching. The army's very appearance, once so proud, lowered its morale and thus its chances for survival.

The cold swept away thousands each day. Bald men died first, because most of the body's heat escapes from the top of the head. Cold lulled men to sleep, and sleep meant death. They'd sit down to rest, fall asleep, and never awaken. Sergeant

Bourgogne's men once saved him from eternal "sleep." He was snoring loudly, in broad daylight, when they pulled him by the ears, slapped his face, and kicked his backside—anything to get him up. After several minutes of this, they succeeded, but he wasn't grateful. "I felt very cross, however, at being roused."

The retreat was doubly hard on prisoners of war. Russian prisoners, like everyone else, had been weakened by hunger. Those unable to keep pace were simply killed by their guards. When questioned about this, the guards denied that they'd done wrong. Sudden death by the bayonet, they said, was merciful, compared to what awaited the Russians. There was some truth in this: most prisoners starved or froze in the enclosures where they were penned up each night.

The cossacks grew bolder as the retreat continued. One never knew when they'd strike. A unit might be passing a forest when suddenly the cry "Urrah! Urrah! Urrah!" pierced the air. Squadrons of cossacks burst from the trees, dashing in among the troops with their swords and lances. Some were cut down on the spot; others became prisoners.

God help anyone who fell into cossack hands! Prisoners were stripped naked and left to freeze in the snow, or left for the peasants. Nearly all were murdered by the peasants; indeed, they'd actually buy prisoners from the cossacks to torture. Sir Robert Wilson saw groups of Frenchmen buried or burned alive. He once came upon sixty naked men whose necks were laid on a log. Russians, men and women singing in chorus, stood over each man and beat out his brains with heavy sticks. Small wonder that captives begged cossacks to shoot them before the peasants could do their worst.

It was now every man for himself. Even Old Guard veterans,

comrades for so many years, lost all feeling for one another. Anyone with food hid himself and ate it in secret. Respect for rank vanished in the equality of suffering. Officers stopped giving orders they knew would be ignored. A grim joke, probably true, began to circulate. It seems that a private thought his officer dead and began stripping him of his clothes. The officer, stirred awake, gasped, "Comrade, I'm not dead yet." The soldier stood up, saying: "All right, my officer, I'll wait a few moments more." Most weren't so patient. Dying men, crying for mercy, were stripped as they lay helpless.

The wounded had little chance of survival. There were no more medicines, and the surgeons were too busy with their own problems to look after those who were doomed anyhow. Those lying in carts suffered constantly as they bumped over rutted roads. Their moans made the drivers jittery; the little food they ate seemed wasted. Drivers often whipped their horses to shake their passengers onto the road, where they were crushed under the wheels of the cart behind or found by the peasants.

New life came into the world even among such frightful scenes. Women, as we know, accompanied the army. Scores of them were pregnant and went into labor during the retreat from Moscow. Something about them struck a chord within the soldiers, reminding them of their humanity. They'd halt in the middle of a snowfield and form a circle, their backs to the woman, sheltering her while she gave birth alone. Madame Dubois, the wife of an army barber, had an easier time than most. At the height of a blizzard, at minus ten degrees Fahrenheit, men built a shelter for her out of pine branches. Nevertheless, her son only lived two days. The father, a private, knelt with him in his arms while a soldier dug a tiny hole in the snow. When the hole was ready, he kissed him and laid him in the grave. They covered it, and the march continued. Very few newborns and their mothers ever made it back to France.

Night was the worst time. As soon as the sun set at four o'clock, temperatures fell further. Survival now depended upon having a fire outdoors, or finding shelter indoors. But that was easier said than done. Soldiers refused each other a place by their fire, or demanded food for the privilege. Early arrivals crowded into any peasant huts or barns that remained intact. They'd bar the doors, stabbing latecomers who tried to push their way in.

Sergeant Bourgogne, a latecomer, described such an incident. Having been driven away from a barn, he and his squad settled down for a night of misery. They were trying to warm themselves by a small campfire when the barn suddenly burst into flames. Someone had been careless and, since its doors opened inward, over 800 men were trapped when they tried to rush through at once. Bourgogne's men saved a few, including an officer, who they dragged through a hole torn in the wall. Others rushed to the scene, not to help, but to warm themselves and admire the blaze. They just stood around, saying, "What a beautiful fire!" As for those inside, when the fire went out, they searched the bodies for any remaining scraps of food.

Food, more than anything, meant life. Men had forgotten what it was like to have a full belly. Except for the emperor, everyone made do with horseflesh. Horses died constantly of hunger and cold. Their meat, though stringy and tasting of sweat, was usually eaten half-raw. Yet, to starving men like Sergeant Bourgogne, it was delicious. One day he made a stew of horseflesh and oats seasoned with salt. It didn't look very appetizing, and it smelled worse. Still "it was the best meal I have ever had in my life." For the rest of his life his mouth watered when he recalled it.

Hunger forced men to be creative. If dead horses weren't available, they'd cut steaks from the haunches of living animals as they passed by. The horses didn't object: numbed by the cold, they couldn't feel the knife going in, dying later when their wounds became infected. Horse-blood soup was another favorite. It was so popular, in fact, that men marched with blood-smeared beards, dipping their fingers into the company pot as they plodded along. Frozen blood, however, did just as well. Ice-blood was collected and sucked like cough drops.

If worst came to worst, men might eat their fellow human beings. This is no exaggeration. Both French and Russian officers saw cannibalism among the retreating troops. Even Sergeant Bourgogne was tempted. He'd once gone two days on nothing but a frozen raven he'd found on the ground. "I am sure that if I had not found any horseflesh myself, I could have turned cannibal. To understand the situation, one must have felt the madness of hunger; failing a man to eat, one could have demolished the devil himself, if he were only cooked."

Napoleon felt no need to share his men's suffering. He traveled with the Old Guard at the head of the column, seeing nothing of the horrors that went in his wake. Most of the time he rode in his coach, bundled in furs from head to foot. In addition to the coach, he had eight wagons full of food, a carriage for his clothes, three cooks, and sixteen other servants. Servants shaved him each morning and made sure he had a fresh change of clothes. At night, if no house was found for him, he slept in his coach on a special bed. There was always plenty of white bread, beef, wine, and his favorite rice with beans and lentils.

The common soldiers—Frenchmen, at least—seem not to have blamed him for their troubles. His servants often went around the campsites, asking for dry wood to warm the emperor. Even the dying gave gladly. "Take what you can for the emperor," they'd say, raising their heads.

———

THE ROAD FROM SMOLENSK led to the Berezina River. Once again General Winter did the unexpected. The Berezina had been frozen solid until late November, when the temperature rose enough to crack the ice. That shouldn't have been a problem, since Polish cavalrymen held the only bridge for hundreds of miles. Unfortunately, the enemy surprised them and burned down the bridge. Worse, 120,000 Russians were closing in from all directions. Napoleon had only 40,000 fighting men and an equal number of unarmed stragglers—the wounded, noncombatants, women, and children. Unless he crossed, and quickly, they'd be trapped at the river and wiped out.

Napoleon feared that the end was near. To prepare for his last stand, he burned all unnecessary vehicles, including several of his own. Battle flags, which he'd given the *Grande Armée* at Boulogne, were burned, along with all important papers. He vowed to die fighting, rather than be captured by the Russians.

Yet luck smiled upon him once again. French cavalry were patrolling upstream when they met a peasant whose horse was wet only up to the chest. *Only up to the chest!* After some hard-fisted "persuasion," he admitted that he'd crossed the river and led them to a ford near the village of Studyanka seven miles north of the ruined bridge.

Napoleon was at his best during those last days of November. The moment he learned of the ford, he issued his orders. Hundreds of men were sent to repair the bridge and make sure that they were seen doing do. This was a bluff to draw enemy attention away from Studyanka.

Meanwhile, 400 *pontonniers* (engineers trained in building bridges) swung into action. Studyanka was torn down for timber and clamps forged out of scrap iron. Each section of bridge was made on land, then dragged into the river and joined by *pontonniers*. Naked, they worked for hours in frigid water up to their necks. Dozens were swept away by the swift current; others were crushed by ice floes. Yet their comrades succeeded in building two 300-foot bridges: a light footbridge for the infantry and a heavier span for cannons and wheeled vehicles.

That night, November 26 into 27, everyone was exhausted. Soldiers huddled around their campfires, waiting for the signal to cross in the morning. The stragglers could have crossed easily; indeed, officers ordered them to leave while the bridges were clear. But they were in no mood to obey orders. It was cold, very cold. The houses of Studyanka had provided them with plenty of firewood. Although hungry, they were warm for the first time in days. They wouldn't budge from their fires.

The army began to cross at dawn. Just then Russian guns opened fire from a nearby ridge, setting the scene for the greatest tragedy of the Napoleonic Wars.

The crowds of stragglers made excellent targets. When cannonballs and shells began to fall among them, they panicked. Thousands of terrified people suddenly stampeded for the bridges. Philippe de Ségur saw it all:

They ran in every direction. They accumulated on the bank. In a second one saw a huge mass, men, horses, carts, laying siege to the narrow entrances to the bridges. Those in front, pushed by the weight of those behind . . . were crushed, trampled on, or forced into the ice-filled water of the Berezina. . . . Some cut a path for their wagons with swords. Others drove their carriages through the helpless crowd, crushing men and women. Still others wept, begged, and collapsed, terror wiping out the little strength they had left. Some, shoved away from the bridges, tried to climb their sides, but most were pushed into the river. Women were seen among the ice floes with children in their arms, holding them higher and higher as they sank. When their bodies were under water their stiffened arms still held the little ones up. Then the artillery bridge collapsed. Those on it tried to turn back, but the stream of men in the rear, unaware of the disaster, heedless of the cries of those in front, kept pushing and forced them over the edge; only to be themselves forced over a second later. Then they swarmed to the other bridge. They thought themselves safe on setting foot on the bridge, but a fallen horse, a missing plank, broke the flow and they fell. . . . Men who had been thrown down and were being smothered attacked with nails and teeth the legs of their comrades who were trampling on them, only to be kicked aside as if they were enemies. . . . In the uproar made by the boom of cannon, the bursting of shells, the shriek of the wind, cries, groans, and curses this soulless mob could not hear the moans of their victims!

Order was restored only after the guns fell silent at sundown.

That night (November 27 into 28), the temperature was twenty degrees below zero. Again the bridges were open, and again the stragglers huddled around their fires. And once again they panicked when the Russian guns opened up in the morning. On the third day, with Russian troops closing in, Napoleon ordered the bridges burned. Thousands of people were left behind. They wandered in groups along the edge of the river, stunned, unable to decide what to do next. Hundreds jumped in and tried to swim or climb onto the ice floes. All of these drowned. Others ran into the flames of the burning bridges, which collapsed under them. Most sat around their fires, waiting for the cossacks, who massacred even the women and children.

Ten years later, Prussian visitors found an island near the Berezina's left bank. It was a new island, formed by bodies that had fallen off the bridges and were covered with mud and sand. The island itself was covered in blue forget-me-nots.

We don't know exactly how many crossed the Berezina. Possibly 30,000. What is certain is that Napoleon lost 25,000 soldiers and at least that many noncombatants. But the army's ordeal was still far from over.

———

SOME WEEKS EARLIER, the emperor learned of the Malet plot. General Claude Malet, a lunatic, had escaped from an asylum and tried to overthrow the government with the help of a few like-minded men. They'd arrested the minister of police, won over several army units, and were about to take over when the plot was exposed and they were shot. Still, it was a close call. Too close.

There was no telling if other, luckier, Malets lurked in the shadows. Besides, bad news travels fast. The loss of the *Grande*

Armée might encourage Napoleon's "allies"—Austria and Prussia—to join Russia and Britain in an all-out war against him. His throne and his empire were at stake. He must rebuild his forces for the struggles to come. And that could only be done from his capital.

On December 3, he arrived at Smorgoni, fifty miles east of Vilna. There he dictated the famous Bulletin Number Twenty-nine in which he admitted serious losses. These were not his fault, but due entirely to the weather, he said. The bulletin ended on a high note. Frenchmen should take heart, for "His Majesty's health has never been better." He left two days later with General Caulaincourt and a small cavalry escort. Marshal Murat was left in command.

Napoleon's journey to Paris was an adventure in itself. His route lay across Poland and East Prussia. The Poles still trusted him, even though he'd lost thousands of their young men. It was otherwise with the Prussians, who'd always hated him. He joked about what might happen if they were captured. The Prussians would sell them to the British, who'd exhibit them in a cage in London, smeared with honey and slowly eaten by flies. This foolish notion made them laugh for the first time in weeks.

There were also serious moments. Napoleon tried to convince his companion that Europe feared Russia more than anything else. Caulaincourt wasn't convinced. Politely but firmly, he told him some unpleasant truths. Europe feared him, resented his dictatorship, and hated his unending taxes. They argued back and forth until they reached Paris near midnight on December 18. The emperor went to the Tuileries, where the guards rubbed their eyes in disbelief. They thought they were seeing a ghost.

In the meantime, the *Grande Armée* was in its final agonies.

The day after Napoleon's departure, the thermometer fell to
an all-time low for December. Temperatures of thirty-six degrees below zero turned the land into an icebound desert.

The army, which had survived other cold snaps, had no
strength left for this one. The cold was absolutely ferocious.
Birds froze in flight and fell to the ground. One night several
Old Guard veterans froze while seated around their campfire.
The next morning, a sentry was found standing at attention—
frozen stiff! For a few minutes' warmth, men would burn entire
houses. A Russian general was stunned by the scene in another
camp: "I saw a dead man inside a horse which he had gutted
and emptied in order to crawl inside and get warm."

Vilna was no refuge. When the army arrived on December
8, it found the city well-stocked with supplies. The soldiers,
however, were beyond reason. Insane with hunger, they
stormed the warehouses, fighting for food, stuffing themselves,
and wasting much of what they found. Then they turned on
the civilians, looting and killing in a blind fury. Civilians were
glad to see cossacks on the city's outskirts and hear the booming
of their guns. Murat resumed the retreat after only twenty-
four hours.

The fugitives reached Kovno on the fourteenth. They were
back where they'd started, only now it was the Russians who
were advancing. Although the Niemen was frozen, they
crossed on the one remaining bridge. Marshal Ney covered
the crossing with a thirty-man rear guard. He fought with grim
determination, giving ground only after the others were safe.
Walking backward, firing the muskets that others had thrown
away, Ney was the last Frenchman to leave Russia.

The campaign of 1812 was Europe's costliest until the twentieth century. Of the vast army that crossed the Niemen in
June, about 5,000 recrossed in organized units. They were

joined by 25,000 stragglers, supply troops, and troops who'd occupied captured towns. Except for the handful who survived in Siberian prison camps, all the others perished. Russian losses were about 150,000.

France went into deep mourning for her lost sons. The color black replaced the cheerful Christmas decorations. Families locked themselves in their houses to brood about the past and worry about the future. Yet it was the returning soldiers who suffered worst. Their wounds were bad enough, but they'd heal in time. The most painful wounds, however, lay deep inside of them—in their minds and souls. Memories tortured them and gave them no peace. They'd wake up at night sweating, shaking, screaming. They saw the faces of lost comrades in those of passersby in the street. Children's tears were like those of other children, left behind on windswept plains.

It was more than human beings could stand. Some lost their minds. General Andoche Junot, who'd known Napoleon since Toulon, began to eat grass and go around wearing only his sword; finally he committed suicide. Others suffered amnesia, forgetting the past in order to live in the present. In time, they dared to remember—and write. Only by writing about the past could they put it to rest within themselves. Sergeant Bourgogne was such a man. He wrote because, "I cannot do otherwise. . . . All these things have taken such possession of my mind that I think if I write them down they will cease to trouble me." They still trouble us.

Napoleon was not troubled. He did not look backward. He looked forward—to more wars.

THE ROAD
TO WATERLOO

*"It has been a damned nice thing—the
nearest-run thing you ever saw in your life."*
—THE DUKE OF WELLINGTON, June 19, 1815

IN DECEMBER 1812, the wreck of the *Grande Armée* reached
Königsberg in East Prussia. The sight of these human scarecrows shocked the citizens of this quiet university city. Although some remained outwardly polite, others, especially the
young, showed their contempt openly. Students marched
through the streets, shouting the latest song:

> Drummers without drumsticks,
> Cuirassiers in women's clothes,
> Knights without a sword,
> Riders without a horse!
> Man, nag, and wagon
> Thus has God struck them down!

Prussia, indeed, was stirring in every city, town, and village.
For six years she'd been humiliated, robbed and oppressed
more than any of Napoleon's other victims. But as long as he
seemed invincible, people could only swallow their anger and
wait patiently for "the Day." Now the waiting was over. The
Russian disaster had cut the tyrant down to human size. It so
weakened the legend of his invincibility that all the hatred
he'd aroused suddenly burst into the open. The time had come
for what Germans call their "War of Liberation."

King Frederick William III gave the signal. Early in February 1813, he called for volunteers to form new army units.

217

The people answered with a spirit like that of France in 1793. Men of all classes and ages came forward to fill the ranks. Their rallying cry was *Freiheit und Vaterland* (Freedom and Fatherland).

Those who could not fight served in any way they could. Some gave money and goods. Others gave their time and skill, as when the elderly replaced teachers who'd joined the army. Women, particularly in Berlin, also contributed to the war effort. Married women exchanged their wedding rings for iron rings with the inscription: "I have given gold for iron." Many joined groups to roll bandages and make splints for the wounded. Teenage girls sold their long braids to wigmakers and gave the money to buy ammunition.

Prussia's army was led by Field Marshal Gebhard Lebrecht von Blücher. A plain man with simple ways, Blücher was crude, loud, and hot-tempered. He spent his nights playing dice and drinking whiskey, seldom going to bed sober. Soldiers loved him because he was really one of them. "Good morning, children!" he'd call to them, even at night. "Good morning, Father Blücher!" they'd reply.

Despite his age (seventy-one in 1813), Blücher was a bundle of energy. Much of that energy came from hatred, the driving force in his life. Blücher hated France, Frenchmen, and every-thing French. Most of all he hated Napoleon, who he saw as the living devil. Sometimes he would draw his sword and lunge at an unseen opponent, shouting "Napoleon!" His one desire was to beat the French and put their emperor before a firing squad. Unlike the sly Kutuzov, who died in March 1813, he believed only in attack. Blücher's orders were usually limited to a single word: "Forward!"—hence the nickname "Marshal Forward." His only strategy was to hit first, hit hard, and keep hitting until the enemy collapsed.

Napoleon felt he could beat a hundred Marshal For-
wards. Although Russia had been a setback, it was surely not
the end of the world. He was master of Italy, the Netherlands,
and all of Germany except Prussia. Austria was still an ally,
albeit a restless one. True, Spain continued to be a problem,
but it was minor compared to the issues at stake in Central
Europe.

The rebuilding of France's war machine began within days
of his return. Once again he was the Napoleon of Austerlitz—
confident, energetic, decisive. He buried himself in work,
putting in twenty hours at a stretch without resting or eating.
Once his secretary, groggy with fatigue, fell asleep while taking
dictation. When he awoke hours later, he saw the emperor
writing at the desk. He began to excuse himself, only to have
his master cut him short. "Why didn't you tell me you were
tired?" he asked. "I don't want to kill you. Go to bed. Good
night." The secretary obeyed, but the emperor worked through
the night.

Napoleon achieved a military miracle. From January to
April 1813, he replaced all the equipment lost in Russia. On
his orders, France's arsenals produced hundreds of thousands
of muskets, bayonets, and swords. Foundries, working around
the clock, made nearly a thousand cannons. These weapons
cost the French people nothing, since Napoleon paid for everything out of his own pocket, in cash. For years he'd kept 158
million francs in gold—most of it taxes collected from his
non-French subjects—in the cellars of the Tuileries for such
an emergency.

The men to use the weapons came from every corner of the
empire. Retired soldiers were called back to duty. Sailors and
policemen were taken into the army. The draft was speeded
up, so that nineteen-year-olds were taken a year ahead of

schedule. Veteran officers were brought from Spain to whip them into shape.

French training camps filled with draftees. The infantry were known as "Marie-Louises," since she'd also joined the emperor at nineteen. Raw youths who'd never been away from home or heard a shot fired in anger, they had to be taught everything from scratch. The cavalry were called "chickens mounted on colts," because there wasn't enough time to train either them or their mounts; horses were in short supply, so many having died in Russia. Enthusiasm, however, made up for lack of experience. Men were proud to serve the emperor, who they'd learned to adore since childhood.

In April 1813, Napoleon led 200,000 men across the Rhine into Saxony, Prussia's western neighbor. It was a bold move, aimed at taking the Prussians and Russians by surprise. The first clash came at Lützen (May 2), where he personally led the Young Guard against Blücher. Napoleon charged with a drawn sword, ignoring the shells bursting all around. Lützen was a costly victory, and an incomplete one, since lack of cavalry kept him from pursuing the fleeing enemy. It was the same at Bautzen three weeks later. He'd won again, but there could be no final victory without cavalry to finish the job.

Napoleon needed time to rest his army and reinforce his cavalry. To buy that time, he asked for a truce, claiming he wanted to begin peace talks. The Austrians agreed to act as go-betweens in the negotiations.

He met the Austrian foreign minister, Count Clemens Metternich, at Dresden toward the end of June. Metternich's proposals, however, were anything but friendly. If he wanted peace, Napoleon would have to return northern Italy to Austria, the Grand Duchy of Warsaw to Russia, and all the territory taken from Prussia. In effect, he'd be giving up all the gains he'd made since 1800. If he refused, Austria would join the allies. She already had 200,000 men under arms, and more were on the way. These, plus the allies' 300,000 men, would tip the scales against the French.

The emperor flung his hat to ground and began ranting like a maniac. He wouldn't surrender an inch of territory! No, not one inch! He'd fight the world, alone if need be, to save his empire and France's honor. The French army was strong—stronger than it had ever been. And he was still Napoleon—the Napoleon who'd never lost a major battle.

Metternich, a sour-faced man with a squeaky voice, stood his ground. "I have seen your troops," he said coldly. "You have nothing but children. You have caused an entire generation to be wiped out. What will you do when these, too, have disappeared?"

Napoleon exploded. Sputtering with rage, he revealed his true nature, perhaps more than he intended. He cared nothing for the world, nothing for humanity. He'd gladly let everything go up in smoke so long as he had his rights. "My honor first, then peace," he shouted, his face flushed. "Monsieur, you are not a soldier. You don't know what goes on in the heart of a soldier. I came of age on the battlefield, and I don't give a damn for a million lives. . . . It may cost me my throne, but I will drag the whole world down in its ruins!" To which Metternich replied: "You are lost, Sire."

Austria declared war, as Metternich promised she would, and a grand alliance was formed against Napoleon. Austria, Russia, and Prussia were soon joined by Sweden and Britain. The allies vowed not to rest until they'd rid the world of the tyrant. It must be a war to the finish.

Britain became the allies' paymaster and chief supplier. Over £4,500,000 (the equivalent of $8,100,000) in hard cash went to pay the allies' bills. Beginning in the summer of 1813, British ships brought everything their armies needed. In addition to weapons, they received such things as: 175,796 pairs of boots, 140,000 shoe brushes, 58,000 linen underpants, 69,624 pairs of stockings, 691,360 pounds of meat, 28,625 gallons of brandy and rum. The latter was greatly appreciated by the hard-drinking Blücher.

From August 26 to 27, Napoleon won a two-day battle at Dresden. Seen by itself, Dresden was a brilliant victory. But it was also part of a larger picture, one that was very bleak. The allies had finally learned how to counter his strategy of dividing their forces and throwing his full strength against one and then the other opponent. Now it was they who attacked weakness and avoided strength. They went after his marshals, but avoided the master himself. Whenever he advanced, they retreated. The result was a series of small, yet smashing, victories around Dresden. French losses rose daily, forcing the emperor to retreat to his base at Leipzig.

The climax came during the four-day Battle of Leipzig, or the Battle of the Nations. From October 16 to 19, the enemies pounded each other with artillery. The allies also unleashed their secret weapon: rockets. A British invention, these were sheet-iron tubes filled with gunpowder and launched from wooden tripods. Unlike today's missiles, they were impossible to aim with accuracy, nor could they travel more than a mile. Still, their effect was devastating. Scores of Frenchmen were killed at a time, their scorched and torn bodies lying in piles where they fell. These were devilish devices, Frenchmen thought. Whenever they saw one coming, whole units dropped their muskets and ran for cover.

Slowly the French gave way. Forced into the city, they retreated across the Elster River on its western side. A corporal, frightened by an enemy patrol, blew the bridge too soon, trapping the rear guard on the wrong side. Hundreds dove into the Elster, only to drown in the swift current. The windows of buildings overlooking the river were filled with women watching the scene below. They hated the French, and seeing so many drowning gave them pleasure. Each time a man began to go under, they cheered and waved "good-bye" with their handkerchiefs. Leipzig cost Napoleon 73,000 men to the allies' 54,000. Even more serious was the blow to his prestige. For the first time an army commanded by the emperor in person had been defeated in a pitched battle.

Bad news poured in from every direction. After Leipzig, all of Germany rose against Napoleon. Saxony, Bavaria, Baden, and Württemberg joined the allies. Jerome Bonaparte's Kingdom of Westphalia collapsed like a house of cards. Cossacks and Prussian cavalry scoured the countryside, hunting French stragglers. The Dutch rebelled and asked for British support.

The Spanish ulcer bled worse than ever, thanks to Sir Arthur Wellesley, who'd become Duke of Wellington. During the summer of 1812, he defeated the French at Salamanca and captured Madrid. The *madrileños* went wild with joy as he led his troops into their city. Bells were set ringing. Laughing *señoritas* waved from balconies. One Spanish greeting, however, was more than the hardbitten Redcoats could take. "Amidst all this pleasure," says Private Wheeler, "we were obliged to submit to a custome so unenglish that I cannot but feel disgust. . . . It was to be kissed by the men. What made it still worse, their breath was so highly seasoned with garlick, then their huge mustaches well stiffened with sweat, dust and snuff, it was like having a hair broom pushed into ones face that had been daubed in a dirty gutter."

Wellington took the offensive after Madrid. Slowly at first, then with growing speed, he advanced northward. On June 21, 1813, he met the enemy's main force at Vitoria on the Ebro River. King Joseph was so sure of victory that he built grandstands and invited local people to watch the spectacle. They did see a spectacle, but not the one he'd intended. The Redcoats shattered his army and sent it racing for the border. Private Wheeler and his friends, all champion looters, had a field day. Soldiers sang, danced, and drank themselves silly on wine from the captured wagon trains. Some put on generals' uniforms heavy with medals, others women's dresses embroidered in gold and silver. The duke was not amused, but he let them have their fun anyhow. They'd earned it.

Vitoria ended both the Peninsular War and the French kingdom of Spain. Wellington, never one to waste time, crossed the Pyrenees into France in October. The allies crossed the Rhine two months later.

British newspapers hailed the New Year with a headline: "He's falling! He's falling!" Napoleon's days as emperor of the French were numbered.

———

ON JANUARY 24, 1814, Napoleon left the Tuileries to join his army. Ahead lay many battles against heavy odds. Before stepping into his carriage, he took a few moments to be alone with his family. He kissed Marie-Louise tenderly, then tiptoed into the room where his son lay sleeping. Leaning over the tiny bed, he kissed the child gently on the forehead. Little did he know that he would never see them again.

During the next eight weeks, Napoleon fought one of the most brilliant campaigns in history. At Brienne, within sight of his old school, he defeated the Prussians and Russians. He moved so quickly that Blücher would have been captured had he not leaped onto his horse moments before the French

Napoleon in 1814. While still pictured in the regal pose of emperor, he shows the effects of years of strain, campaigning, and overeating. From a painting by Jean-Louis-Ernest Meissonier.

arrived. Other battles were fought at places that would become famous during the First World War: Château-Thierry, Verdun, La Rothiere, and Rheims. In February, he won six battles in nine days. Although he slowed down the invaders, it was like trying to halt a tidal wave with a broom.

Napoleon decided on a desperate gamble. Rather than defend Paris, as everyone expected, he planned a wide sweep to the southeast. Slipping behind the enemy, he'd cut their supply lines and intercept their reinforcements, leaving their field forces high and dry.

It was a fine plan and might have worked, had he not written about it to his wife. On March 23 his letter was captured by a cossack patrol. The allied leaders were amazed when they read it. What should they do? Their headquarters were only a hundred miles east of Paris. Should they ignore Napoleon and march on the capital, or fight him before he took action? That same day Czar Alexander received a secret message from Talleyrand. The former foreign minister had waited years to avenge Napoleon's insult, and this was his chance. The allies, he said, must strike while the iron was hot. People were tired of war and wanted only peace. Let them advance quickly and Paris would be theirs for the taking.

Talleyrand's message settled the issue. The allies closed in from all sides and overran the meager defenses. On March 30, their guns commanded Paris from the heights of Montmartre. The population was terrified, since Blücher made no secret of his wish to burn their city to the ground. Czar Alexander, however, had had enough of such outrages. A civilized man, he promised that Paris would be spared; it wouldn't even be looted. The city promptly surrendered and was occupied by allied troops.

Napoleon realized his plan had backfired only when it was

too late. Upon learning that the allies were marching on Paris, he hurried back to organize its defense. On the evening of the surrender, he met a troop of cavalry on the city's outskirts. "Why are you here?" he asked an officer. "Where is the enemy? What about Paris?" Only then did he learn that it had fallen hours before. He was stunned. His empire was gone, and now he'd lost his capital. Silently, with downcast eyes, he rode to the nearby Château de Fontainebleau.

A few days' rest convinced him that all was not lost. He still had 60,000 troops. He'd keep fighting.

His marshals, however, disagreed. They'd had a bellyful of war. After twenty years of fighting, they wanted to live quietly with their families and enjoy their wealth. Napoleon's plan meant only more lost battles, further retreats, and probably the destruction of Paris itself. Enough was enough. There must be peace—*now!*

On April 4, after a parade of the Old Guard, they told the emperor how they felt. He simply brushed them aside with a sneer. So, they wouldn't fight! Very well, he'd appeal directly to the army. His soldiers were still loyal, even if their commanders weren't. He'd lead them to bigger, better victories.

Marshal Ney stepped forward. No one had ever questioned his loyalty, and he resented such a remark. "The army won't march!" he announced, his voice quivering with rage.

"The army will obey me!" Napoleon snapped.

"Sire, the army obeys its generals."

That came as a slap in the face, but it brought Napoleon to his senses.

"Well, then, what is it you want, Messieurs?" he asked softly.

"Abdication."

On April 6 he gave up his throne unconditionally.

The work of twenty years lay around him in ruins. Worse, it was clear that the allies meant to keep him from his family. Being too weak-willed to resist, Marie-Louise had allowed herself and the young Napoleon to be taken to Vienna. The emperor was desperate, desolate, heartbroken. A week after abdicating, he swallowed a vial of poison he'd been carrying since leaving Moscow. It made him sick, but wasn't strong enough to be fatal. After nine hours of vomiting, he fell asleep, resigned to living his life to its natural end.

It promised to be a very dull life indeed. The allies were not as bloodthirsty as he'd imagined. Instead of shooting him, they'd decided to exile him to the island of Elba. Napoleon knew all about Elba—the ninety square miles of land whose outline he used to see from his native Corsica. The would-be emperor of the world would be emperor of Elba. The creator of the *Grande Armée* would have a toy army of 400.

On April 20, Napoleon bid farewell to his followers at Fontainebleau. The remnants of the Old Guard were drawn up in the courtyard near his coach. They stood at attention in silence, many with red eyes and tears rolling down their cheeks.

His words were aimed at their hearts. "*Adieu, mes enfants!* (Good-bye, my children!) I would like to press you all close to my heart; let me at least kiss your flag!"

The honor guard stepped forward, carrying the square of silk with the eagle insignia. Names were embroidered on it in gold: Marengo, Austerlitz, Jena, Eylau, Friedland, Wagram, Vienna, Berlin, Madrid, Borodino, Moscow. Proud names. Names to stir men's hearts.

Napoleon grasped the flag and kissed it gently. The Guardsmen wept openly. He then raised his hand and said, "Goodbye, once again, my old comrades. May this last kiss pass into your hearts!"

It did.

After his coach had passed through the gate, they burned the flag. The enemy could take anything he wanted, except this symbol of their manly pride. Some, unwilling to be without it, ate the ashes.

The emperor of Elba's coach rolled across France, escorted by four allied representatives. Things went well at first. In town after town he heard the familiar "Vive l'Empereur"; an old lady even hung onto the coach window and blessed him. But as they neared the Mediterranean coast, the mood changed. People in that area, an old royalist stronghold, had always resented him as an upstart. Now they told him so.

As the coach passed, they lined the road to jeer and throw stones. When it stopped, mobs gathered round, spitting, shaking their fists, and howling for Napoleon's blood. He turned pale with fright and began to tremble. As we've seen, he'd always been terrified of mobs, of "the human beast," as he called them. But this time was special, for he alone was the target. In his terror, he disguised himself in an Austrian uniform. This was the only time in his life that he showed cowardice, and it made him ashamed.

One night Napoleon and an English escort rode ahead to have dinner at a country inn. The owner, a childless widow, opened her heart to the "Austrian." She'd heard that Bonaparte was traveling toward the coast. Lord, what she'd give to have him in front of her carving knife!

"You have a good deal of hate for the emperor. What did he do to you?" Napoleon asked.

"What did he do? Ah, the monster! It was because of him that my son is dead—and my nephew, and so many other young people!"

Something in her voice touched him deeply. For once he understood what he'd been doing to plain people for so many years. He went into a corner and sat by himself, lost in thought, his head in his hands. An onlooker said he saw tears on his cheeks. Too bad the experience wore off so quickly.

Napoleon was glad to board the British warship *Undaunted* at the port of Fréjus. He quickly made friends with the ship's crew by his easy manner and gifts of gold napoleons, each worth three months' pay. On May 4, as *Undaunted* anchored at Elba, the sailors sent him a brief note: "Good health, your Honor, and better luck next time."

Meanwhile, word of his abdication sped across the Continent. Except for one short break, Europe had been at war for a full generation. At last peace had come. That Easter of 1814 was the sweetest within living memory. The churches were jammed, as people everywhere thanked God for peace and prayed it would last forever.

As spring turned to summer, weary men in ragged uniforms plodded toward France's borders from every corner of Europe. They were prisoners of war making their way home after years in captivity. They came eastward from Spain, northward from Italy, and westward from Russia. Still others moved south from Belgium, where they'd come ashore from British transports. Most of this group reached the border by way of the main road from Brussels. Eight miles from the Belgian capital, the road crossed a low plateau called Mont Saint Jean. Set back from the plateau's edge, amid farms and cornfields, stood a village with an English-sounding name: Waterloo.

It was a name they would hear again.

———

NAPOLEON BUSIED HIMSELF as he thought an emperor should. He modernized the Elban government, improved the island's roads and ports, and strengthened its defenses. His army had grown to a thousand with the addition of Imperial Guard volunteers who'd come at their own expense. There was also a "navy" of a half-dozen small vessels.

The small world of Elba also allowed the emperor to relax as he hadn't done for years. He took long walks and amused himself by playing practical jokes on his staff. A favorite trick was to slip a rotten fish into an officer's pocket, and then ask to borrow his handkerchief. He played cards with his mother and sister, Pauline, who'd arrived for a long visit. He'd cheat. Letizia would catch him and rap his knuckles, then everyone had a good laugh.

France's new ruler was Louis XVIII, brother of the executed Louis XVI. A grotesquely fat man who belched constantly, he'd never forgiven Napoleon for crowning himself emperor. There was nothing he wouldn't do to make "that monster's" life miserable. The king refused to send him money, as promised. His agents were forever spying on him and there were rumors of assassination; given the Cadoudal plot of 1800, these rumors had to be taken seriously. There was even talk of removing Napoleon to a place far from Europe. Elba, royalists believed, was too close for comfort. They'd never feel safe until he was out of the way—permanently.

Napoleon had his own agents operating in France. Peace, it seemed, was not an unmixed blessing. Their reports told of the public's anger over increased taxes. The end of the Continental System had brought a flood of British goods, harming French businessmen and causing unemployment. Most importantly, soldiers still loved Napoleon and despised Louis XVIII. Lack of money had forced reductions in the army. Men who'd grown up in barracks felt lost in civilian life; without professions, many drifted into poverty. Thousands of officers

were retired on half-pay and their posts given to royalists who'd
fought against their country. Even the marshals, who'd forced
the emperor's abdication, were badly treated. Here the issue
wsa not money, but respect. Royalists scorned these low-born
men, who'd risen through their own efforts. Marshals' wives
were treated as servant girls. Marshal Ney's wife, the daughter
of a chambermaid, was snubbed by royalist ladies. Ney told a
friend: "I have had enough of seeing my wife come home in
tears after a day of snubs. Clearly the King doesn't want us;
only with Bonaparte shall we be respected."

Napoleon at forty-five was as ambitious as ever. He was
rested, at the height of his mental powers, and growing bored.
Destiny, he felt, didn't intend him to rule a make-believe
empire on a tiny island. He belonged at the center of things—
in France.

On February 26, 1815, the Elban "fleet" set sail with the
emperor and 1,200 men. After a three-day voyage, it anchored
near Cannes. Napoleon's boldest adventure had begun.
Known as the Hundred Days, it would end in one of history's
greatest battles.

Avoiding royalist areas, with their bitter memories, he led
his force through the Maritime Alps. How would the French
people greet him? What would the army do when ordered into
action against him? Napoleon couldn't be certain. He could
only hope for the best and trust his luck.

The moment of truth came outside the city of Grenoble.
When Napoleon drew near, he found the road blocked by
troops of the Fifth Regiment. They stood in line, silently,
bayonets fixed, muskets ready. One false step and old comrades
would be at each other's throats.

Napoleon was fearless. Calmly, he ordered his men to lower

their weapons—no need to make the others nervous. He then rode alone toward the waiting line. It was the best performance he'd ever given. At fifty feet he dismounted and walked forward slowly, to allow the impression to sink in. He was wearing his cocked hat and gray overcoat, familiar to every French soldier.

"There he is! Fire!" cried an officer.

Silence.

Napoleon stopped and called out: "Soldiers of the Fifth! I am your emperor! Recognize me!"

Silence and fidgeting.

Taking a few more steps, he threw open his coat, pointed to his chest, and shouted: "If there is one soldier among you who wants to kill his emperor, here I am!"

Kill their emperor! Kill their Little Corporal! Never! A tremendous shout of "*Vive l'Empereur!*" burst from the ranks. The soldiers broke formation and, tossing their hats on the points of their bayonets, rushed forward. They crowded around him, knelt at his feet, stroked his boots, kissed his hands, cried like babies. It was the same in every town after Grenoble. Wherever he appeared, the soldiers joined him. In less than a week, his tiny force became a mighty army.

When word of this reached Paris, a jokester hung a sign near the Tuileries. It read: "From Napoleon to Louis XVIII, My good brother, you needn't send any more troops. I have enough." Louis took the hint and fled, taking his royalists with him. His worst regret was that he'd left his bedroom slippers behind; it had taken him years to break them in.

On March 20, Napoleon was carried up the steps of the Tuileries by a cheering crowd. Jean-Roch Coignet, a retired captain on half-pay, couldn't contain his delight. He cheered so loudly that, "I must say that I just about ruptured my spleen."

The French welcomed their hero, but not his dictatorship. In order to win their full support, he enacted various reforms. The constitution was revised to allow more people to vote in local elections. Freedom of the press was granted, along with other liberties borrowed from the American Bill of Rights. Yet, deep down, he remained the same undemocratic Napoleon. After defeating the allies, he intended to send the legislature packing and abolish the reforms.

———

THE ALLIES WERE FLABBERGASTED at Napoleon's return. In London, screaming headlines announced "The Devil is Loose!" In Berlin and Vienna, the common people went into mourning. Many wore black armbands and flocked to the churches to beg God's mercy. Their rulers branded him an outlaw and "the enemy and disturber of the peace of the world." Solemnly they pledged to crush him and drive him from Europe once and for all.

The allied plan called for 794,000 men in four armies— British, Prussian, Austrian, and Russian—to invade France simultaneously. Their main difficulty was time: it would take several weeks for the Austrians and Russians to gather their forces and march west. Only Blücher's and Wellington's troops were close at hand, in Belgium. Blücher's men were a rough bunch who knew their business. The duke's army, however, was a hodgepodge of Belgian, Dutch, German, and British units. The first two were not noted for bravery; the Germans were good, but too few; the Redcoats were mostly raw troops backed by a handful of Peninsular War veterans. Britain and the United States had been at war for the past three years. After the fall of Paris in 1814, the best regiments left for

America, and their meeting with Andrew Jackson's frontiersmen at New Orleans.

Napoleon could follow one of two strategies. The first was defensive: he could make the allies come to him, wear them out in defensive battles, and then force negotiations on his terms. Or he could strike a crushing blow against the Anglo-Prussian armies before their friends arrived. He chose the second course, because it promised quick victory and would spare France another invasion.

Surprise was the key element. On the night of June 13, he secretly concentrated his army opposite the Belgian border city of Charleroi. His aim was to drive a wedge between Wellington and Blücher and destroy each in turn.

At first, everything went according to plan. On June 15, he captured Charleroi in a lightning move. He then advanced in a huge Y-shaped formation; that is, two wings backed by a central reserve. The right wing headed for the Prussian base at Ligny, the left for Quatre-Bras, a vital crossroads on the way to Brussels. Thus, with a single blow, he'd split the allied armies.

That evening the Duke of Wellington attended a ball in Brussels. He was having a good time, until a messenger brought word of the French capture of Charleroi and their advance on Quatre-Bras. The duke sat up with a start, exclaiming, "Napoleon has humbugged me, by God!" Beckoning for his aides to follow, he went into another room and unrolled a map of southern Belgium. The army, he said, must concentrate at Quatre-Bras. But if it couldn't hold out there, "I must fight him here." As he spoke, he pointed to Waterloo.

In the early hours of June 16, bugle calls echoed across the sleeping city. Instantly drumbeats mingled with the skirl of bagpipes. From all over Brussels, troops rushed to their

assembly points. Youngsters who'd never seen action were
eager for a crack at the French. Veterans, who knew the score,
said good-bye to their wives and children with tearstained faces.
One poor Redcoat wept openly; he kissed his baby, handed it
to his wife, kissed her, and ran after his company.

Once formed, each regiment marched through the city gates
and disappeared into the chill morning mist. Scores of officers
left for battle in their dancing shoes and silk stockings. Fifes
and drums set the pace with a snappy tune, "The Girl I Left
Behind Me." Its words were loved by all, because they spoke
to the soldier's deepest feelings:

> Kind Heaven pray mind me;
> And send me home, safe back again,
> To the girl I left behind me.

The duke's advance units arrived at Quatre-Bras, known to
Redcoats as "Quarter Brass," later that morning. Napoleon
ordered Marshal Ney to pin them down while he attacked the
Prussians at Ligny. There soldiers on both sides fought as if
they were settling personal scores—savagely. Blücher galloped
into action shouting, "Vorwärts, meine kinder, vorwärts!" (Forward, my children, forward!) While leading them, he was
thrown from his horse and badly bruised. Later he soaked his
aching feet in brandy, drinking the leftovers to soothe his
insides.

This was not Blücher's only close call. Strong French reinforcements were nearing Quatre-Bras when a note from the
emperor ordered them to Ligny. There is no doubt that their
timely arrival would have finished the Prussians. But they were
saved when a more recent note from Ney ordered them to
continue on to Quatre-Bras, thus failing to arrive in time for
either battle and allowing Blücher to retreat with his army
intact. The next morning, Napoleon sent a 30,000-man force

in pursuit, while he joined Ney. The Prussians, he felt, were out of the picture. They wouldn't trouble him again anytime soon.

Upon learning of the Prussian defeat, Wellington swore— like a gentleman. "Old Blücher," he said, "has had a damned good spanking." There was nothing to do now but retreat to the plateau of Mont Saint Jean. He'd already made head-quarters at Waterloo and sent word to Blücher that he'd risk a battle if at least some Prussian divisions could come to his support. Blücher promised to send them as soon as possible. If they arrived in time, Napoleon would be caught in a giant vise and crushed. If not . . .

The British retreat began at dawn on June 17. It was hell; pure, simple hell. The French, who were held off by a strong rear guard, were not the problem. Throughout the day and much of the night, rain fell in buckets, turning roads into streams of mud. Reaching their destination, the Redcoats made camp in the open. Everyone had his personal tale of woe. Lieutenant James Hope wrote in a letter home:

> Fancy yourself seated on a few small twigs, or a little straw, in a newly ploughed field, well soaked with six hours of rain; your feet six or eight inches deep in the mud; a thin blanket your only shelter . . . cold, wet, and hungry. . . . Imagine yourself placed in such a situation and you will have a faint idea of what we suffered on the night of the 17th and the morning of the memorable 18th of June.

Ensign William Leeke of the 52nd Infantry had joined the army upon turning seventeen a month earlier; his mother had begged him not to choose such a dangerous career. Now he remembered her words. He and a friend were lying in the mud when some horses, terrified by the lightning, broke loose.

The animals galloped about all night, making the youngsters jump up every few minutes or be trampled. Peninsular War veterans turned up their noses at such hardships. "Lord have mercy on your poor tender carcass!" they'd tease. "What would you have done in the Pyrenees?" Or "Oho my boy! This is but child's play to what *we* saw in Spain."

William Wheeler, a sergeant at last, gave up trying to sleep altogether. He and his squad sat on their knapsacks without a campfire, the water running in streams from the cuffs of their jackets. Huddled under sodden blankets, smoking their short clay pipes, they passed the long hours until dawn. Still, they were content, for in Spain the rain had been an omen of victory. The nights before Salamanca and Vitoria were also full of rain, thunder, and lightning. Besides, it was nice to know that the French were just as miserable. Rather than wallow in the mud, many of Napoleon's infantrymen stayed on their feet all night. Cavalrymen slept on their horses' backs, a mistake, given the uphill charges the next day.

6:30 A.M.

Daybreak, Sunday, June 18, found officers and men blue-lipped from the cold. A two-days' growth of beard made them look seedy; the dyes had run from their wet uniforms, staining their bodies various shades of red and blue. As the sun appeared, they busied themselves with necessary chores. Wood was gathered, fires lit, and clothes hung to dry. There was little to eat, except some lumpy porridge and a tiny portion of meat. Private William Clay of the British Guards received a chunk of pig's head "in its rough state." He was glad to have that much; most of his friends ate nothing and fought the battle on empty stomachs. Everywhere men were cleaning muskets, sharpening bayonets, and checking ammunition. There was a

constant *pop, pop, popping* as muskets were fired to get rid of
the charges that had stayed in them during the rainy night.

Warriors of more than five nations had come together to
slaughter one another. Napoleon with 71,947 men and 246
guns faced Wellington with 67,711 men and 156 guns; Blücher
with his 61,000 men and 40 guns was still fifteen miles to the
west. The duke had placed his army on the plateau and on
the gentle slope leading up to it. His positions can still be seen
today. Unfortunately, the Belgian government, in its eagerness
to commemorate the battle, dug up part of the battlefield and
heaped it into a giant earthen cone topped by a stone lion. It
is ugly. Uglier still are the parking lots, fast-food shops, and
souvenir stands that block the view.

Wellington's front line ran just below the plateau's southern
edge and followed a country lane with thick hedges on either
side. Men could stand behind the hedges, invisible until the
enemy was practically on top of them. Openings had been cut
in various places to allow cavalry to pass through easily. The
duke's main line, however, was on the plateau itself. His reserves waited behind the crest, safe (mostly) from falling shot
and shells, just as they'd been in Spain. In addition, two groups
of buildings stood among the fields below, each of which
became a vital outpost. The first group, on his right, was the
Château de Hougoumont, a large manor house, farm, and
garden surrounded by a six-foot wall. If left unguarded, the
French could easily slip behind the entire British positon; there
was no way to defend the plateau without Hougoumont. La
Haye Sainte, the second group, was a farm just 200 yards in
front of his first line, concentrated fire from there could blow
a hole right through the center. Napoleon's positions were on
the opposite ridge, across a shallow valley. These were not
meant for defense, but as staging areas for the attack. Gun

batteries were placed on the ridge. Masses of infantry waited at the ridge's base and in the fields behind.

The emperor's plan was simple: break the enemy's first line, charge up the slope, and sweep him off the plateau. It was *too* simple. Although he'd never personally fought the British, he made no effort to study the duke's methods. Officers who'd served in Spain warned that Redcoats in formation *"c'est le diable"* ("are the devil"). But once again wishes replaced facts in Napoleon's mind. "Because you have been beaten by Wellington, you think him a great general," he told doubters. "I tell you Wellington is a bad general, the English are bad troops, and that this affair is nothing more than eating breakfast." The Englishman, however, had no illusions. Nor did he have a battle plan. He meant to take things as they came, and act accordingly. And he'd pray for Blücher to arrive in time.

Once they'd prepared, the allies waited for Napoleon to make the first move. The morning passed slowly. Soldiers sat on the ground talking, or lay dozing with their heads on their knapsacks, enjoying the sun. They talked of different things: home, loved ones, past fights, comrades "gone west." No one talked of fear, since fear was considered unmanly. George Keppel, a sixteen-year-old ensign in the Fourteenth Infantry, spoke for many during the hours of waiting: "I wished the fight was fought."

At about eleven o'clock a breeze brought the sound of cheering from across the valley. Those in forward postions peered out to see what was happening. All they could see was a mass of men moving forward, then dividing to the right and left when it reached a small crossroads. "There he is on his white horse!" said an officer with a spyglass. Everyone knew who he meant.

Napoleon sat on his favorite charger, Marengo, reviewing

his army for the last time. It was a gorgeous spectacle. Drums throbbed. Trumpets blared. Regimental bands played marching songs. Flags fluttered in the breeze. As the troops passed, each outfit greeted him in its own fashion. Cuirassiers trotted by, waving their swords over their heads. Infantrymen raised their hats on the points of their bayonets. Gunners twirled their rammers. All shouted "*Vive l'Empereur!*" Wellington's men watched the glittering display, heard the cheers, and gave their weapons a final check.

11:30 A.M.

The Battle of Waterloo began at Hougoumont late in the morning. The château was defended by nearly a thousand Scots Guards and Coldstream Guards. Big men with broad, ruddy faces, enemies said they were too stupid to know when they were beaten. That was both a joke and a compliment, since these Scottish Highlanders were famous for their stubborn courage. They might be outnumbered. Their positon might be hopeless. But you could count on two things: they'd fight to the end and sell their lives dearly.

Today they showed their "stupidity" at its best. Attacked by 13,000 Frenchmen, they refused to give an inch. When Frenchmen burst through the gate, they shot them all down, except for a little drummer boy. Anyone trying to scale the wall was met with axes, musket butts, and bayonets. Exploding shells set fire to the farm buildings, which were filled with wounded. Since their comrades couldn't be spared to rescue them, those who couldn't crawl out on their own were burned alive. The air in the yard was thick with smoke and reeked of burning flesh and manure. Everyone was black with soot and scorched by embers; men's hair caught fire. Sergeant Wheeler never forgot what he saw there after the battle. "I went to the

The Duke of Wellington, in a portrait by Francisco Goya. A brilliant general, Wellington first overcame Napoleon's troops in Spain, and would oversee the emperor's final defeat at the Battle of Waterloo. BELOW, the battle begins at the Château de Hougoumont. Though outnumbered thirteen to one, its defenders would repulse all French attempts to seize this key position. From a drawing by Thomas Sutherland, 1816.

farm house, what a sight. Inside the yard the guards lay in heaps, many who had been wounded inside or near the building were roasted, some who had endeavored to crawl out from the fire lay dead with their legs burnt to a cinder." But the Highlanders held Hougoumont.

——————

1:30 P.M.

Hougoumont was burning when Napoleon made his next move. Early in the afternoon, an eighty-gun battery began to soften up the British center. *Baroom-boom. Baroom-boom.* The earth shook as the guns poured out a deluge of shot and shell. Clouds of smoke drifted across the battlefield, completely hiding it for minutes at a time. Although most of the duke's men kept under cover, several units were exposed on the slope— and these suffered horribly. Those who survived that day had the experience burned into their memories.

Ensign Leeke was carrying the regimental flag when the bombardment began. He stood in a field, proudly holding the flag, as the first shots *whooshed* overhead. "There, Mister Leeke, is a cannon shot," said a sergeant, "if you never saw one before, sir." He'd see plenty of them before the day was done.

At first Leeke was excited, since everything was new to him. But excitement turned to terror when he noticed two men of his regiment lying dead under a tree; he had to try hard not to cry. He later saw a rare sight—and wished he hadn't. While glancing at the French positions, a single gun caught his eye. Fascinated, he watched the crew load, aim, and fire it at his unit. A veteran had told him that the only time you saw a cannonball was if it came head-on. Suddenly he saw a round black dot leave the gun's barrel—and come straight at *him.* Leeke became a man during the next few seconds. "I thought,

Shall I move? No! I gathered myself up, and stood firm, with the [flag] in my right hand." He'd die, but he wouldn't disgrace himself by ducking. The shot missed him and wounded four men standing to his right.

Leeke was lucky in that he never saw someone hit squarely. Cannonballs did not simply kill; they smashed their victims to pieces. Sergeant William Lawrence of the Fortieth Infantry saw a shell fragment cut a friend in half and take off the head of a soldier he knew. Nearby, Lieutenant Wray was talking to Captain Fisher when a ball struck: "At the same time poor Fisher was hit I was speaking to him, and I got all over his brains, his head was blown to atoms." Single cannonballs were known to strike anywhere from one to twenty-five men. The wounded were not supposed to cry out, since that might unnerve their comrades. "O man, don't make a noise," an officer would shout, and usually the fellow pulled himself together and was quiet. Some poor souls quietly bled to death rather than disobey an order.

The bombardment halted after a half hour. Time seemed to stand still in the eerie silence that followed. But old-timers knew what that silence meant: gunners ceased fire only to avoid hitting their own advancing infantry. The worst was still to come.

Suddenly drums began to throb in a strange rhythm:

The rum dum. The rum dum.

The rummadum dummadum, dum, dum, dum.

Veterans of Spain remembered it well, and told puzzled youngsters about the *pas de charge*. Peering from cover, they saw that the valley floor had come alive with marching men; more men, in fact, than they'd ever seen in one place at one time.

Three columns, totaling 18,000 men, advanced in formations 200 across and 30 deep. The columns passed to the right of La Haye Sainte, human steamrollers that seemed irresistible. As the drumbeats increased in tempo, officers shouted *"En Avance!"* ("Advance!"), and the men answered with a triumphant roar. They had reason to cheer. The only allied troops visible were some Belgians, and they were running away. Redcoats weren't to be seen anywhere. Ahead loomed the hedges. Wellington's main line and victory lay beyond.

Then it happened. The columns were forty paces from the hedges when they heard a command shouted in English, "Up Gordons! *Fire!"* Instantly 3,000 Gordon Highlanders sprang up as if from the earth and fired across the hedges. It was impossible to miss such a large mass, and Frenchmen toppled over in droves. Others, dazed by the sudden hail of lead, broke ranks and tried to escape. But there was no place to go; the columns were so tightly packed that men could only knock into one another, spreading confusion as they went.

Before the muskets' noise died away, there came another shout: "Charge! Charge! Hurrah!" Frenchmen saw the Gordons, a swarm of "women soldiers" in tartan skirts and long woolen stockings, burst through the hedge. The kilted Highlanders came at them with gleaming bayonets. Their bagpiper, a six-foot-six mountain of muscle, stood on a hillock, urging them to move faster. Again and again, his pipes played a hurry-up tune: "Johnny Cope, Are Ye Waukin' Yet?"

But the French rout had only just begun. They were falling back in disorder when the sound of hoofbeats rose above the din of battle. Nearer it came, until the Scots Grays, one of Wellington's best cavalry regiments, leaped over the hedges at breakneck speed. Swords flashing, they shouted their war cry: "Scotland forever!" The Highlanders answered with, "Go at

them, Grays! Scotland forever!" Many were so excited that
they grasped the stirrups and dashed ahead with the cavalrymen.

The Grays literally sliced their way through the French.
Sergeant Charles Ewart went straight for the flag of the Forty-
fifth Regiment, the "Invincibles." A first-class unit, its flag
bore the names of past victories at Austerlitz and Jena. The
flag's guard fought bravely, but Ewart wouldn't take "no" for
an answer. "I cut him through the head," Ewart said of his
first victim; the second "I cut from the chin upwards, which
cut went through his teeth"; the third was nearly decapitated.
As Ewart rode off with the bloodstained trophy, his comrades
called, "Well done, my boy!"

A kind of infectious lunacy took hold of the cavalrymen.
The bugle sounding Recall was ignored as they swept across
the valley and up the far slope. Napoleon's guns stood there,
and they'd killed many a fine fellow. Now their crews would
taste cold steel.

The Scotsmen slashed the crews and disabled the guns. Even
their mounts joined the fight. Corporal John Dickson's horse,
Rattler, bit and tore at everything in her way. By then, however, horses and riders were exhausted. Squadrons of French
cavalry blocked their retreat, butchering them as they tried to
break through. Of the 2,500 horsemen who charged, less than
half returned to their lines. Wellington congratulated their
commander, but warned him never to try that stunt again.

———

3:30 P.M.

Napoleon had tried artillery and infantry against the allied
line, but it still wouldn't break. By midafternoon, Marshal
Ney, his battlefield commander, saw men and vehicles heading northward, off the plateau. We know that they were

wounded soldiers and empty ammunition wagons moving to the rear. Ney, however, decided that a retreat was underway. Eager to finish the job, he sent his cavalry into action without asking the emperor's approval.

Wellington was astonished. In the valley below were lines of horsemen—12,000 in all—in blue uniforms, plumed helmets, and steel breastplates. Each line came at a steady trot, 500 abreast, riding stirrup to stirrup. They flowed like ocean waves across the folds of the valley and up the gentle slope ahead. French guns bombarded the plateau's crest to cover their approach.

"Prepare to receive cavalry!" redcoated officers shouted. Infantrymen, lying down behind the crest, stood up and formed hollow squares three ranks deep. The soldiers in front dropped onto one knee, their musket butts firmly set on the ground and their bayonets slanting outward, forming a hedge of steel; the rear ranks stood ready to shoot over their heads. The squares were arranged in a checkerboard pattern, with cannons in between. For some unknown reason, Ney, who certainly knew better, had made a basic mistake. If cavalry attacked squares, they had to be supported by infantry and light artillery. Sending them in alone was like committing suicide. Squares could not be broken by cavalry because horses, unlike men, will not dash into massed bayonets.

Wellington's cannons were double-loaded with solid shot topped by a container of grape. The French came steadily onward, spurring their mounts into a gallop. When they came within range, the gunners fired as fast as they could. Salvo after salvo ripped through the forward ranks, knocking down men and horses. Their comrades rode by without pausing.

Now the squares were only thirty yards away. Cavalrymen went at them with bloodcurdling yells, firing pistols and slashing with swords. Redcoats crumpled to the ground, their places immediately filled by those behind. Dead and wounded were dragged into the center of the square where their blood formed puddles. Private John Lewis of the Ninety-fifth Infantry was surrounded by death:

> My first-rank man was wounded by part of a shell through his foot, and he dropt. . . . I covered the next man I saw, and . . . a musket-shot came sideways and took his nose clean off . . . Just after that, a man that stood next to me on my left hand had his left arm shot off by a nine-pound shot, just above the elbow, and he turned around and caught hold of me with his right hand, and the blood ran over my trousers . . . and he dropt directly. The man on my right hand was shot through the body, and the blood ran out at his belly and back like a pig stuck in the throat; he dropt on his side; I spoke to him; he just said, 'Lewis, I'm done' and died directly.

Finally the order came: "Fire!" Volleys of musketry lashed out from the squares at point-blank range. The bullets made a strange noise against breastplates; one soldier compared it "to the noise of a violent hail-storm beating upon panes of glass." Riders toppled to the ground, rolling and bouncing like rag dolls flung by an angry child. Horses collapsed and fell on their riders, crushing them. Riderless horses plunged and reeled, adding to the confusion. The survivors charged around and past the squares, only to retreat down the slope, reform, and come back for more.

Again they ran into a hail of bullets. This time, however, the duke unleashed his cavalry as well. Those in the squares were amazed at the battle that swirled around them. Horsemen fought as the knights had done during the Middle Ages, sword against sword. Sergeant Tom Morris of the Seventy-third Infantry saw an Englishman give a backhanded sword stroke that sent a cuirassier's helmet flying with his head still in it. The horse galloped away with the headless rider sitting erect in the saddle, "the blood spurting out of the arteries like a fountain."

Napoleon was furious at Ney; his attack had been reckless, useless, dangerous. But once committed, he had to be supported. Rather than take his losses, the emperor ordered more cavalry into action. And the result was always the same. Twelve times the French charged, and twelve times they fell back before the unbroken squares. The squares were surrounded by heaps of dead and wounded, men as well as animals.

The duke watched everything with keen interest. Mounted on his favorite horse, Copenhagen, he rode along the crest. He was perfectly calm, even as men were blown to bits before his very eyes. If he needed to send a message, he scribbled it in pencil on slips of paper kept for the purpose. If things became too hot, he'd take refuge in one of the squares. While pausing near a gun battery, an officer saw Napoleon and asked if he should fire. "Certainly not," the Duke snapped. "It is not the business of commanders to fire upon each other." Gentlemen still considered it unsporting to shoot deliberately at enemy commanders. The emperor, for his part, watched the action through a telescope from the inn of La Belle Alliance, well behind the fighting lines. It's a wonder that he saw anything through the smoke.

6:00 P.M.

The next ninety minutes decided the Battle of Waterloo and Napoleon's fate. During a lull in the fighting, he learned that Prussian troops had been sighted to the east. Prussians! He was stunned. After their defeat at Ligny, he'd dismissed them as a real threat. Now, with Blücher nearby, he needed to win quickly or face certain defeat. Ney was ordered to take La Haye Sainte at any cost.

The defending Redcoats fought bravely, but were overrun by swarms of Frenchmen. Ney quickly turned La Haye Sainte into an advanced fire base. Wellington's center was blasted by scores of heavy guns. At such close range, there was no telling how long he could hold out. He'd already lost thousands killed and wounded; the others were exhausted after a sleepless night and a day's fighting. Grim-faced, he rode back and forth along the line, hoping against hope. "Night or the Prussians must come," an aide heard him say.

Seeing the enemy weaken, Ney sent an urgent appeal to Napoleon for the Imperial Guard. The moment of decision had come. As at Borodino, the Guard had taken no part in the battle thus far. Its men were rested, well-fed, and raring to go. Victory was certain, if the Guard came at once, Ney insisted. If not, Wellington would scrape together his last reserves and wait for the Prussians. It was now or never.

Once again Napoleon hesitated at the crucial moment. "Troops?" he asked sarcastically. "Where do you expect me to find them? Do you expect me to make them?"

With these words he threw away any chance of victory.

By seven o'clock that evening, Blücher's advance forces were going into action on Wellington's left. Only then did Napoleon decide to use the Guard. It was a gambler's last fling of the dice, and it failed.

The sun was setting when Ney led the Guard into action. What a spectacle! It came in ranks sixty abreast, rank after rank, covering the valley floor. As it passed, wounded men stood up to cheer. A soldier sitting on the ground with both

legs crushed kept shouting, "This is nothing, comrades. Forward! *Vive l'Empereur!*"

Wellington stood behind the units that would bear the brunt
of the attack. Although they knelt and could not see the enemy,
he had a clear view from atop Copenhagen.

The Guard moved slowly, deliberately, sure of its strength
and mission. Victory was its heritage; after all, it had never
been defeated in battle.

The duke waited until its tall bearskin hats came over the
crest. "Now!" he shouted. "Now is your time! Up! Make ready!
Fire!" Redcoats leaped to their feet and let go with a crashing
volley. Napoleon's Guard, his invincible Guard, suddenly
halted. Its front shattered, men falling right and left, it began
to fall back.

"*La garde recule!*" ("The guard retreats!")

The cry swept from one end of the valley to the other. Fear,
like a disease, is contagious. Once it takes hold of a group of
people, it spreads beyond control. The Guard's retreat triggered
a general panic in which the French army collapsed. There
was no longer anyone to give orders, nor anyone to follow
them. Soldiers ran for their lives, throwing away guns, knapsacks, and whatever else might slow them down. It was every
man for himself.

The sun was only a glow in the west as Wellington watched
from the top of the slope. Everyone who could see through
the smoke had his eyes glued to that spot. The duke stood in
the stirrups holding his hat above his head. At last he waved
it three times in the direction of the French. There was no
need for orders. The whole allied line gave three cheers and
charged. And at that very moment, the Prussian main force
poured onto the battlefield.

The pursuit continued southward, along the Charleroi road. Blücher's cavalry were fresh, and they were out for blood. Few Frenchmen who came near their blades lived to tell the tale. One squadron made its fortune by taking Napoleon's own coach, a rolling palace on wheels. Its furnishings included golden plates and cutlery, a writing desk, a folding bed, a set of golden toilet articles, and a silver chamber pot. Best of all, they found diamonds worth two million francs sewn into the lining of a spare uniform. His Imperial Majesty always traveled in style.

NIGHT

Wellington rode back to Waterloo across the moonlit battlefield, saying nothing as he passed through that tormented land. The bodies of 47,000 men and 10,000 horses lay within an area of two square miles.* The living, numb with fatigue, had simply fallen to the ground and slept without blankets, surrounded by corpses. The wounded were everywhere, shrieking in pain and begging for water. Few were helped, and it took four days to find and treat them all. Many a hero died for lack of prompt medical attention.

Wellington returned to his headquarters for a late supper. The table was set for his staff, but he ate alone; most staff members were either dead, wounded, or busy elsewhere. After eating, he lay down to sleep on the floor, for one of his favorite officers was dying in his bed. The young man died about three o'clock in the morning. When the surgeon woke Wellington with the news, he cried. He was later heard to remark: "I hope to God that I have fought my last battle. . . . I never wish for

*Wellington lost 15,000 men, Blücher 7,000, and Napoleon 25,000, plus 8,000 prisoners and 220 guns.

any more fighting." Napoleon's conqueror had seen enough of war.

About this time, a French lieutenant named Martin reached Quatre-Bras. Scattered over the countryside were the remnants of a once-great army. Up ahead, he saw a campfire in a forest clearing. Hoping for a little food and rest, he walked toward the fire, which some of the Old Guard were fueling with sticks. Off to the side, among the trees, he saw a lone figure: the emperor. Napoleon stood still and silent, his arms crossed on his chest, staring down the road to Waterloo. Martin turned away without a word. There was nothing to say.

The Napoleonic Wars were over.

EAGLE ON THE ROCK

"I have made noise enough
in the world already,
perhaps too much."

—NAPOLEON, October 1, 1816

ON JULY 20, 1815, HMS *Bellerophon* met a sister ship cruising off the French coast. Captain Frederick Maitland, her commander, hailed the vessel's captain with the words, "Well, I have got him!"

"Got him? Got whom?"

"Why, Bonaparte—the man who had been keeping all Europe in a ferment these twenty years."

"Is it possible? Well, you are a lucky fellow!"

Napoleon's fall had been swift and total. He'd hurried back to Paris after Waterloo, intending to gather another army. But the French people were unwilling to sacrifice any more of their sons to his ambition. The legislature, sharing their feelings, forced him to abdicate on June 23. Later that day, Joseph Fouché, his former police chief, formed a temporary government that invited Louis XVIII to return. No hard feelings, Fouché explained. The nation had gone temporarily insane during the Hundred Days, but had returned to its senses.

The fallen emperor had become a man without a country. What could he do? Where could he go? Royalist agents were anxious to get their hands on him. Many Frenchmen, blaming him for loved ones' deaths, would gladly slit his throat. And that mad Prussian, Blücher, still meant to put him before a firing squad.

Fouché suggested an escape to the United States. The Americans, however, wouldn't hear of it; President James Madison had no sympathy for a has-been dictator. At last Napoleon decided to throw himself on the mercy of Great Britain. The British were a generous people, always willing to let bygones be bygones. Surely they'd find a place for him, since he no longer threatened them. He'd retire to a country estate, become a gentleman farmer, and spend his free time writing his memoirs. It was a nice dream, with all the permanence of a soap bubble.

On July 14—Bastille Day—Napoleon made his way to the Île d'Aix—an island in the Bay of Biscay—where he saw *Bellerophon* patrolling offshore. The next day, he surrendered and went on board with several aides. From that moment on, his life as a free man ended.

During the voyage to England, he was on his best behavior, and Captain Maitland treated him as an honored guest. He quickly became the center of attention. Always courteous, he put on an outward show of good spirits, although inwardly he worried about the future. Eager to learn about so famous a warship, he poked his nose into everything, visiting the holds, inspecting equipment, and asking questions. Sailors were questioned about the battles they'd fought in, especially Trafalgar, where "Billy Ruffian" had been severely damaged. Officers got a thorough grilling. "How many arms have you cut off?" he asked the surgeon. To the paymaster he'd say: "How much do you steal?" During a review of marines, he charged into the ranks, took a musket out of a man's hands, and showed how Frenchmen presented arms.

Bellerophon arrived at Plymouth on July 31. No sooner did she drop anchor, when the docks filled with people hoping for a glimpse of the frightful "Boney." When sailor George

Home stepped ashore, he was mobbed by inquisitive school-girls. "What is he like?" they asked. "Is he really a man? Were his hands and clothes covered with blood when he came on board? Aren't you afraid of him?"

People came from as far away as London to see the fallen dictator. Soon *Bellerophon* was surrounded by rented boats packed with tourists. Captain Maitland counted over a thousand boats in a single day, each with about eight passengers, all wearing their Sunday best. His crew kept them informed by hanging out a board on which were chalked notices such as : "He's at breakfast"; "He's gone back to his cabin"; "He's coming on deck."

Napoleon was pleased by all the attention. He often came on deck dressed in his favorite outfit, the green uniform of a colonel of the Imperial Guard and a cocked hat with a tricolor insignia. The tourists, amazed that he was human after all, applauded and waved. He'd smile and tip his hat to the ladies. "What pretty women," he told an aide, winking. After a week at Plymouth, he was transferred to the *Northumberland*, which was put to sea to avoid the tourists. The British government didn't want him to become too friendly with its people.

Meanwhile, the allied leaders had decided to send him far from Europe. His home was to be St. Helena, a British-owned island named for an early Christian saint. St. Helena was nothing like Elba. Located in the middle of the south Atlantic, thousands of miles from any continent, it was an escape-proof prison without bars. Napoleon would no longer be shown the respect due an emperor. From now on he'd simply be "General Bonaparte," a retired officer abiding by his captor's rules. He'd have his own aides and servants, and live in his own house. But all communications with the outside world must be through the British governor. Every visitor would need the

governor's pass, every letter would be read and sent only if it
met with his approval. Redcoated officers would check on the
"general's" whereabouts once a day. If he went for a ride or
a walk, an officer must accompany him beyond his front gate.
Military outposts would look down from every hilltop. A small
fleet of warships would circle the island day and night.

Napoleon had a tantrum when told of his fate, only to have
the British officials reply with cold politeness. They hadn't
come to hear his complaints, they explained, but to give him
the facts. End of interview. If he chose to rant and rave, that
was his business.

On August 9, Napoleon and his companions left England
aboard *Northumberland,* escorted by seven other vessels. His
companions were three generals who'd volunteered to share
his exile. Generals Bertrand and Montholon brought their
wives and children; General Gourgaud was a bachelor. There
was also a secretary, Emmanuel Las Cases, whose *Memoirs of
the Emperor Napoleon* is one of the best firsthand accounts of
his years on St. Helena.

The voyage, though not unpleasant, was long. Napoleon
spent the daylight hours pacing the deck with his hands clasped
behind his back. Hours would pass without his uttering a word;
he'd only stare at the blue Atlantic. At night, he'd read, or
have others read to him. He was most interested in a biography
of Horatio Nelson, the man who'd done so much to ruin his
plans.

St. Helena came into view on the morning of October 15.
The French dressed quickly and hurried on deck to see their
new homeland. It was worse than anyone had imagined; even
Englishmen were shocked on seeing it for the first time. There,
rising from the deep, was a gray mass of volcanic rock. High
cliffs, bristling with cannons, came down to the water's edge;

there was no beach or dock, only stairs cut into the rock. The island's capital, Jamestown, was simply a few tar-roofed houses huddled at the base of two cliffs. "The devil must have spawned the island as he flew from one world to the other," one of the ladies said in disgust. Napoleon stared in silence and, after a few minutes, returned to his cabin.

St. Helena is only ten miles long by seven wide. Its population numbered 7,000, half of them soldiers assigned to guard the exiles. Most civilians were Chinese and Indians; three-quarters of the blacks were slaves brought from Africa to do the heavy work. The whites made their living by repairing ships sailing between Europe and the Far East, and supplying them with fresh water. The Duke of Wellington knew the island well—and hated the very sound of its name.

For the first seven weeks, while his house at Longwood was being prepared, Napoleon stayed at the home of the Balcombe family. William Balcombe, a prosperous merchant, lived there with his wife, daughters, servants, and slaves. The girls, Jane, sixteen, and Betsy, fourteen, trembled at finding themselves under the same roof as the child-eating "Boney." Napoleon soon calmed their fears. Having lost his power, for the first time in his adult life he was free to enjoy himself.

As if by magic, the "Corsican ogre" changed into a fun-loving uncle. Betsy, a pretty, high-spirited girl, had never had such a playful friend. Language was no barrier, since she was studying French. They played cards (at which he cheated), blindman's buff, and hide-and-seek. Some of their games, however, were at the expense of others. Shortly after his arrival, a neighbor's girl, Miss Legg, came for the day. She'd heard such horrible stories about Napoleon that, when told he was in the next room, she became terrified. Betsy excused herself and told him of her fears, begging him to play a little "joke" on her. He walked up to the child and, brushing up his hair with his hands, made a horrible face and let out a savage howl. Miss Legg was scared out of her wits. She promptly hiked up her skirts and ran from the house screaming.

Betsy's idea of fun could also be dangerous. One day, she asked Napoleon to show her his sword. The moment he put it in her hands, she drew the blade and began swiping it over his head. Amazed, he backed up until she pinned him in a corner, telling him to say his prayers, for she meant to cut him to ribbons. The noise finally brought her sister, who scolded her and promised to tell their father. When she lowered the blade, Napoleon took his revenge. He grabbed hold of her ear, which had been pierced the day before, and gave it a firm pinch. She called out, and he then grabbed her nose, smiling as he pulled it.

But the past was never far from his thoughts. One day Betsy's father locked her in a dark cellar for misbehaving. The cellar had rats, and she cried. Napoleon came to the grated window to cheer her up by mimicking her long face.

"You see," he said, "we are both prisoners and you cry. I don't cry."

"You have cried?"

"Yes, I have, but the prison remains nevertheless, so it is better to be occupied and cheerful."

The good times were not to last. On December 9, Napoleon and his party moved into Longwood House, a twenty-three-room building shared by fifty people: generals, wives, children, and servants. Longwood is built on a windy plateau that is always damp. In winter, there is cold, piercing dampness; in summer, hot, suffocating dampness, as in a steambath. Green mold covered the walls and mildew gave clothing a foul, musty odor. Brown rats scampered about; you could even hear them running in the walls. They got into the provisions, scared the children, and ate the eggs in the chicken coop. Once, when Napoleon took his hat from a table, a large rat sprang out and ran between his legs. The servants killed as many as twenty rats a day, but there were always others to take their place.

Life was made doubly miserable by the island's governor, General Sir Hudson Lowe. A former infantry officer, Lowe was a fussy, ignorant man terrified of displeasing his superiors in London. Lacking common sense, he took himself too seriously, insisting that everything be done by the book. Somehow he always managed to say the wrong thing at the wrong time, even to his fellow Englishmen. Wellington, who'd known him for years, called him "a damned old fool." No one, then or since, has challenged the Duke's description.

A more secure man might have gotten along with Napoleon. As it was, they were like fire and gunpowder. Whenever they met, there was an explosion of tempers. Nothing was too petty to argue about. Napoleon refused to answer to any title other than "Emperor"; Lowe refused to call him anything but "General." When Lowe wanted to trim his household expenses, Napoleon called him a boor and a barbarian. "You do not know how to conduct yourself towards men of honor," he shouted, "your soul is too low." Lowe, not to be outdone, used some pretty underhanded tricks. For example, he read Napoleon's mail and repeated the contents, however private. He and Lady Lowe would amuse their guests with a toast:

> God save the King
> God save the Queen
> Damn our Neighbor.*

*"The Neighbor" was their nickname for Napoleon.

The worst quarrels concerned security measures. Lowe wasn't taking any chances with this slippery fellow. Security, already tight, was further tightened, until Napoleon complained he could hardly breathe. He must show himself to British officers at least twice a day. When he took to his rooms, refusing to come out, Lowe made a captain climb up to the window of his room to watch him naked in his bath. At sunset, seventy-two soldiers entered Longwood's garden and took positions under the windows. Anyone—French or English—caught without a pass had to spend the night in the guard-house.

We know today that these precautions were unnecessary. Napoleon's European followers would gladly have rescued him, but decided the risks were too great. Joseph Bonaparte had moved to Philadelphia, where he became a wealthy businessman. In 1817, he contacted several Frenchmen who'd come to America after Waterloo. They worked out a plan to settle *Grande Armée* veterans in southern Alabama. The settlement, known as Champ d'Aisle (Field of Refuge) was to be a copy of Napoleonic France transplanted into the wilderness. Only the emperor himself was needed to complete the picture. Rescue plans were made, only to be canceled when a spy reported that his guards had orders to kill him at the first sign of an invasion.

Napoleon lived in two small rooms with used furniture bought by his jailers at bargain prices. The bedroom had a dressing table and camp bed, the same one he'd used during ten years of campaigning. The study was lined with bookcases and decorated with family portraits. These were the closest he'd ever get to his loved ones. Already his wife and son were fading memories. Marie-Louise was living with another man,

whom she eventually married; she died in 1847. Little Napoleon was being raised as an Austrian nobleman; his tutors
spoke only German to make him forget French and that he
was an emperor's son. Always sickly, he died in 1832. Letizia
lived until 1836, dying in her eighty-fifth year. Long blind,
she spent her days caressing the emperor's marble bust and
whispering into its deaf ears.

Time hung heavily upon the inmates of Longwood House.
With nothing important to do or think about, their tempers
became frayed. Grown men, brave soldiers, bickered over
trivia. Their wives gossiped and told tales behind each other's
back. General Gourgaud records a typical week in his diary:

Tuesday, 25th: Boredom! Boredom!

Wednesday, 26th: The same.

Thursday, 27th: The same.

Friday, 28th: The same.

Saturday, 29th: The same.

Sunday, 30th: Grand boredom.

Napoleon passed the time as best he could. One project was
to turn Longwood's small garden into a big garden. Dressed
in a cotton shirt and trousers, slippers and a straw hat, he'd
lead the servants in digging up the ground and transplanting
trees. He tried to keep up his spirits by continuing the customs
of the Tuileries, which made him feel that he was still emperor.
Dinner became the high point of each day's activities. The
generals came to dinner in full dress uniform, and their ladies
wore floor-length gowns of the finest silk. Uniformed butlers
served them on silver plates; tall silver candlesticks lit the tiny
dining room. After dinner the ladies would play the piano and
sing. Napoleon might read poetry or a play, which made everybody yawn, for he read in a flat, toneless voice. At about ten

Exiled on St. Helena, Napoleon gazes out to sea. Though
Napoleon still wears the dress of emperor, the guard at right,
who accompanied Napoleon whenever he went outside, attests
to his status as a prisoner. A drawing based on a painting
by L. Kratke.

o'clock, he'd stand up and bark: "What time is it? Bah! What does it matter? Let's go to bed."

Above all, Napoleon talked—and talked. His purpose was not merely to waste time, but to make the world remember him as he wished to be remembered. Always an actor, he used his exile to create a legend that would live through the ages. He knew that everything he said would be written down, becoming raw material for future historians. In effect, he'd be guiding their pens from the grave.

Napoleon portrayed himself as a martyr persecuted because of his concern for humanity. A peace-loving man, he'd always been forced to fight by selfish monarchs fearful of reform. His conquests were meant to bring about European peace and unity; indeed he'd always wanted a "United States of Europe." Endless explanations of Waterloo showed how he'd planned the perfect battle, only to have Wellington blunder into victory. Any mistakes that had been made were not his fault, but due to others who'd "failed him." These explanations, however, were so much nonsense and lies. In the end, his actions spoke louder than his words.

His words also show that he never changed. Cynical and callous, he still worshiped force and despised his fellow human beings. Although he said he loved the French and hoped to be buried among them, he really held them in contempt. In 1816, for example, he told Las Cases what Louis XVIII should do to control the people. "There is nothing like summary courts-martial to keep the lower classes and the rabble in line. Only by terror can the Bourbons maintain themselves in France. . . . The harder they are on the French, the better for them. Hang, exile, persecute—that's what they must do. . . . The French nation has no character. . . . " As for his old soldiers, those who'd served him so faithfully, he said the king could never trust them. Louis "ought to send one hundred thousand veterans to Santo Domingo and let the climate and the blacks take care of them, thus getting rid of both the soldiers and the blacks."

In the summer of 1820, Napoleon's health began to fail. He became nauseous and felt a stabbing pain in his right side. The pain grew worse as the months passed, causing him to vomit and lose weight. These symptoms were familiar to him: they pointed to stomach cancer, the same disease that had killed his father. Nothing the doctors did helped; indeed, their medicines caused him to roll on the floor in pain. Too weak even to walk, he took to his bed, moaning, "Poor me!"

By April 1821, he was living only on sugared water. Coffee, a favorite drink, was forbidden. General Bertrand, who kept a diary of Napoleon's last days, was heartbroken. "Tears came into my eyes as I watched this man, who had inspired such awe, who gave his commands so proudly . . . pleading for a spoonful of coffee, begging permission like a child, and not being given it, returning again and again to the same requests, always failing, but never getting angry. . . . This was the great Napoleon: pitiful, humble." How the mighty had fallen!

Napoleon died on May 5 at 5:49 P.M., three months shy of his fifty-second birthday. A few days before, feeling the end near, he ordered an autopsy to determine the true cause of death. He also ordered that his heart be sent to Marie-Louise, although one wonders what she would have done with it.

The seven doctors who performed the autopsy failed to agree. The Englishmen reported cancer of the stomach. It was a "convenient" cause of death, for, if true, it absolved their country of responsiblity for his death. Napoleon's own doctor, a Corsican named Antommarchi, blamed ulcers brought on by the harsh climate of St. Helena, thus putting the blame squarely on his jailers' shoulders. We may never know who was right—or indeed if any were right.

In 1978, Dr. Sten Forshufvud, a Swedish expert on poisons, offered a third explanation. After reading accounts by Napoleon's aides, Forshufvud decided that the emperor had been poisoned with arsenic—murdered. Since arsenic leaves traces in the hair, Forshufvud collected hair samples the emperor had given as souvenirs to various people. Tests showed that, at the time he died, his hair had thirteen times the amount of arsenic normally found in humans. British scientists have challenged these findings, and a lively debate continues. The only way to know for sure would be to examine the body itself, something the French government refuses to allow. Even if murder could be proven, the murderer's reasons and identity will probably never be known.

Napoleon was buried in a little valley with a beautiful view of the ocean. He'd picked the site years earlier, during a stroll with General Bertrand. Lowe refused to send the heart to Marie-Louise, one of his more sensible decisions.

A squad of British soldiers guarded the grave for nineteen years. Still there were those who refused to believe that their emperor was gone. Rumors circulated that a soldier named Roubeaud, his exact double, had taken his place, allowing him to escape. Some declared that he died selling spectacles in Italy, others that he ended his days in Philadelphia. It was even claimed that he was ruling a kingdom of blacks in "darkest Africa."

In 1840, during the reign of King Louis-Philippe, it was decided that Napoleon's remains should be brought to France for reburial. A ship called *La Belle Poule* (the Beautiful Hen), was sent to take them from St. Helena.

Paris greeted the remains with all the honors once given the living man. On December 15, the hearse, drawn by sixteen black horses, passed under the Arc de Triomphe, built to celebrate his victories, and down the great avenue of the Champs-Elysées. Hundreds of thousands of people, including uniformed veterans of the Imperial Guard, lined the route. The sun shined—the "sun of Austerlitz"—and banners fluttered in the cold breeze. Bands played the old marching songs. Cannons boomed in salute. Again the capital echoed to the familiar cry, "*Vive l'Empereur!*" By day's end, Napoleon lay under the golden dome of the Invalides.

During the following weeks, politicians gave long speeches about France's greatest lawmaker and statesman. Poets outdid themselves in flowery tributes to the "Man of Destiny." Veterans recalled bygone days, when they were young and followed their Little Corporal across burning deserts and lofty mountains. Perhaps he supplied the best epitaph when, as he lay dying, he sighed: "What a story my life has been!"

SOME MORE BOOKS

There are thousands of books on Napoleon and the Napoleonic Wars. Here are a few of the ones I've found most helpful.

Bourgogne, Jean Baptiste François. *The Memoirs of Sergeant Bourgogne, 1812–1813*. New York: Hippocrene Books, 1979.

Brett-James, Antony, ed. *1812: Eyewitness Accounts of Napoleon's Defeat in Russia*. New York: St. Martin's Press, 1966. This and the following books by this editor have invaluable accounts by participants in the Napoleonic wars.

———. *Europe Against Napoleon: The Leipzig Campaign, 1813*. New York: Macmillan, 1979.

———. *The Hundred Days*. New York: St. Martin's Press, 1964.

———. *Life in Wellington's Army*. London: George Allen & Unwin, 1972.

Brownlee, Walter. *The Navy that Beat Napoleon*. Cambridge: Cambridge University Press, 1980. A useful survey for the younger reader.

Butterfield, Herbert, Sir. *Napoleon*. New York: Collier Books, 1962.

Castelot, André. *Napoleon*. New York: Harper & Row, 1971.

Cate, Curtis. *The War of the Two Emperors: The Duel between Napoleon and Alexander, Russia 1812*. New York: Random House, 1985.

Caulaincourt, Armand Augustin Louis. *With Napoleon in Russia*. New York: William Morrow, 1935.

Chandler, David G. *The Campaigns of Napoleon*. New York: Macmillan, 1966.

———. *Dictionary of the Napoleonic Wars.* New York: Macmillan, 1979. Invaluable. The best reference book available on this subject in the English language.

Costello, Edward. *The Peninsular and Waterloo Campaigns.* Camden, Conn.: Archon Books, 1968. A firsthand account of these bloody campaigns by one of Wellington's soldiers.

Cronin, Vincent. *Napoleon.* New York: William Morrow, 1972.

Delderfield, R. F. *Imperial Sunset: The Fall of Napoleon, 1813–1814.* Philadelphia: Chilton Book Co., 1968.

———. *The Retreat from Moscow.* New York: Atheneum, 1967.

Dupuy, Trevor N. *The Battle of Austerlitz: Napoleon's Greatest Victory.* New York: Macmillan, 1968. For the younger reader.

Durova, Nadezhda. *The Cavalry Maiden: Journals of a Russian Officer in the Napoleonic Wars.* Bloomington: University of Indiana Press, 1988.

Elting, John R. *Swords Around a Throne: Napoleon's Grande Armée.* New York: The Free Press, 1988.

Forester, C. S. *Nelson.* London: John Lane, 1952.

Forshufvud, Sten, and Ben Weider. *Assassination at St. Helena.* Vancouver: Mitchell Press, 1978.

Glover, Michael. *The Peninsular War, 1807–1814: A Concise Military History.* Camden, Conn.: Archon Books, 1974.

Guérard, Albert. *Napoleon I.* New York: Knopf, 1969.

Herold, J. Christopher. *The Age of Napoleon.* New York: Harper & Row, 1963.

———. *Bonaparte in Egypt.* Harper & Row, 1962.

———, ed. *The Mind of Napoleon: A Selection from His Written and Spoken Words.* New York: Columbia University Press, 1955.

Hibbert, Christopher. *The Days of the French Revolution.* New York: William Morrow, 1981. The Revolution as it really was, horrors and all.

Holtman, Robert B. *Napoleonic Propaganda.* Baton Rouge: Louisiana State University Press, 1950.

Howarth, David. *Sovereign of the Seas: The Story of the British at Sea.* New York: Atheneum, 1974.

———. *Trafalgar: The Nelson Touch.* New York: Atheneum, 1969.

———. *Waterloo: Day of Battle.* New York: Galahad Books, 1974.

Keegan, John. *The Face of Battle*. New York: Viking, 1976.

————. *The Mask of Command*. New York: Viking, 1987.

————. *The Price of Admiralty: The Evolution of Naval Warfare*. New York: Viking, 1989.

Laffin, John. *Women in Battle*. London: Abelard-Schulman, 1967.

Lewis, Michael. *A Social History of the Navy from 1793–1815*. London: Allen & Unwin, 1960.

Lloyd, Christopher. *Nelson and Sea Power*. London: The English Universities Press, 1973.

Longford, Elizabeth. *Wellington: The Years of the Sword*. New York: Harper & Row, 1969.

Lovett, Gabriel H. *Napoleon and the Birth of Modern Spain*. New York: New York University Press, 1965.

Markham, Felix. *Napoleon*. New York: Mentor Books, 1963.

Martineau, Gilbert. *Napoleon and St. Helena*. Chicago: Rand McNally, 1968.

Masefield, John. *Sea Life in Nelson's Time*. Freeport: Books for Libraries Press, 1969.

Napoleon, *The Military Maxims of Napoleon*, ed. David Chandler. New York: Macmillan, 1987.

————. *Napoleon's Letters*, ed. J. M. Thompson. London: Dent, 1954.

Nastyface, Jack. *Nautical Economy*. London: W. Robinson, 1836.

Naylor, John. *Waterloo*. New York: Macmillan, 1960.

Nicolson, Nigel. *Napoleon 1812*. New York: Harper & Row, 1985.

Oman, Carola. *Napoleon at the Channel*. Garden City: Doubleday, 1942.

Palmer, Alan. *Napoleon in Russia*. New York: Simon & Schuster, 1967.

Palmer, R. R. *The World of the French Revolution*. New York: Harper & Row, 1971.

Rogers, H. C. B. *Napoleon's Army*. New York: Hippocrene Books, 1974.

Rothenberg, Gunther E. *The Art of War in the Age of Napoleon*. Bloomington: Indiana University Press, 1980.

Ségur, Count Philippe-Paul de. *Napoleon's Russian Campaign*. New York: Time Inc., 1965.

Terraine, John. *Trafalgar*. New York: Mason Carter, 1976.

Warner, Oliver, *Nelson's Battles*. New York: Macmillan, 1965.

———. *Victory: The Life of Lord Nelson*. Boston: Little, Brown, 1958.

Weider, Ben and David Hapgood. *The Murder of Napoleon*. New York: Congdon & Lattès, 1982.

Wheeler, William. *The Letters of Private Wheeler, 1809–1828*. Boston: Houghton Mifflin, 1951.

Wilson, Sir Robert. *General Wilson's Journal, 1812–1814*, ed. Antony Brett-James, London: Kimber, 1964.

INDEX